JEWELS

of Mind and Mentality

DUTCH JEWELRY DESIGN

1950 – 2000

JEWELS
of Mind and Mentality

DUTCH JEWELRY DESIGN
1950 – 2000

Edited
by
Yvònne G.J.M. Joris

Introductions
by
Antje von Graevenitz
and
Jaap Huisman

Het Kruithuis, Museum of Contemporary Art, 's-Hertogenbosch/NL
010 Publishers, Rotterdam 2000

JEWELS
of Mind and Mentality

DUTCH JEWELRY DESIGN
1950 — 2000

CONTENTS

7 Foreword
Yvònne G.J.M. Joris

9 Communicating mentalities: A rhetoric of Dutch jewelry 1950-2000
Antje von Graevenitz

49 New Jewelry for a Renewed Country, 1950-2000
Jaap Huisman

81 Jewels of mind and mentality

307 Biographies and bibliographies

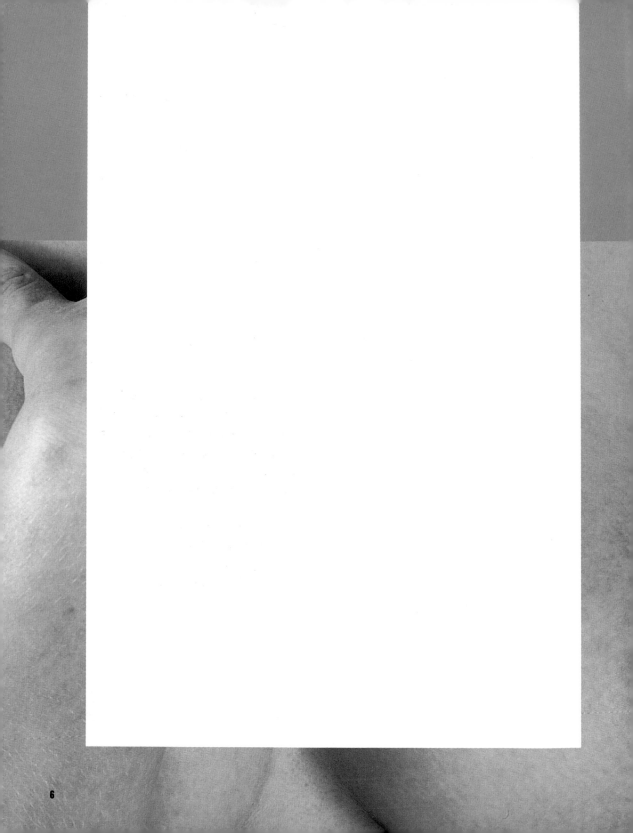

Foreword

The Netherlands is a sober and serious kind of place. Ornament and decoration do not sit well with the Dutch character. Holland is the product of design. It is a country of logical lines and layouts – an overwhelmingly cerebral character that also typifies Dutch culture. This may help explain the high quality of Dutch design, whether in architecture, fashion, interior design, graphical work or jewelry.

The past five decades have been exceptionally important, not least in the field of jewelry design. The rug has been well and truly pulled out from beneath "traditional" jewelry, the function and meaning of which have been rethought. The goldsmith's craft has given way to jewelry design, while jewelry has been elevated to the status of an art form. Dutch designers have led the way in this process, standing in the front line of a development that has had international repercussions.

It was a period dominated by conceptualism. However, the diversity of approach displayed by the various designers was sufficiently strong to provide a constant flow of new impulses and to prevent the discipline from getting bogged down in dogmas or rigid styles. The conceptual element, which peaked in the 1960s and 70s, shifted somewhat into the background in the 1980s, before moving back into the spotlight in the 90s – a tendency that looks set to continue in the years to come. This wealth of ideas forms the thread running through the developments of the past fifty years. Intellectual conviction, evident craftsmanship and a strong, pioneering spirit have combined to give Dutch jewelry design a leading role on the international stage.

Recognition of this fact is overdue. The present publication is the first to review the role and significance of Dutch jewelry over the past half century. This is not only important in terms of its own art-historical position, but also to do justice to the influence that Dutch jewelry has exerted on international developments in this field in the course of five decades.

Yvònne G.J.M. Joris
Director Museum het Kruithuis

DUTCH

JEWELRY

DESIGN

1950
—
2000

JEWELS
of Mind and Mentality

JEWELS
of Mind and Mentality

DUTCH JEWELRY DESIGN
1950 – 2000

COMMUNICATING MENTALITIES:
A RHETORIC OF DUTCH JEWELRY 1950-2000

Antje von Graevenitz

DUTCH
JEWELRY
DESIGN
1950
–
2000

JEWELS
of Mind and Mentality

"I will show you something that will change your mind" Janis Joplin sang in the 1960s. "Mind" had taken the place of the old idea of the "soul" as a description of the "self", of consciousness, and the ability to perceive, to feel and to think. Joplin's music arose in the era of hippies and flower power. They wore flowers – some real, some printed or stitched onto fabric – and long strings of ethnic-style chains as the physical signs of a different mentality. These things signified tolerance of the other and the other's culture, a preference for the natural, idyllic life, and love for all – a sense of life that Janis Joplin and her generation believed in. Jewelry in that period was an eyecatcher that conveyed a more optimistic message than at any time since the war. It may even have been the most positive mentality that jewelry had ever communicated.

In essence, jewelry always conveys a mentality, even if the context is not always as striking, or as politically and socially engaged as it was in the hippie era. Its maker has certain intentions, linked to mind and mentality, but so too does the customer, who wears the jewel in his or her own way. The design reflects the mentality from which the piece arose, shifting attention away from the pure beauty of the work and onto what it wishes to say. In the process, the jewel no longer simply bestows its beauty on the wearer but a mentality too, which, in some cases, is even more important. The aesthetic element is a given, and every maker and all wearers make their own choices, which are scarcely open to debate. However, the mentality represented by the modern jewel is a valuable, and thus far neglected, point of discussion.

What kind of jewelry does the woman of the world wear today? And who now qualifies as a "woman of the world"? The television newsreader? She remains a half-figure – an upper body – that addresses us in a neutral tone so as to reduce the world's calamities to the status of dry facts. She must be as interchangeable and impersonal as possible. Apart from the buttons on her standard-issue clothes, there is rarely any sign of jewelry, other than the occasional glitter in the hollow of her throat, where something may hang from a chain. She has to project a modest and business-like image, stripped of any trace of luxury, power or sex. She must arouse no more than a flicker of interest on the part of the viewer – just enough to hold his or her attention. A businesswoman's neck is allowed a little more decoration – a string of white pearls, perhaps, with each pearl representing an oyster's tear, recalling the oyster's pain. After all, the business world can be a vale of tears, too. This is as far as the conveyed mentality goes. The desire to be seen functions as the existential basis for the role played by the jewel. A simple chain offers the certainty and relative anonymity of a uniform. On other times of the day, that uniformity can be set aside and greater individuality can be displayed, according to the personality of the wearer. Jewelry is rare on the beach, for instance, where the sun is supposed to reach your body unhindered by anything more than the odd tattoo or piercing, ear-ring, hair-clip or comb. Men prefer gold chains, which they often cherish like a talisman (even athletes like to display them during their sporting performances). That is basically it for beach jewelry. At other times, individuals are much more emphatic when it comes to the mentality expressed by a piece of jewelry. The jewel is then allowed to fulfil its spiritual function as a means of communication – a token of *joie de vivre*, identification, power or non-conformity.

Conveying zest for life is a fundamental principle of all jewelry – its primary *raison d'être*. Its meaning shifts, however, as soon as it comes to be seen as the vehicle of a specific spirituality or mentality. Walter Benjamin called this the "double power" of jewelry, citing an image of his mother. She had a large and heavy brooch that she could no longer wear on her chest and had to attach to her belt instead. Benjamin remembers admiring the glittering stones: green, blue, yellow, pink and purple, while the sparkle reminded him of dance music. At the same time, the brooch gave off an aura of protection – a representation of society, "which truly resided in my mother's belt; I also saw truth in the talisman, which protected her from all that could threaten her in the outside world."[1] Jewels say something, therefore, about ways of living, impact on the outside world, and the visible form that all this ought to assume. This makes them a means of communication that embodies total eloquence.

Benjamin cites several important aspects of jewelry: the eroticizing, the magical and the status-enhancing, the latter capable of conferring dignity and, to Benjamin's mind, truthfulness. Traditionally, jewelry has not only been worn as a token of wealth, luxury or status, or as the finishing touch to a costume worn on a particular occasion – mayors, for instance, wear their ceremonial chains as a symbol of their office when receiving important guests. A similar function is fulfilled by the pendant with a large silver square and circle that Gijs Bakker made for Professor Fons Elders.[2] The piece suggests the ability to "square the circle" and refers to the professor's field of philosophy. Jewelry can also be tasked, however, with conveying a general message to mark a particular style, such as the long, floppy chains that gyrated along with the Charleston dresses of the 1920s – a period in which dynamism and movement were highly esteemed. The Futurist Manifesto and the movement's fascination with technology (which underpinned the rise of Kinetic Art) no doubt also contributed to this attitude. What is more, jewelry served to convey spirituality and mentality in the past, otherwise we would no longer feel the urge to view the finest pieces in museum collections. Take the beautiful Jugendstil comb, which

JEWELS
of Mind and Mentality

resembles a plant with round, white fruit. Combs like this continue to express the value that was placed upon nature around 1900 as a metaphor for a beautiful woman.

Given this background, might it be argued that a shift has taken place, whereby attention has moved from beauty towards mentality? This is the question we intend to discuss in this essay. Beauty is not the primary requirement, yet it is far from unimportant. To put it more strongly, there is evidence of a distinction being drawn between attractive, luxurious jewels, such as those set with precious stones, and another category that seeks deliberately and now primarily to convey a specific mentality. This is the objective with which jewelry of the latter type is designed and produced. It is possible to interpret this second type as being less about ornament and more about decoration. According to an old tradition, the notion of "decorum" relates especially to its significance relative to the piece's surroundings. Since classical antiquity, decoration has been viewed as an aesthetic addition. Primed with rhetorical meaning, it must be an important and visible addition to something that would in itself be incapable of explicitly conveying that meaning – the wearer's body, for instance. This sums up the difference between the jewel that is intended to express magnificence and splendor, and the "decorum" that is bestowed by a mentality that shuns such display.[3] Without a degree of rhetoric, this mentality will not be apparent either to the wearer or to others. The decorative jewel must, therefore, make a perceptible statement. So what has Dutch body decoration been talking about since 1945? What follows is an attempt to reconstruct the conversation via a series of examples.

Style, conceived as the ultimate distillation of the formal cultural idiom of a given period, ceased in the second half of the 20th century to be the only valid, synthesizing concept. Fashion, furniture, houses, works of art and ornaments can no longer be fitted into a universal formal idiom. Style has given way in recent years to lifestyle, which can best be considered in clusters – lifestyles that center on work, on leisure or on body culture. The attributes to accompany these lifestyles are offered for sale in an endless variety of form, expression, material and utility. Dutch designers of body decoration have avoided being driven by such market mechanisms every bit as much as their customers have. They are suspicious of current fashion, and those who wear their designs have sufficient imagination to choose body decorations that have not been pre-digested by some marketing operation. Belief in the value of individuality and the expression of identity is decisive when choosing jewelry.

When it comes to describing the mentality from which this jewelry has arisen, the old notion of a *Zeitgeist* or "Spirit of the Age" is no more helpful than that of "style".

JEWELS
of Mind and Mentality

A more useful starting point nowadays is the intention of the maker, his or her interest in particular works of art and concepts from native or ethnic cultures, and his or her strategies and ideas about human beings, the body, posing, and so on.

Nobody these days would attempt to portray the development of jewelry in a given period as a linear process, let alone a progressive one. The pattern tends instead to be presented in terms of a wide-ranging, parallel and non-hierarchical history, in which points of orientation and shifts of focus may be identified. These points and shifts can only be discerned, moreover, in relation to individual pieces of jewelry. A practiced eye and experience of dealing with jewelry allows us to extract a number of ideas relating to the consciousness of the maker and his or her customer (spirituality/mind), and to the mentality (attitude) being conveyed. In his 1969 exhibition "When Attitudes become Form" at Berne's Kunsthalle, Harald Szeemann was the first to present art history as a succession of different attitudes. Since that time, it has also been possible to discern a similar shift of emphasis (paradigm change) in the discipline of jewelry design.

Gerrit Rietveld's famous "Red-Blue Chair" (1918) may be a piece of furniture, but it is also intended as a work of art. When tagged in this way, different aspects of the chair draw our attention. The painted wooden planks become vectors that cut through space in all directions, while the colored surfaces at the ends seemingly refer to autonomous energies – the "bloodstream" of the construction, which flows in space. Sitting on the chair, one is at once part of the work and the critical viewer of its synergy – not merely the active agent, like an astronaut in the MIR space station, but a reflective one, too.

Something very similar has been going on within Dutch jewelry. Its wearers become part of a "higher endeavor" – an idea that has long since shed any religious connotations, but is linked instead to the pursuit of compelling perception. You take your place, as it were, in the story evoked by the body decoration. The wearers become an integral part of a particular presentation and are able to look at themselves from a distance, as part of a story. They participate with their bodies in the aesthetic performance offered by the jewel. The pure "consumer" need for the pleasure of being beautiful lapses and the wearers are obliged to open up their minds to a new sensation, mood or fiction, in which they participate with every fiber of their being. Their aesthetic attention fixes on the intention – the intended and the perceived mentality of the jewel. There is no point, therefore, in viewing decorative pieces like this as autonomous objects, as they can only fully develop their meaning in dialogue with the wearer – just like Rietveld's chair, in which furniture and person collude in the metaphysical performance.

JEWELS
of Mind and Mentality

The orientation points or parameters cited in the literature on the development of Dutch jewelry since 1945 are, first and foremost, the use of new, previously neglected and inexpensive materials,[4] followed by the focus on body-related objects and the idea of the jewel as a kind of veil for the body. These were strong arguments, which were customarily used when identifying key figures, their teaching methods and their schools. We will avoid that kind of approach here, not to mention the contextual, sociological and biographical angles as well. Our focus is, after all, on the mentality and the associated rhetoric that have developed in Dutch jewelry since 1945. Looking back, we discern other orientation points relating to the paradigms mentioned earlier. On closer inspection, all the points listed above basically skirt the most important question: what is the relationship between body and decoration, and how does jewelry define this relationship so that a particular mentality can be rendered visible? A definition of this kind is based on rhetorical elements, but which ones?

"You put on jewelry and you're seen", wrote Gijs Bakker to illustrate the contrast with an ordinary work of art: "You hang a painting on the wall and you can ignore it."[5] Person and jewelry together – provided, of course, that the jewel has been given a message – form a kind of "Bildleib". This "image-body" exists in the synthesis between the two forms. As a figurative body it is artistic, while as a physical body it is an object.

The idea that the work and the viewer or wearer physically belong to a shared image-body dominates much of the international art production of the 1920s and 30s and also that of the period since the 1960s. Duchamp, Brancusi, Acconci, Morris and Bruce Nauman, to name just a few, viewed their work as envelopes for the active viewer, who placed his or her body and mind in an empty space offered by the work of art. A jewelry maker, who is concerned with propagating a new mentality, uses the wearer to flesh out the jewel, both materially and spiritually. As soon as the empty space has been occupied, a shared "image-body" arises.[6] The mentality is revealed in this new world by the interplay of jewel and body and the accompanying rhetoric.[7]

The mentality of body decoration would not be discernible if it were not presented with such clarity. And this is where the power of post-war Dutch jewelry lies. For the most part, this jewelry is very outspoken in its display of a particular mentality. It "speaks out" about its function for the mind, at least to those who are receptive to the suggestions that the piece evokes. These have often been deliberately caused by the maker, in which case the design is attuned to the legibility of the intention. Less pre-programmed associations can, however, also prompt the wearer or viewer to recognize a particular mentality, provided that they are related to the "statements"

fig. 1
Archibald Dumbar
Perpetuum mobile
brooch 1955
white and yellow gold, silver

DUTCH

JEWELRY

DESIGN

1950
—
2000

JEWELS
of Mind and Mentality

15

made by the jewel. The intended mentality has to "speak" through the piece, otherwise it will be lost. In ensuring that it can do so, the maker uses a particular rhetoric, which makes the transmission of the mentality possible. Reception of this rhetoric plus the association of the wearer (or viewer) thus combine to determine the mentality of the jewel.

In order to perceive the mentality of a jewel, the viewer has to develop a membrane capable of functioning as a filter for the most pronounced aspects. Photography is a useful tool in this regard, as we see in publications on international and especially Dutch jewelry. The illustrations focus on the most obvious aspects, which are cited below as subjects of jewelry's rhetoric. Points of interest form clusters – the rhetoric of movement, technology on the body, the jewel as work of art, aggression and, finally, the rhetoric of ethnic solidarity with other cultures. The examples of post-war jewelry discussed here can, of course, be viewed as works of art, although the analysis will focus primarily on the rhetoric of a particular mentality and not on a quality judgement. We will, however, consider whether the rhetoric supports the piece in terms of shifting the boundaries towards the categories of painting, sculpture or drawing. In those cases, the rhetoric of the jewel as work of art serves as the defining factor in the process of consideration.

THE RHETORIC OF MOVEMENT

Movement is an innate property of the body and a chain responds to that movement seemingly by itself. It is different, however, when the jewel itself defines the movement – if, for instance, it displays a twist or shift, or if it evokes the memory of movement through its creation process. Language has many verbs to describe movement and these can provide jewelry designers with fundamental prompts: slide, fold, pierce, oscillate, combine, roll, spread out, exchange, and so on. All these verbs are found in the post-war development of Dutch jewelry, the true beginnings of which lie in the early 1950s, and the high point in the 1980s and 90s.

Archibald Dumbar set the tone in 1955 with a brooch design. His "perpetuum mobile" referred to one of humanity's oldest dreams, which had first been given concrete shape with Foucault's Pendulum (fig. 1). In 1913, Marcel Duchamp commented on the dream of perpetual motion by fixing a bicycle wheel to a kitchen stool, in what was also an ironic reference to the Futurists, who were loudly singing the praises of movement and speed at the time. The dream returned in the 1950s – the old laws and dreams had not disappeared, even though the Second World War had made the transience of things brutally tangible – when Dumbar and Chris Steenbergen picked up the thread once again. In 1957, Steenbergen managed to capture the tension that immediately precedes movement. This law of nature will have been perceptible via the jewel to its wearer. Later, recalling her training as a dancer, Emmy van Leersum and her husband Gijs Bakker designed a series of white leotards for a 1969 show at Amsterdam's Galerie Art & Project. They called it "Clothing Suggestions" and used hemispheres or rings to emphasize the knee and elbow joints and other elements underneath the leotard (fig. 2).[8] They were unlikely to win any fashion prizes, but the clothes looked sporty, dynamic and even elegant.

Van Leersum and Bakker continued to develop the idea of formal transformations and began to concentrate on metamorphoses. Inspired by the art of Ad Dekkers, Emmy van Leersum designed a steel "bracelet" in 1968, part of which was angled to suggest a different form (square), though this remained dominated by the round "bracelet". Gijs Bakker, by contrast, tried to treat the circle and square even-handedly, making a stainless steel bracelet (p. 105) that mutated from a circle to a right angle to create a surprising form. It was a metamorphosis with something of a poetic charge. Ovid told how Daphne turned into a tree while being pursued by Apollo. For his sculpted group, Gian Lorenzo Bernini chose the moment just before Daphne completes her transformation, when she is still part human and part tree. Bakker's bracelet is in a similarly intermediate stage. Does the wearer want to fit the square to his or her arm (because the angle of the square is annoying) or, conversely, has the bracelet had enough of the wearer and is it trying to extricate itself from its adapted form? Could this have been the "struggle" that Bakker presents? Whatever the case, the work is indeed the visual manifestation of a poetic metamorphosis. The monumental sculpture that Ad Dekkers made for Amsterdam's Wibautstraat displays a similar metamorphosis. However, that work lacks the extra presence of the wearer, which, in Bakker's case, lends a strong narrative element.

The same applies to another source of inspiration. In 1953, the Swiss artist Max Bill made a kind of elongated loop in red granite, which, as a symbol of perpetual motion, represented endless return. (The piece was, sadly, destroyed by vandals). With this work, Bill put forward an example of both concrete and absolute art. The meaning of a loop of this kind alters as soon as a human neck, arm, finger or ear is inserted in it. In 1965, Emmy van Leersum used yellow gold to make a tie-holder in the shape of a loop, an element that was to remain present in her work until 1979. She gave the same shape to a large collar (p. 108-109), although this required a fastener to make it wearable. Gijs Bakker designed his first variation on the loop in 1967, when he combined two ellipses to create a loop encircling the arm. He used the shape again in 1969 for a wide collar. Since that time, the motif has appeared regularly, also in the work of others: Paul Derrez produced an amusing, twisted

fig. 2
Emmy van Leersum and Gijs Bakker
clothing suggestions 1970

DUTCH

JEWELRY

DESIGN

1950
—
2000

JEWELS
of Mind and Mentality

collar (p. 212-213) from folded black plastic (held together by a steel spring), as if an old-fashioned, pleated lamp-shade had been magically transformed into a high-class jewel, the wearer of which acts as an eternal light. In 1985, Maria Blaisse designed a special felt hat that borrowed the loop's twist. But a hat remains more independent of the body than, say, the twisted collar that Lous Martin made in 1992. The lemniscate he placed on the wearer's shoulders refers to an idea of Oskar Schlemmer, who decorated one of the figures in his 1920 "Triadisches Ballett" with a recumbent figure eight, which he christened "The Absolute".

Progressions and/or degressions of expanding and/or contracting elements symbolize, through their movement, either evolution or decline. Absolute value has been ascribed in the 20th century to progression. Consequently, its visual representation by means of geometrical elements had been a common method in art. This systematic design principle was already being applied during the Bauhaus period in Weimar and in the work of Theo van Doesburg. It cropped up again after 1945 in Constructivist and Systematist art, and among the 50 artists of Europe's Nouvelle Tendence (1961–65). In the second half of the 1960s, Ad Dekkers and Peter Struycken also used progressions and degressions of formal elements to suggest continuous movement. Emmy van Leersum applied the principle of progression to the system of incisions in her steel bracelets (p. 155-156-157). This seemed to be a contradiction, for why should such heavy steel rings appear so fragile? She interpreted the progression or degression of incisions as a principle allowing an exceptionally durable material to be attacked.

Jewelry designers were attracted to dualities of this kind, such as that between durability and fragility. Beginning in 1980, for instance, Hans Appenzeller produced a whole range of pieces for his "American Series", in which geometrical metal grids had their perspective distorted and were pushed in from two sides. The distortion of perspective in these pieces was caused by a progression from regular, square cut-aways to elongated diamond shapes. The two extremes represented duality. In this way, Appenzeller picked up the thread established by a necklace made by Esther Swart-Hudig in 1963 (fig. 3).[9] The same principle was applied once again in the 1980s, by Maria Hees in 1986 and Frank van Zwicht in 1987. The latter designed a bracelet in which the two ends are linked by a progression from dark to light (in steadily increasing parts). It typifies the tradition of conceiving Constructivism in terms of dualities. In the examples cited here, however, the makers of the jewelry have sought to bring the oppositions of two extremes close together, without having them merge completely. Thesis and antithesis remain visible in their synthesis.

The spiral is a solution for a progressive or degressive movement, which need not be structured from specific elements, but which gradually grows bigger or smaller. It is surprising how often this precise form appears in Dutch jewelry in the 1980s and 90s. In 1982, Willem Honing began with a papier-mâché spiral that wound around the arm (p. 214). Bakker followed in 1984 and Birgit Laken in 1987 with steel, gold and silver coils,[10] Paul Derrez designed a red, spiral collar in aluminum and plastic, with a sphere fastener as if this were an object from an ironmonger's – a bicycle lock, for instance – to be worn round the human neck. His idea is reminiscent of Pop Art. In 1986, Gijs Bakker made a spiral out of torn Japanese paper, laminated in PVC, while in 1991, Annelies Planteijdt made a spiral from gold and torn paper: "Infinity, notions of movement, repetition and endlessness in space"(p. 265). This combination of materials seemed surprising. From time to time, she produced variations on the spiral, in which she abandoned the taut line in order to allow it to swing more or less freely. The form also crops up occasionally in Marijke de Goey's work, although she bent the continuous form into squares.[11]

The form of all these spirals seems absolute and hard, and in no way suitable for adaptation to the irregularly sculpted and soft human body. This is particularly evident in Gijs Bakker's filigree-like necklace "Dahlia" (1984). That flower's fine lancet leaves are placed in a spiral of transparent PVC laminate, strictly arranged from small to large. As soon as the spiral is wound around the neck, the three-dimensional body is seemingly reduced to flatness. Nature is dissected and subjected to order. This idea can be traced back to a neo-classical thought. The leaves are laid out for a possible study of nature. Just like the art works made of leaves that Herman de Vries often arranges on tabletops. In Bakker's "Dahlia", the body makes way for the higher value of the contemplation of nature, for which the spiral provides the model. It is perhaps significant that the apocalyptic symbol of the spiral should be adopted in the final years of the 20th century. The evolution symbol can be interpreted as both negative and positive, depending on the direction in which the viewer "reads" it. By linking natural leaves with the abstract symbol of the spiral, Bakker may have been seeking to give his work a critical, ecological charge. The dahlia is, incidentally, the flower that is traditionally placed on graves in Germany.

Jewels sometimes represent verbs of motion like "slide". Frans van Nieuwenborg, who trained as an industrial designer, and Martijn Wegman produced a belt in 1972 made out of transparent plastic. It could be made to fit waists of any size by sliding the end of the belt into the aluminum fastener. It was an ingenious solution that fitted in perfectly with the themes of the early 1970s: the fastener provides meaning. One year later, Hans Appenzeller designed a bracelet made out of two Perspex rings fixed in place with rubber caps (p. 144-145-146-147). Sliding the disks caused the

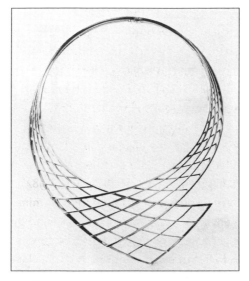

fig. 3
Esther Swart-Hudig
necklace 1963
white gold

JEWELS
of Mind and Mentality

fig. 4
Chris Steenbergen
ring 1969
perspex

DUTCH

JEWELRY

DESIGN

1950
—
2000

bracelet to click off. In the 1980s, Gijs Bakker, Maria Hees (in 1986) and Lous Martin also used "sliding" as a method and subject in their work.

The purpose of "exchanging" or "swapping" elements of the jewel is primarily to encourage the wearers to participate by making choices (an idea honored by Nouvelle Tendence artists like Karl Gerstner). Chris Steenbergen introduced the principle into Dutch jewelry in 1969 (fig. 4).[12] He returned to the idea in 1976 and 1984. Bruno Ninaber van Eyben also used the swap method in a wristwatch, for which the wearer could choose from a series of identically shaped but differently colored Perspex straps (p. 169). Wearers could thus be aware of their physical status: what emotion, mood or image did they have at that particular moment? By what motives was the choice made? In this way, wearing became a conscious act — once again, something that was entirely in keeping with the spirit of the time.

"Rolling" as a special form of movement was expressed in a Richard Walraven chain from 1982, in which dark triangles were rolled up to form little tubes. Rolling as a sculptural action is familiar from the Post-Minimalist work of Richard Serra, who used it to make the working process, the status and the tension of lead the art work's only subject. Material characteristics constitute the story. Walraven followed suit. In a sense, the process of rolling up triangles naturally recalls the spiral, though this analogy is not directly legible.

"Joining" represents another principle of movement. In 1980, Chris Steenbergen connected two differently colored metal sheets by dovetailing them together. This carpentry technique takes on a more visual character because of its essential alienness to metal. "Repetition", meanwhile, is an ancient mode of movement on which Beppe Kessler has placed particular emphasis in her jewelry. As she has said: "little crosses repeat rhythmically. They are set with the same movement, yet are different each time. The simplicity of a repetitive action reveals a form."[13]

"Revealing" is another verb of motion, and one that might be applied, for instance, to Nel Linssen's work. Her folded-paper jewelry only reveals the colors concealed within when it is worn. The surprise associated with wearing it adds a glowing and erotic play of color, that is only released when spread across the neck or arm.[14] The "melting" of ice also represents concrete movement: in 1992, Dinie Besems' chain of ice-cubes on a nylon cord only took five minutes to disappear on the wearer's body. Fortunately, a video recording was made. Process Art brought metamorphosis into art as a literal event. Yet a chain that disappears by melting has to be interpreted as an act of rebellion against the lovely, precious and charming jewel. In its place, a woman presented herself as performance, as a form of real theatre.

The material can be deliberately selected for its suppleness, tension or flexibility. Appenzeller made a series of gray rubber necklaces and also came up with a strange type of leather bracelet containing rigid rings that pressed through the soft material (they also recall Emmy van Leersum and her husband's "Clothing Suggestions"). Lous Martin followed in 1975 with an acrylic and metal cuff that seems knitted – a fitting extension for a sweater (fig. 5). This piece also conceals a rigid ring. Sliding the cuff up the arm – literally rolling up the sleeve – changes the shape and color.

An oscillating movement appears to be one of the most natural ways of generating dynamism. Once again, it was Chris Steenbergen who first explored oscillation in 1970. With two curved silver bands and a Perspex fastener, he created a bracelet in which the oscillating movement lay at the jewel's heart. Hans Appenzeller also adopted this principle in 1981. Françoise van den Bosch famously made a bracelet (with three variations) in 1971 (p. 140),[15] in which she bent two aluminum circles (one anodized black and the other silver colored) into semicircles and hooked them together as links. In this way, she created a kind of basic "chain" that suggested eternal movement. The two colors accentuated the twin circles in this perpetual motion machine and betray the duality that was so familiar at the time from the Chinese Yin and Yang symbol. Like many other jewels, this bracelet has a metaphysical charge that enables the wearer to participate in a cosmic meaning within the tradition of "decorum".

THE RHETORIC OF TECHNOLOGY ON THE BODY

A lot of body decoration that accentuates or merely suggests movement offers an unusual angle on technology, mostly with a positive slant. Technology has been embraced, with the jewelry maker behaving almost like an industrial designer. Some of them – Bruno Ninaber van Eyben and Frans van Nieuwenborg/Martijn Wegman, for instance, and, to a certain extent, Gijs Bakker – have developed further in that direction, while others – Marion Herbst, Paul Derrez and Onno Boekhoudt, among others – have deliberately distanced themselves from designer status. This development towards design was initiated in the 1950s by Chris Steenbergen, Archibald Dumbar and Riet Neerincx. They began by processing inexpensive, industrial materials like alpaca and fairly rigid aluminum. Their successors swapped these materials for steel, Perspex and even nylon. Industrial materials like this came to define the special look of contemporary Dutch jewelry. There were periods in which a particular technical solution could provide the starting point for making a piece of jewelry. This is chiefly the case in the 1960s and 70s, when Emmy van Leersum, Françoise van den Bosch and Hans Appenzeller began to work. The value

JEWELS
of Mind and Mentality

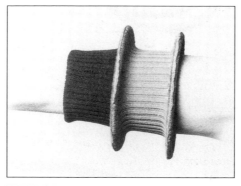

fig. 5
Lous Martin
Cuff bracelets 1975
acrylic and metal

DUTCH

JEWELRY

DESIGN

1950 —
2000

JEWELS
of Mind and Mentality

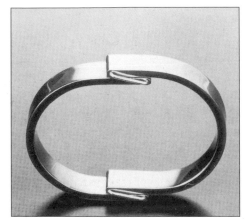

fig. 6
Hans Appenzeller
Folding bracelet 1975
silver, gold and brass

DUTCH
JEWELRY
DESIGN
1950
—
2000

JEWELS
of Mind and Mentality

26

of innovation was so highly regarded at the time that technical advances – as soon as these were pushed forward as an important element of the piece itself – could be a message in themselves. A technical solution was the prompt, the subject, and the actual value of the piece.

Wrists vary in shape and they also need to retain their freedom of movement. Chris Steenbergen solved this problem by making the two fastenings between two half-bracelets the core of his design. He began by studying the fundamental question of what it means to be a designer rather than a traditional goldsmith or silversmith working for the social elite. One of the implications was that the physical features of the jewel now also became the point of the work in terms of its content. The fastening of a bracelet, which, as a special surprise, only needed to be twisted and which fastened ingeniously on the forearm, was, in itself, a source of pleasure for the wearer. An example is the "Folding Bracelet" that Hans Appenzeller designed in 1975 (fig. 6). He returned to the theme in 1982, with his "Twist and Wave" collection, in which the fastener was actually set with diamonds.[16] The fastener: That's it... Like a number of his Dutch colleagues, Appenzeller spent several decades searching for new technical solutions to use as the primary motif of a given piece. Following in the tradition of the now long-closed Staatliche Bauhaus in Dessau, these designers engaged in laboratory-style research: how far can you take the material, the human body, the technique or production method? While Appenzeller was busy assembling a bracelet from two Perspex elements attached with rubber knots in 1973 (thereby updating Steenbergen's design), Lous Martin arrived at a similar solution using plastic and steel wire, placing the fasteners outside the bracelet.

Dutch jewelry makers operated as veritable body engineers, paralleling the working methods of designers in search of innovative products. It comes as no surprise, therefore, that it should be a designer like Bruno Ninaber van Eyben who, in 1976, conceived the now famous watch that you could hang round your neck from a rubber band (p. 173). The watch moved with the body and could always be seen by wearers who had to keep both hands free – nurses, for instance. The face of the watch was upside down, so that it could be read by them. "I like to give things an element of movement – because of their static existence, to overcome their gravity," he said in an interview. "The kinetic element makes it possible to have movements of surprise. I am delighted if I can do something along those lines. It provides another dimension, it stimulates the imagination."[17] It also demonstrates that the application of technical know-how need not be the sole ambition of the designer-jewelry maker.

Nylon tape provided the raw material for a loop around Emmy van Leersum's neck. She transformed this everyday packaging material (the stuff used to tie up bundles of newspapers, for instance) into a necklace, which, with its different colors, looked as regular as it was entertaining. Around 1970, Hans Appenzeller decided to use rubber – a supple and, in his hands, even elegant material, though one that has the disadvantage of growing steadily warmer on the skin. The one-off pieces that are customary in the world of precious objects[18] had to give way in part to series of multiples. The wearer was interested in the idea behind the piece, rather than its rarity. Jewelry design thus borrowed an idea from the development of art. Daniel Spoerri's EAT-ART series was the first to introduce the public to the idea of multiples. From 1966 onwards, artists dreamed of unlimited runs of serial objects. It was not until Takis, however, with his double lamp that this was actually achieved. The dream not only reflected a marriage between art and industry, but above all the idea that it would be possible for the buyer to participate in the work of art. Reasonable prices and the mentality with which it was created would make the art work more accessible.[19] The multiple was a manifestation of a great utopia. Venues like Galerie Sieraad fell over themselves to incorporate multiples in their program, alongside the traditional one-off. Many artists sought to refer to industrial products in the content of their work. In 1967, Gijs Bakker put stovepipe around a woman's neck and wrists (p. 110-111-112). Construction and plumbing materials became a lucky dip for some designers. In 1971, Marion Herbst made a bracelet from pieces of chrome-plated shower hose (p. 138-139).[20] Industrial products and semi-finished goods became important sources of inspiration, in addition to the interest in the everyday that Pop Art had cultivated. The tide soon turned, however. Although characteristic works have continued to be produced in series, the trend at the moment is towards one-off pieces which – as in the world of haute couture – lend themselves better for show and for photographs in magazines. This development had been influenced by the prevailing trend – the desire for painting and sculpture-like features and the need for narrative and one-off entertainment.

THE RHETORIC OF THE JEWEL AS WORK OF ART

In 1969, an exhibition of contemporary Dutch jewelry toured the United States. The title of the show was very apt: could these "Objects to Wear"[21] really be worn? What about the wearer? Many of the new objects were too heavy to be worn. The pieces announced the emancipation of body decoration from the wearer – at least that's how it seemed. In reality, it was less a practical issue than a question of the right definition. The compilers of the exhibition – museum director Jean Leering, artist Ad Dekkers and curator Wil Bertheux – established a tight, cool line, requiring that each piece should be clearly worked out in terms of a formal problem and in accordance with a preconceived plan. This approach was wholly in line with what was viewed in contemporary culture as a Dutch identity. The decorative aspect – however that notion might have been interpreted – was not the point of departure. Art counted for more than the jewel. So it was that "The Dutch School" (David Poston) came to be born for the outside world.[22] Shortly afterwards, Ralph Turner organized an exhibition of work by Emmy van Leersum in London's Ewan Philips Gallery, to which he gave the even more explicit name "Sculptures to Wear".

The "object to wear" fitted into the evolution of jewelry towards apparently autonomous works of art – a process that had been underway for some time. Chris Steenbergen drew inspiration from a Russian émigré in Britain, Anton Pevsner, while Riet Neerincx (another pioneer of the new Dutch jewelry after the Second World War) looked to British sculpture – a natural orientation for a designer who had trained in London.

The difference between the two sources of inspiration was not especially big. In their "Realist Manifesto" of 1920, Anton Pevsner and his brother Naum Gabo were the first to praise time and space as part of the work of art, an idea that was then adopted by the British. The space in between now became an important element – not as a break or void, but as the location of time and space, present in the air that flows in between. It was here that reality could make its true entrance into the work of art, transforming art and life into a unity. It functioned, of course, as a rhetorical form that promulgated an ideal unity between the relative (the actual space) and the absolute (the work of art). Henry Moore and Barbara Hepworth accepted irregularly shaped holes in their sculpture, and Neerincx too made a biomorphic gold brooch in 1964, which features funny holes in its cellular form (p. 99).[23] The fabric of the dress – the support beneath the jewel – also functioned as part of the composition. Neerincx elaborated on this idea with her rings, drawing fingers and skin into the work as well – life flowing through the jewel.

Emmy van Leersum looked more to the work of Frans Zwollo Jr., than to that of older Dutch jewelry makers like Esther Swart-Hudig, Nicolaas van Beek and Riet Neerincx. And more than that, she was inspired by international art, which she saw at big exhibitions like documenta in Kassel and in the museums of Paris and Amsterdam. She was particularly interested in the work of Naum Gabo and Max Bill. Characteristic of her ambition to work as a sculptor on behalf of the human body, is the fact that she used very heavy or else very light materials of the kind that also played a part in the autonomous art of the time (light materials, for instance, began to crop up in the late 1960s in movements like Arte Povera and Soft Sculpture). This led Van Leersum and Bakker to exhibit their work in an art gallery for the first time in 1971.

DUTCH
JEWELRY
DESIGN
1950
2000

Their show at Amsterdam's Galerie Swart brought them into contract with artists like Ad Dekkers, Peter Struycken and François Morellet, whose fundamental exploration of areas like the relationship between nature and reason and that between chance and calculation, raised themes that were familiar to the jewelry designers. Their work also touched upon the designer's world in terms of technique, while in their constructions, these artists viewed the geometrically calculated organization of their work as a high aesthetic value. Like them, Emmy van Leersum believed that the nature of the construction ought to be legible in her work, no matter how surprising an effect her solution might have. An understanding of the process of artistic decision-making became part of the credo of virtually all the artists grouped around Galerie Swart. The couple exhibited bracelets in progressive series based on a clear geometric construction. Those who wore one of the heavy bracelets were able in their imagination to take part in an idea that only took shape with all the other wearers. It was not the individual that counted but the system.

In reality, Emmy had simply designed these jewels. The often highly labor-intensive manufacture was done by Gijs Bakker, with occasional workshop assistance. The idea was, however, infinitely more important than the craft. Van Leersum chose steel, even though other materials were easier to work with. The weight of the steel jewelry was an essential aspect of her work's individuality and lack of compromise: these truly were "sculptures to wear". In 1971, she designed a steel bracelet, part of which was galvanized. Another weighty piece, it was to have a significant influence on several Dutch jewelry designers. Steenbergen had, in fact, made a very similar, pierced bracelet in gold shortly before, but it did not have the same effect.

Both Marion Herbst and Onno Boekhoudt produced variations on Van Leersum's idea decades later. Boekhoudt made eight silver rings (p. 291-292) with galvanized sections, which were like minimalist sculptures. Meanwhile, Van Leersum's technique of incising steel – as Ad Dekkers did with wooden sheets – was reprised by Richard Walraven in 1990. To mark the 15th anniversary of the VES (Vereniging van Edelsmeden en Sieraad-ontwerpers – Association of Goldsmiths, Silversmiths and Jewelry Designers),[24] he designed a "Crown for Each Finger" using the same technique.

Although jewelry makers like Onno Boekhoudt and – until her death – Marion Herbst continued to see themselves as plastic artists, the tone of their work changed. Like the Post-Minimal artists, they responded to the temptation of material experimentation. Leather and copper, soft and hard, matte, smooth and shiny – in other words, purely physical properties – determine the story of their often dualist design.

fig. 7
Jacomijn van der Donk
ring 1991
glass, copper

DUTCH

JEWELRY

DESIGN

1950
2000

JEWELS
of Mind and Mentality

31

The ambition of conceiving body decoration as art has been discussed, among others, by the British sculptor and goldsmith David Watkins.[25] He cites Boekhoudt in the sculptural line,[26] LAM de Wolf in connection with textiles and Philip Sajet with paintings. Whether these jewelry makers are the only representatives of the trend towards crossing boundaries into other categories of art is open to dispute. Watkins' list is undoubtedly much too short: other designers could equally well be cited, even for categories like drawing, photography and the object. And why Philip Sajet should have been picked in relation to painting is curious to say the least.

The category of virtual sculptors includes Marion Herbst (one of her humorous pieces is the 1975 "Salad Basket", which was ironically transformed into a jewel in the era of Pop Art and the rise of feminism),[27] and Françoise van den Bosch, who died prematurely. Together with Onno Boekhoudt, the sculptor Berend Peter Hogen Esch and Karel Niehorster founded the Bond van Oproerige Edelsmeden ("League of Rebellious Goldsmiths"). The BOE, founded in 1973–74, preached contrariness and offered playful resistance to the austere and dogmatic culture promulgated by the dominant strand of contemporary Dutch jewelry. The lid of "BOE Box" produced in 1974 bears the following words: "The BOE is a group of four goldsmiths and one sculptor who wish, through the more personal presentation of their work, including the necessary information, to broaden the normal manner of exhibition, to make it a manifestation of ideas (p. 160)." This step was considered necessary in order to shift the boundaries of jewelry design. At the same time, they wished to approach the wearer in a spirit of humor and play. The group made little boxes containing all manner of objects and texts – not so much jewelry, but things like packets of seeds with playful instructions. You could explore them, use your hands and discover your body – as was also the case, in fact, with other jewelry.[28]

Seven years later, Jacomijn van der Donk designed her "Ring 91" in glass and copper (fig. 7). A small icicle of beads sticks into the wearer's palm. Physical intimacy had become commonplace by that time, but Van der Donk appears implicitly to be referring to the products of the 1970s revolt. The icicle, although intended as a piece of jewelry, can also be viewed as a toy – a kind of *Handschmeichler* (hand-stroker).

Play long remained the favorite domain of Marion Herbst, who liked to experiment with materials (newspaper and metal, for instance, in 1973–74). Shortly before her death, she constructed small reliefs on the elongated needle of a brooch (p. 278). The result was a series of small, linear landscapes reminiscent of children's toys. These works come close to Auke de Vries' sculptures.

The odd one out in this list is Ruudt Peters. The jewelry that he produced in 1995

fig. 8
Ruudt Peters
Wunstorf ring 1994
silver, marcasite, gold leaf

under the collective name "Ouroboros", comes the closest to a series of small sculptures (fig. 8).[29] Spikes or balls on an icicle shape produce sensations in the palm of your hand, as in Van der Donk's work. The tactile element in a ring like this is very important. Wedged between two fingers, only a small fragment of the ring protrudes above the hand. In each case, this "upper world" tells a different plastic story than the object concealed in the palm. What is more, the hand is taken over almost entirely by the demands imposed by the jewel. It is virtually impossible to do anything other than grip, show and feel, which takes some getting used to.

Peters is very interested in the secret idiom of alchemy — that ancient language of the parallels that exist between the material and the spiritual/mental world. The equivalence of matter and spirit can be demonstrated through "maneuvers of exchange". Much of Peters' recent work — the 1997 series "Lapis", for instance — derives from alchemical metaphors, like the minimal alembics (vessels), in which matter used to be cleansed in laboratories using chemical processes. Linking elements in Peters' work are clasps made of copper-wire — a material which, according to the alchemists, reflects female beauty (it represents Venus) and conducts electricity/energy. It might seem odd for a goldsmith to be attracted to secret teachings, yet alchemy has become such a familiar language and open discipline in 20th-century art that it is actually hard to describe it as secret any more (Kounellis, Beuys, Abramovic, Yves Klein, Pieter Laurens Mol, Thom Puckey and others have all drawn on it). Artists have sought to restore old relationships like this, which have been shattered by science and the rise of electronic media. Use of the alchemist's idiom is only partly to do with esoterica. It also relates to the place that the tangible, visible, thinkable and imaginable occupy in the world, where they form a counterweight to and against the development of a media-oriented culture.

Although it is stretching things somewhat to link the calculated, geometric-abstract work of Emmy van Leersum to the esoteric creations of Ruudt Peters, there are similarities all the same — some of which they also share with other colleagues. Both, for instance, work according to the principle that there must be a specific language capable of conceptually underpinning the designer's decisions. Body decoration without an underlying argument has no reason to exist. It is a principle that has typified the post-war development of Dutch jewelry.

While it is natural for jewelry makers to have links with sculpture and to engage in groundbreaking exploration in that field, the links with painting are less obvious. LAM de Wolf paints fabrics before turning them into jewelry (p. 198), while Beppe Kessler decorated her 1987 collar with brushstrokes worthy of the "Mülheimer Freiheit" group. Members of that group, including Walter Dahn and Georg Jiri Dokoupil, introduced the figurative "Wild Painting" around 1979, with its self-important gestures of the paintbrush. Because Kessler uses the human body rather than a painter's canvas for her support, the overall effect says "let it be how I want" – a phrase that sums Kessler up perfectly. The body is concealed behind the call for greater expressiveness. The statement is extreme and theatrical in the context of the rather sober Netherlands. It leads body decoration in the direction of costume design. Other designers have only partially adopted the influence of painting. The bits of cardboard that Lous Martin painted in acrylics in 1989 and then joined together to make a golden chain, display a more controlled "wildness". The same goes for the collage-like necklaces and brooches of Robert Smit, who frequently paints or scratches whimsical and irregular structures in an unhierarchic field onto small sheets of precious metal, which he then assembles to form complete jewels (p. 243-244-245). His way of working is rounded off with wild, blue lumps of paint. The result looks deliberately uncontrolled, painterly and yet precious – as if a maverick painter or sculptor had turned to jewelry as a tiny mode of expression. This gives Robert Smit's work a fresh and spontaneous appearance, which can be communicated to the wearer.[30] New distribution channels were required for work like this.[31] The existence of specialist jewelry galleries and the promotional work they undertook, extended the movement's base. Attention was also drawn to the development of jewelry design by the prizes awarded by the Françoise van den Bosch Foundation to commemorate the designer who died in 1977. Above all, they have offered support to radical designers.

The relationship between jewelry and drawing has received considerably less attention in the Netherlands than that between sculpture and painting. Emmy van Leersum took the first steps in this direction, possibly because it was her husband who did the actual smith's work, while she tended to work at the drawing board. Once again, the source of inspiration was Ad Dekkers, who drew on both sides of pieces of transparent paper, suggesting a non-existent space. Emmy opted for semi-translucent Perspex to make stiff and very wide bracelets (which fastened rather laboriously around the forearm), on which she generally combined a black line, as the only decoration, with an incision in the shape of a triangle or part of a circle. In this way, the incision was made to function as a variation on the line, and she used the two to divide up the curved surface of the bracelet. Her later nylon necklaces (p. 210-211) can be interpreted as further developments of these line drawings, just as her gold-wire bracelets from the late 1970s also belonged to the tradition of line drawing (p. 184). Ruudt Peters produced a drawn decorative jewel in the true sense of the word in 1983, with his drawings of Renaissance architectural ornaments. He took the capital and base of a column from an old drawing, stiffened them with

DUTCH

JEWELRY

DESIGN

1950
2000

acrylic and attached them to a double metal pin. When worn, the pin vanished into the wearer's clothing, leaving just the ornaments visible and causing the body to function as a column.[32]

Emmy van Leersum showed the way towards a new perspective on the goldsmith's ancient craft. She tried with all her might to avoid traditional associations, seeking instead to tell a kind of story with her work – a story about the importance of formal exploration, in which the body directly participates. After all, "heavy" is only truly heavy on the body and "transparent" only becomes so when the pink skin underneath is visible. A line around the arm, meanwhile, is a challenge to the irregular shape of the forearm. The line was a guiding principle in her work. It seems always to have been her point of departure, visible in incisions or drawn lines, or given physical form in bars. It varies between disruption and basso continuo, but is always the most calculated form. Everything had to look austere, and this was aided by the straight or curved line. In this way, the line took on an almost moral function. The body offered irrefutable proof of the synthesis of her rational analysis and physical irregularity and sensitivity. To Van Leersum, it was an abstract-constructive story. Nowadays, by contrast, the content of that story is once again permitted to be narrative – a principle that she, in her time, was absolutely unable to share.

Annelies Planteijdt, for instance, has golden lines undulate back and forth over a hand. They curve only halfway round a finger, and move freely in the air as if the moving hand were formed by the flow of air (p. 256/261). Dinie Besems' 1994 chain also has a real and a narrative side. It seems at first sight to be made simply from matte white balls, held together by little knots like a string of pearls (p. 280). The pay-off comes a moment later, when you notice that the little balls have been cut from a piece of chalk and then polished. If you were to hang the necklace around your neck, the chalk would leave traces on the skin or fabric. To put it in semiotic terms: the signifier and the signified combine to form the actual meaning. The Dutch word for pinstripe ('krijtstreep') translates as "chalk stripe", and if the piece were worn, as intended, with a suit of that material, it would leave further, irregular "chalk stripes" on it. Being and appearance combine to form the story for as long as the balls of chalk last. The story ends when they wear out.

THE RHETORIC OF THE STORY

Gijs Bakker has taken the invention of stories for the body to particular extremes in recent decades.[33] This development reflects the important place that entertainment has assumed in society, even as a yardstick of quality. Straight after our evening meal, the television provides our daily dose of disaster, football, crime and

melodrama. Yet to get through with a story, that story has to have a point and ought preferably to be somewhat titillating. In 1982, Lily van Ginneken coined the idea of the "New Frivolity", which fits Bakker's work in the 1980s and 90s perfectly.[34] The function of his photograph of a woman wearing a laminated photo of a man around her neck is to deceive. The man seems to hold her in his arms. It seems to be a profound embrace, a natural gesture between people who have known each other for years and who, for a moment, are wholly separate from the world. It is this impression that makes the image annoying. You wonder how this deception is possible and whether it can really be an embrace. The wearer seems to be in conversation with her "necklace man". Real and unreal merge. The decoration is not really a necklace you could wear outside or at a dance, because it makes other partners unwelcome. It is an autistic image that seems to have come from a dream or a performance.

That goes for many stories of this kind. Pieces like this necklace are similar to the kind of 1980s photography in which carefully staged images reveal how the truth and reality of a scene can be manipulated (examples being Bill Wegman and Jeff Wall). The "Fotografia buffa" exhibition at the Groninger Museum in 1986 brought together the work of artists, primarily Dutch, in this field. Gijs Bakker first began to explore the technique around 1977/79, when he combined large collars with photographs, including one of a beautiful red rose, to which two drops of dew cling like large teardrops (p. 205). The head of the woman wearing the collar seems to complete the flower, as if she were part of a fairy tale. Emmy van Leersum herself was photographed as the rose's radiant centerpiece.[35] The droplets of water have seemingly taken the place of diamonds. The piece is, indeed, intended as a commentary on a 1960 design by Cartier for a brooch with a coral and diamond rose (fig. 9).[36] In 1989, Bakker placed real yellow sapphires on a photographed bouquet of flowers, playing with tradition once again (p. 259). He took his game a great deal further, however, through a variety of brooches to the habit of telling stories or expressing a state of mind via T-shirt or badge slogans (those painted by Keith Haring, for instance). In 1998, he attached two apparently falling babies to a football in order to mock the "sacred" game. The little figures resemble the tumbling musclemen in a Hendrik Golzius print, who manage to show off their physique even while falling. Bakker substituted babies for famous images, with results that either amused or scared the viewer.

The work of Dinie Besems is no stranger to the autistic gesture either. Although her humor is expressed with a touch more refinement that the Bakker necklace we have just described, the theme is no less grim: "This Space is Mine" is the title of

fig. 9
Cartier
brooch ca. 1960
form of a rose in coral and diamonds

her chains, which offer two possibilities (p. 286). You can either place them on the table on four legs, in which case the silver cord demarcates the resultant spot as if it were a piece of private land, or else hang the cord around your neck, in which case the 8 cm high legs dangle like ordinary pendants, blurring their function. However, those who are aware of the twin functions now also view the wearer's neckline as a piece of private property... In the early days of Land Art, Dennis Oppenheim marked out a square piece of ground with poles and rope, though he also added some watchful German Shepherds. Fortunately, Dinie Besems' work is not accompanied by any barking or growling, yet the idea behind it is equally strict – "Keep off!"

Whenever a story is told, quotations from movies will not be too far away. Jacomijn van der Donk made a filigree silver necklace in 1994 that suggests two hands resting on the wearer's shoulders and a constant threat to her neck (fig. 10).[37] The immediate association is with classic thrillers like Hitchcock's "Strangers on a Train" (1951), which begins with murder by strangulation, followed by the simulated throttling of a richly decorated woman's neck at a party. A girl observes the simulation and suddenly makes the psychological link. The wearer of Van der Donk's necklace would play a similar role of near-victim, were it not for the fact that the Art Deco-like form of the hands and their filigree technique suggest such little strength, perhaps rendering them bearable. Gijs Bakker also plays his game with the ladies with a great deal of irony. He has, for instance, placed a sinister chain made of photographs of gradually erecting phalluses around a woman's neck, creating an impression of a vast, emasculatory orgy that has just finished and is now being celebrated ("Johnny Awakes", 1998). Another piece of neck jewelry has photographs of the heads of two fighting bulls. Perhaps the wearer is being cast as Europe, with the two bulls having to do combat before the winner can carry her off over the water? In this way, the old myths are brought, with a chuckle, back to life. On another occasion, Bakker had ladies – or rather would-be ladies – wear photographed necklaces in the manner of crown jewels (p. 239). The title, "Queens" is no less ambiguous.[38] Herman Hermsen picked up the baton, narrowing his focus to the "Madonna". His photographed halo (once again laminated) turns the wearer into a secularized Madonna, with, of course, a nod towards the American pop star. There is a great deal of theatre here, as Ralph Turner and Gert Staal have already noted.[39] The body becomes part of a solo exhibition.

"Representation" and "simulation" were the period's magic words, into which the reality of the body was subsumed. The trend eventually began to take on some extreme features. Philip Sajet (in 1990, together with G. Meeussen) created a silver necklace to which gold, red, blue, yellow and green musical notes were attached,

fig. 10
Jacomijn van der Donk
necklace 1994
silver

DUTCH
JEWELRY
DESIGN
1950 2000

JEWELS
of Mind and Mentality

40

hopefully scoring out a cheerful tune around a woman's neck ("La Zingara"). At the other end of the spectrum was Ted Notens' necklace "Princess" (1995), which consisted of a plastic pendant in which a dead mouse with a string of pearls round its neck was laid to rest.[40] Stories as gruesome as this were rarely told by jewelry designers, although the method had been explored to some extent by Art Nouveau and Art Deco. Perhaps it was a revival of the Punk idiom, which saw bloody children's heads being worn as body decoration, safety pins pushed through noses or lips and Rover's collar worn round his master or mistress's neck. Symbols for the terrible tales of the No Future youth in the utopias of Ronald Reagan and Margaret Thatcher. Horror stories like this were told with a smile rather than pent-up fury in the Netherlands. This was tongue-in-cheek rebellion. After all, in the 1960s, the symbol of Amsterdam's Provos, which they left as their calling card all over the city, was a little apple with a dot. The barbarity of a dead mouse worn decoratively around the neck is an exception.

THE RHETORIC OF AGGRESSION

The relationship between jewelry and the body does not always have to be a loving one. In his series of engravings, the English artist William Hogarth did not conceive of "Marriage à la Mode" as a paradise – plenty of shrapnel flies around the battlefield of fashion. Many designers in recent decades have wondered whether the jewel actually caresses or torments the body. Exploring this idea was clearly seen as a challenge. It is virtually unheard of before 1968. Body decoration could occasionally be far from ornamental (take Steenbergen or Dumbar's spiky brooches, or the holes in a Neerincx brooch), but they were not intended to torment the wearer. It was not until the period of Body Art (1969–77) and within the realm of unusual expressions of body decoration like tattooing, piercing and Post-Punk jewelry, that Dutch designers too began to think differently about the sacredness of the body. A similar development occurred in art. Artists like Vito Acconci, Bruce Nauman and Dennis Oppenheim, who used and abused their bodies as a kind of modeling clay, began to draw attention. The exhibition "Sonsbeek buiten de perken" in Arnhem (1972) and performances at Stichting de Appel in Amsterdam (from 1975) brought their work to the attention of the Dutch public. Shows followed at the main museums in Amsterdam and Rotterdam, while "New York Body Covering" and "Bruce Nauman" were among the exhibitions staged at Eindhoven's Van Abbe Museum. Those with a more discerning eye could trace the development of this movement in art back to the early 1970s and art magazines like "Avalanche" (at the Art & Project gallery in Amsterdam).

Emmy van Leersum and her husband Gijs Bakker set the tone in this area, too. Both designers sought to alter the image of the woman, by means of such things as the large, heavy collars in anodized aluminum that they designed between 1967 and 1969.[41] The effect was that of the wearer's severed head resting on a plate. They looked like closely guarded ladies-in-waiting, and this on the eve of Women's Liberation in the early 1970s![42] It was a strange sight indeed when, at the First Biennale for Constructive Art ('Elemente und Prinzipien') in Nuremberg, 1969, Lin Dekkers walked proudly, if not very comfortably, through the galleries with one of these collars round her neck. What everybody saw was first and foremost the high, blue and gleaming collar, to which her body was subordinated. In 1974, Bakker made a profile jewel for his wife Emmy, which not only probed the contours of her face – and closed her mouth – with a steel wire, but also restrained her face with a horizontal line. It was like a tailor-made muzzle. Anyone wearing such an object would be totally silenced. Emmy was a difficult woman, he said much later. She always knew best and decided what had to be done in the workshop, even when her demands seemed impossible. In the only known photograph of the piece, Emmy van Leersum looks distinctly unhappy and wary in what looks like a facial chastity belt. It is an extraordinary piece, which perfectly expresses the love-hate relationship between jewel and body.

Wearing a bracelet from Emmy van Leersum's 1975 series of plastic cylinders could be hazardous, especially if you had small children. A sharp triangle protruded from them, on which you could seriously hurt someone.[43] Van Leersum was not, however, interested in the practical side of wearing jewelry. The important thing to her was the definition and unconventionality of a solution, and she was well aware of the fact. She once told the art-historian Dolf Welling: "I've worked with triangles a lot. There's something aggressive about them... A fundamental thing for me has also been linking a function with an action to create a form."[44] In 1973, she and her husband wound metal wire around an upper arm, left it there for a while and then removed it again. Provided it was done for long enough and sufficiently tightly, the arm would retain the marks for some considerable time. In this way, they created "shadow jewelry" that looks fabulous in photographs, but the process whereby it is created can still be felt, even through the photo. Pain can, however, be less important than a cultural statement. The realization of this shadow play was necessary to penetrate to the core of what jewelry can mean: more of an operation on the body than a decoration. Changing the body – performing an operation on it – brings to light a specific mentality that can conflict with the demand for bodily perfection. Breaking open the customary perfection and implanting a surprise, in order to be able to say something new, can represent an extraordinary stimulus. In the case of Van Leersum and Bakker, however, the shadow play was primarily intended to convey something new about the jewel itself. They were philosophers among designers. Their operations gathered a following. In 1979, for instance, the Swiss designer Otto Künzli embarked on his own windings. Aggression had been accepted, the floodgates had opened.

In 1986, Philip Sajet made a chain out of prickly balls made of black, sulfered silver and gold, with a diamond clasp. It makes the wearer's body as inaccessible as that of a medieval knight – a true delight for anyone capable of embracing it.[45] Herman Hermsen developed a ring with a double spike, and Ruudt Peters a necklace with a "Bullet Rose" (1992), the size and weight of which, with its black pearls on patinated silver, give it a martial character.[46] As always, the work of Maria Hees, who adapted an *objet trouvé*, has a more comic personality. She cut the handle off a plastic brush and had the wearer push it through a coarsely knitted jumper, so that only the bristles were visible (p. 180-181). It proved a great success and, among Amsterdam's gallery-goers in particular, it remained part of the fixed "opening repertoire" for many years. If you were brave enough to embrace one of the women wearing these "brooches", the plastic turned out to be not so painful after all, and the jewel immediately became a talking point that put a smile on people's faces. The same applied to the famous zip-fastener that Frans van Nieuwenborg/Martijn Wegman presented as a chain (p. 161). If you were to zip it up entirely, the wearer would be unable to breath. But a half-open zip? The jewel may have been too decorative for Punk, but aggression was gradually accepted.

Dinie Besems was the only designer to think about the pain that the ring could inflict on its wearer without anyone else noticing. Her ring, which she called "Blood Knickers" is shaped like a pair of underpants. With its three openings, it can be placed on the finger in a variety of ways. The shape is not the only thing that reminds us of a pair of women's knickers. It also contains a piece of red coral (known in Dutch as "bloedkoraal" or "blood coral") that can scrape the finger. It might even begin to bleed. No one sees it or knows about it. The wearer keeps the pain and the significance to herself.

A chain she made in 1995 reproduces all her scars and blemishes at that moment on small silver plates, so that someone else can now wear them as decoration. The maker evidently wished to pass them on in order to be rid of them. Scars can be a decoration. Her jewel is ugly, literal and figurative. The chain is an act of "outing" – the opposite of the "Blood Knickers" ring – with which the brave wearer has to identify.

DUTCH

JEWELRY

DESIGN

1950
2000

THE RHETORIC OF ETHNIC SOLIDARITY WITH OTHER CULTURES

The world is getting smaller, thanks not least to tourism. World citizens in the late 20th-century traveled en masse to the furthest corners of the world. The trend may have begun in earlier centuries, but the travellers of that period – who brought back foreign influences that artists were happy to seize on – can hardly be termed "globetrotters". These days, there is a flourishing trade in travel goods, while shops selling exotic furniture and accessories make a living responding to the desires of those who stay at home. The same romantic desire for far-away places can also be expressed through jewelry. European beads were once used as a means of exchange in Africa – now we are buying them back. Dutch porcelain has been produced after the Chinese model since the 17th century, but these days, shops offer tourists industrially manufactured necklaces with beads printed with Delft Blue windmills or flowers, all "typically Dutch".

Serious jewelry has, however, also been produced in this idiom. Nowadays, the Netherlands dispatches travelling exhibitions round the world to show how body decoration in our country has arisen through the transformation of foreign influences. This new direction has been conveyed through exhibitions like "Getooid versierd" (1991) and "Novidades da Holanda. Estudo sobre joias" (1990).[47] Essentially, the ethnic-looking jewel interiorizes the cross-culture aspect. Beppe Kessler has been working for a long time with dualistically selected hard and soft materials, with colorful, almost exotically exuberant fabrics. Some designers have looked to Japanese materials and methods, including Rian de Jong, Nel Linssen and Paul Derrez. Typical of this entire strand is the use of paper or textiles – a technique that dates back to 1967 with Paco Rabanne's paper dress.

Nowadays, the texture and structure of the fabrics are more important than ornamentation. Folds and creases rule the roost. This gives fabrics a tactile effect, to which the jewelry is attuned. Beppe Kessler's "Spinnaker Cloth" (1986) would not be immediately identified as "ethnic", because it uses cheery round patches from a frayed sail to form an entire strip around the neck. All the same, its soft and simple effect is reminiscent of ethnic costume. The entire strand is diametrically opposed to "The Dutch School", and seems to be a protest against its industrial, geometrical, austere and plasticized look. LAM de Wolf, for instance, has draped a jungle of painted silk chains over the wearer's back (1983) (p. 216-217),[48] while Marion Herbst makes small pieces of jewelry, in which she incorporates little feathers as a tribute to Native Americans. In other brooches, the rich colors of her textile "runners" seemingly refer to impressions of Mexico or Peru. Turned into brooches, they suddenly assume the significance of royal medals. The effect is comical, precisely

DUTCH

JEWELRY

DESIGN

1950
2000

because the ethnicity of the colorful ribbons seems to imply the uprating of the other culture. Herbst has also combined silver with gaudy threads and little bells or boats of unknown origin, which suggest some indeterminate ritual function (p. 187). Whatever the case, these objects certainly seem rooted somewhere other than the Netherlands. With her little leaves of carved ivory (taken from piano keys), meanwhile, Jacomijn van der Donk has introduced an African formal idiom into her work, giving her rings a winged appearance.

Although this jewelry is frequently extreme and not comparable with the traditional version from Africa, Peru, Mexico or India, the originals and copies of which are sold here in many shops, it no longer apparently wishes to duck the issue of "beauty". There has been a degree of formal exploration, but the process does not now seem to have been strictly calculated and controlled. Wearability and beauty are no longer notions that have simply been replaced by the concept or the technical idea of the construction. The ethnic jewel loves the body and its sexual aura, and does not oppose it. The earlier neutrality is no longer acceptable. What is more, ways have been found to allow free experimentation with unfamiliar materials, colors, methods and technical solutions – something that poses a challenge both maker and wearer.

Certain facets of the rhetoric discussed here, such as the urge to tell stories and the pull of other peoples are also present with certain variations in other countries. It is only in the Netherlands, however, that the mentalities I have described have featured so prominently in the pattern of development. Dutch designers have been constantly preoccupied by a different set of virtues, which they wished to convey by means of body decoration. In some cases, they have toyed with the expression of vices – Gijs Bakker being the chief protagonist in this respect. In so doing, he has essentially confirmed the almost pedagogical cult that his colleagues have attached to the making of jewelry. Beauty was introduced to its opposite – terror, or terrible beauty. The aggressive side of jewelry raised the human being's other side to the level of decoration, rendering it comprehensible through a kind of "outing" process. The image of the body was not always polished to perfection, but made recognizable as an ambiguous and hence enigmatic entity. Finally, the rise of ethnic jewelry has apparently put an end to the desire to formulate virtues (or vices) in this way.

Are these really obsessions, as Helen W. Drutt English and Peter Dormer would have us believe – passions even?[49] Explanations of this kind merely stress the psychological motives behind the process of creation. Obsessions and passions are based on single-mindedness and a sense of being unable to do otherwise. Viewed in this light, objectivity, freedom and choice all become superfluous. The development of Dutch jewelry, by contrast, has been the result of both sides of this mentality: obsession and objectivity. The work is certainly characterized by the obsessive pursuit of the most explicit possible mentality. Yet there is also a sense of objectivity – a pronounced interest in generating a debate about the work. Illustrations show that the general wearability of the piece is no longer an issue. More important is the uniqueness of the idea and the authenticity of the innovation, as, incidentally, has been the case in fine art for centuries. In this case, however, the primary purpose has been to use pictures to kick-start a debate about the art of jewelry as such. The wearer – ideal or otherwise – is encouraged to contribute to this debate. In this way, the wearer too can participate in a passionately communicated mentality and in a detached narrative concerning the potential for body decoration to "express itself" beyond its own boundaries.

[1] Benjamin, Walter: Berliner Kindheit um Neunzehnhundert, Gesammelte Schriften. Bd IV, Frankfurt a.M. 1950, quoted in 13 Goldschmiede p. 85.

[2] Cat. "Tekens & Ketens". Amsterdam 1993

[3] Cf. Mildner-Flesch, Ursula: Das Decorum. Herkunft, Wesen und Wirkung des Sujetstils am Beispiel Nicolas Poussins. Diss. Köln. Sankt Augustin 1983

[4] Jewelry Redefined. The 1st International Exhibition of Multi-Media Non-Precious Jewelry 1982. British Craft Center. London 1982

[5] Gijs Bakker: statement in: Tien jaar RA. Amsterdam 1986

[6] Cf. Schmitz, Hermann: Der Leib, der Raum und die Gefühle. Ostfildern vor Stuttgart 1998

[7] Cf. Barthes, Roland: Systeme de la mode. Paris 1967

[8] Emmy van Leersum, Gebroken Lijnen, 1930–1984. Museum het Kruithuis. 's-Hertogenbosch, Provinciaal Museum voor Moderne Kunst, Ostend 1993

[9] Holland in vorm. Design in Nederland 1945–1987. Gert Staal and Hester Wolters (eds.). The Hague, p. 205, no. 347

[10] Birgit Laken. Works in Mokumé. Metal in Motion. Amsterdam 1990

[11] Marijke de Goey. Blaricum 1997

[12] Chris Steenbergen. Edelsmid. Museum Boymans- van Beuningen Rotterdam 1985

[13] Quoted in: Tien jaar RA. Op cit.

[14] Nel Linssen 1986–1991. Nijmegen 1991

[15] See the publication by Stichting Françoise van den Bosch. Text by Victoria Bishop van Tuinen and Jerven Ober. Amsterdam 1987 and Ober, Jerven: Françoise van den Bosch 1944–1977 Naarden 1990

[16] Staal, Gert: Hans Appenzeller. Sieraden/Jewelry. Amsterdam 1982

[17] Von Graevenitz, Antje: Against Gravity, the Design of Bruno Ninaber van Eyben. In: DAAT, Dutch Art + Architecture Today. Bureau Beeldende Kunst Buitenland.12, 1982 p. 29

[18] Cat. Unica. Vereniging voor Edelsmeden en Sieradenontwerpers. Stedelijk Museum Amsterdam 1988 and Nederlands Goud- en Zilver- en Klokkenhuis, Schoonhoven 1988

[19] Multiples. Heden Verleden. Uitgave VES. Amsterdam 1986

[20] Marion Herbst, een overzicht 1969–82, prompted by her award of the Françoise van den Bosch Prize. Naarden 1982

[21] Cat. Objects to Wear. Featuring work by Emmy van Leersum and Gijs Bakker, Nicolaas van Beek, Bernard Laméris and Françoise van den Bosch. Smithsonian Institute, Washington DC, 1969. Toured the US after first being seen in Eindhoven, Rotterdam and The Hague, Staten.1969

[22] Mokveld, Monique: Een gesprek. Amersfoort 3.10.1985 in: Images, Sieraden, Schmuck, jewelry. Jubileumtentoonstelling VES (Vereniging Edelsmeden en Sieradenontwerpers, to mark the organization's tenth anniversary). Utrecht 1985 p. 21

[23] Turner, Ralph: Jewelry in Europe and America, New Times, New Thinking. London 1996 p. 21

[24] Uitgaven VES. View Review. Exhibition marking the VES's 15th anniversary. Amsterdam 1991

[25] Watkins, David: The Best in Contemporary Jewelry. London 1993

[26] The interaction between jewelry and sculpture is also discussed in: Onno Boekhoudt: Why not Jewelry? Text: Koos van Zomeren. Published by Reyn van der Lugt. Groninger Museum. Groningen 1998

[27] Cf. Cat. Marion Herbst 1968–93. Mag het iets meer zijn. Wijk and Aalburg 1993. The rebellious strand within this development was promoted by the exhibition and collection policy of Riet Neerincx, who was curator of the Gemeentemuseum in Arnhem until 1986.

[28] When Ralph Turner invited the group to show their work at London's Electrum Gallery in 1974, they were accept as equals by their colleagues.

[29] Cat. Ourobouros. Ruudt Peters. Introduction Jan Hein Sassen. Amsterdam 1995

[30] Robert Smit. Text by Theo van Gogh. Hrsg.v. Martin Pietribiari. Zurich 1997

[31] Smit showed his work, which swings like a pendulum between painting/drawing and jewelry, at the Amsterdam art gallery of Wim van Krimpen on several occasions. In the early 1990s, the latter's wife, Carin Delcourt, opened a gallery in Rotterdam, which rapidly began to specialise in art jewelry. By then, Galerie Swart had been actively tracking the shifting boundary between "free" and "decorative" art for some time. Galerie Seriaal, run by Wies Smals and Mia Visser, began to exhibit multiples by fine artists and serial works by jewelry designers in the late 1960s. Several jewelry galleries now exist: Galerie Sieraad in Amsterdam (founded by Lous Martin and Hans Appenzeller in 1959) followed by Galerie Ra (founded by Paul Derrez in 1976), Galerie Louise Smit and Leeuwarden's Galerie Ekster (run by Jullus Wijffels and Ruudt Peters).

[32] Ill. in : Dormer, Peter and Ralph Turner: The New Jewelry. Trends and Traditions. London 1985 no. 152

[33] Examples in: Staal, Gert: Gijs Bakker, vormgever. Solo voor een solist. The Hague 1989

[34] Lily van Ginneken in: Kunstschrift OKB Jg. Nov./Dec. 1982 p. 208 (special issue on Dutch jewelry)

[35] Drutt English, Helen W. and Peter Dormer: Jewelry of Our Time. Art, Ornament and Obsession. London 1996

[36] See Rizzoli Eleuteri, Lodovica (ed.): Twentieth-Century Jewelry. Art Nouveau to Modern Design. Milan, New York 1994 no. 120

[37] Cat. Jacomijn van der Donk. Text by Onno Boekhoudt. Waregem, Belgium 1995/96

[38] The Industrial Art of Gijs Bakker. A Dutch Production. Crafts Advisory Committee Gallery. London 1998

[39] Dorner, Peter and Ralph Turner: The New Jewelry. Trends & Traditions. London (1986), 1987; Staal, Gert: Beauty is a Story. Museum voor Hedendaagse Kunst Het Kruithuis, 's-Hertogenbosch, The Netherlands 1991

[40] Ted Noten. Amsterdam (1996)

[41] See Rodrigo, Evert: Body-Related Objects/Objets corporels. In: Concepts Comments Processes. Dutch Jewelry 1967–1987, Le bijou néerlandais. Rijksdienst Beeldende Kunst, Amsterdam, The Hague 1987 p. 8

[42] Cat. gijs bakker. d.h.r. ingenieursbureau dwars heederik en ver hey n.v. amersfoort 1972 afb.1 (Cat.6)

[43] Von Graevenitz, Antje: Instrumenten van radicaal denken. In: Emmy van Leersum/ Gebroken Lijnen 1930–1984. Op.cit. p. 14/15

[44] Haagsche Courant 15.4.80

[45] Philip Sajet: Elf Colliers. Amsterdam 1994

[46] Watkins Op.cit.

[47] Cat. Getooid versierd. Parure et Enjolivure. Adorned in Finery. Zierde und Schmuck. Organized by Gijs van Tuyl. Haarlem 1991; Cat. Novidades da Holanda. Estudo sobre joias. News from the Netherlands. A Jewelry Survey. Text by Marian Unger. Fundacao Calouste Gulbankian, Lisboa. Dutch Form, Foundation, Amsterdam 1990

[48] Cat. LAM de Wolf. ICC/ Internationaal Cultureel Centrum. Antwerp 1986

[49] Drutt English, Helen W. and Peter Dormer: Jewelry of Our Time. Ornament and Obsessions. London 1966 – Passion and Profession. Sieraden toen en straks, twintig jaar, Jewelry in Past, Present and Future. Introduction: Gert Staal. Amsterdam 1996

JEWELS
of Mind and Mentality

JEWELS
of Mind and Mentality

DUTCH JEWELRY DESIGN
1950 – 2000

NEW JEWELRY FOR A RENEWED COUNTRY, 1950-2000

Jaap Huisman

DUTCH
JEWELRY
DESIGN
1950
2000

JEWELS
of Mind and Mentality

Onno Boekhoudt lives in isolation in the Frisian countryside, where he searches and searches for the shape of his "things", as he describes his jewelry. Foraging, sampling and tinkering lead to a ring, from which he saws out the shape of a little wooden house (p. 277). The name of the ring – Room for the Finger – describes the extra layer the designer has given the piece. It is an intensely personal quest for a thing intended as decoration for its wearer. Or is it? Although Boekhoudt's work is labeled as jewelry, it could equally well be called art. He slips a ring onto the finger in precisely the same way that he hangs a sculpture in the form of an elongated iron on the front of a house in Norway. The ring, or rather the circle, is the leitmotif in his work, to which he attaches all kinds of meaning.

The city-dweller Gijs Bakker is Boekhoudt's opposite. He skips from perspex to laminate and from diamonds to plastic, producing jewelry that looks as if it has been manufactured industrially, but which actually has an artisanal background. Where Boekhoudt sought to fathom the essence of jewelry at the Kunst- und Werkschule in Pforzheim, Germany, Bakker shattered the conventional ideas about jewels by choosing materials and forms that had never previously been associated with the human body. His chief interest is in the combination of everyday images with extremely precious stones, like diamonds. He makes jewelry because he wants to convey a message.

These are two designers out of the many that the Netherlands has produced since 1950. Both have attracted followers and have trained a whole series of pupils, in whose work the nature and extent of their influence has yet to become clear. It says a great deal that their former pupils – Boekhoudt's at the Rietveld Academie, Bakker's at the Hogeschool voor de Kunsten in Arnhem – have tended to work in their teacher's spirit until they were able to find their own formal idiom. Without that influence, they would not have embarked on the same road and would not have had the same ideas. Having set off on their own, they evolved towards a more personal style, as we see in the work of Annelies Planteijdt, a former pupil of Boekhoudt, who gave her necklaces a similarly poetic eloquence, but became more and more affected by the craft tradition of the goldsmith. Or Maria Hees and Herman Hermsen, who, having studied under Bakker, went on to produce industrial-looking "multiples" in limited series, but with their own character and presence. The tone was established around 1975 and the result was a procession of designers determined to produce individual jewelry.

No matter how variegated that landscape, Boekhoudt and Bakker might reasonably be taken as models of the different strands within Dutch jewelry, even if

the appearance of their designs is somewhat deceptive. In reality, the spectrum is both wider and more nuanced. All the same, it is arguable that they both seek the extremes of the jewel, one in terms of its poetic, cerebral aspect, the other in those of its business-like and communicative element. Extremes yes, but there are similarities, too. They both stress, albeit in widely divergent ways, their fascination for that small object on which you can unleash your ideas. Jewelry offers a miniature canvas for a miniature brush. Another thing they have in common is a lack of interest in prestige – still a crucial aspect of goldsmithing in the 1950s. When it comes to expressing form, anything goes. Wood or corroded iron for one, laminate or diamonds for the other.

As I have suggested, Dutch jewelry cannot be tied down to two founding figures. It has been nourished since the 1960s by a much more varied company than that. It has expanded, it has become polymorphic, it is ingenious and rooted in the present – more compulsively in some cases than in others.

SCULPTURE

The roots of the impetuous growth experienced by modern jewelry lie in the 1950s. Esther Swart-Hudig, Archibald Dumbar, Chris Steenbergen and later Nicolaas van Beek all produced progressive jewelry – an unusual choice at a time when everything still revolved around gold, silver and precious stones. Their work was progressive in the sense that it gradually broke with the conventions of the goldsmith's craft as taught at the Rijksvak- en Kunstnijverheidsschool in Schoonhoven since 1920. In many cases, inspiration did not come from the world of jewelry itself, but from the sculpture of Naum Gabo and Henry Moore and their plastic, organic forms. The conservative Gold and Silver Federation looked on warily at the new crop of jewelers emerging from the academies in Amsterdam, Arnhem and Maastricht – students who were more interested in form and concept than in technical mastery.

The modern jewel had to blaze its own trail. There was no craft tradition in the Netherlands worth speaking of, and ever since the 17th-century "Golden Age", Dutch people have been conditioned against flaunting expensive jewelry. Luxury and ornament flourished in the home and not on the body. In the 1950s and early 60s, there was only one mode of expression – the traditional jeweler's craft with its necklaces and strings of pearls. That monopoly was shattered in 1967 by the sensational "Sieraad III" show at Amsterdam's Stedelijk Museum, in which Gijs Bakker and his wife and designer Emmy van Leersum, had women walking around with stovepipes round their necks (p. 110-111-112). These were objects that were not immediately identifiable as jewelry, and materials that had no relationship with ideas

DUTCH

JEWELRY

DESIGN

1950
–
2000

of "decoration". The exhibition set the tone for what came afterwards.

The movement preached the "exaltation of form", to which the material was more or less subordinate. Bakker: "Form follows concept. That's how it has always been with me." The movement set sail towards industrial jewelry, which it defined as formal products linked to the formal and conceptual art of the period and the prevailing ideas of democracy. The aim was to make things that a wide and socially varied public could understand and perhaps also afford. In this respect, Bakker and Van Leersum were children and mirrors of their time. They adopted the principle that form should always be linked to the body and that it should always function as the packaging of an idea. Decoration and prestige for their own sake were not acceptable, as they interfere with the direct link between clothing and jewelry. What's more, to focus attention on the jewel, Bakker and Van Leersum designed provocatively large wearable objects and experimented with reproduction – the only way for designers to present themselves to a wide audience. They were assisted in this by the first large-scale exhibitions, which were held at a wide range of venues, including the Kapelhuis in Amersfoort, Galerie Nouvelles Images in The Hague, the Van Reekum Museum in Apeldoorn and the Stedelijk Museum in Amsterdam.

The conceptual element that remained dominant for many years – virtually until 1980 – underpinned the "object to wear" – a state of affairs that came in for a degree of criticism. When Hans Appenzeller opened a gallery and shop in New York in 1983, enabling him to compare attitudes there with those in the Netherlands, he realised that decoration is actually taboo for Dutch people – something superfluous. "That's why they seek refuge in the concept."

DEMOCRATIC

You do not only wear what you can afford, but also what you dare to wear. The message being conveyed was that jewelry had to be for everyone. Democracy was the watchword. This was the spirit in which Hans Appenzeller and Lous Marin opened Amsterdam's Galerie Sier(r)aad in 1969, the focus of which was on formal, serially produced jewelry in materials like perspex, aluminum and rubber, which had not hitherto been associated with body decoration (p. 142/151).

Before long, however, the style became somewhat debased, with disciples of Van Leersum and co. beginning to churn out multiples – serially produced jewels lacking any personal signature. The sober, geometric design earned this jewelry the title of "Dutch Smooth" (Hollands Glad) – a name that called out for a reaction, which wasn't long in coming. Marion Herbst in particular sought to resist it, beginning in 1968 with her "Jewelry Action Group", which she christened the BOE – the Bond van

Ontevreden Edelsmeden ('League of Rebellious Goldsmiths'), to which Onno Boekhoudt, Françoise van den Bosch, Berend Peter Hogen Esch and Karel Niehorster also belonged. In 1974, the group issued its "BOE Box". It served as a manifesto, containing as it did miniature works by a wide variety of artists who wished to break the monopoly of "Dutch Smooth" – "smooth" being understood to mean impersonal, anonymous and neutral (p. 160). Herbst and her group wanted jewelry capable of expressing perspective through humor and statements. In so doing, they gave a clear signal – grayish-white is not the only color on the palette.

GROWN-UP

The split in the jewelry world had begun. At the same time, a realization was growing that a professional organization was needed to defend designers' interests and to promote design. The VES (Vereniging van Edelsmeden en Sieraadontwerpers – Association of Goldsmiths, Silversmiths and Jewelry Designers) was duly founded in 1975. Regular exhibitions at the Stedelijk Museum and abroad emphasized the fact that the discipline was growing up and that it was, indeed, possible to get a group of individual designers to pull together. This was the period in which Dutch design flourished – a fact that did not go unnoticed outside the country. Exhibitions abroad, including "Objects to Wear" in 1969, showed that there was a market for pioneering, formal and conceptual jewelry.

The strict, and perhaps dogmatic, elements of the 1960s were now left behind. Different flowers could bloom. In the work of people like Bruno Ninaber van Eyben, Frans van Nieuwenborg/Martijn Wegman (p. 141-165-168-169) and Gijs Bakker, jewelry design came close at this stage to industrial design. This was a logical development at a time when industry in the Netherlands was beginning to develop an eye for the intrinsic value and appearance of its products. Burgeoning interest in this regard also fed through into restrained jewelry designs: a taste for luxury could also be expressed in a "less is more" product in aluminum or plastic. Marion Herbst and, a little later, LAM de Wolf, introduced a sculptural and expressive element. Meanwhile, as the emancipation of jewelry advanced, the variety of materials used by makers increased. In 1976, Robert Smit presented brooches made from Polaroid photographs, while the early 1980s saw the rise of textiles, influenced by British colleges (in the work of Herbst (p. 187), De Wolf (p. 217) and Joke Brakman (p. 222)), and combinations of papier-mâché and rubber in a bracelet by Willem Honing (p. 214) and the early work of Annelies Planteijdt.

In spite of the best efforts of the VES and the promotional work carried out by galleries and museums, modern jewelry remained the preserve of the privileged few after its breakthrough around 1967. All the same, no matter how neat its categorization, jewelry remains a reflection of fashions in society. The jewel measures the pulse of its period, adopting meanings and layers. It is here that the discipline derives its power. The way the jewel developed from a piece of "decorative art" into an autonomous mode of artistic expression is sufficient in itself to illustrate the changing position of designers in society. Having found it difficult to persuade industry to produce serial jewelry, designers returned to their workshops in the period after 1975, to make one-off or limited edition jewels. As one might expect in a society that was focusing increasingly on appearance and effect, the source of inspiration was fine art rather than fashion or design.

In 1978, the Netherlands was overtaken as the main center of pioneering jewelry design by Britain, where a playful approach to the jewel had arisen. More color, more collages of unorthodox materials and, above all, less dogma. The supply of innovatory Dutch designers dried up and the Netherlands entered the 1980s in a spirit of fragmentation, reflection and inward-looking works, which lacked the classic aura of the earlier, formal jewelry. Where the 1970s had focused on the potential for producing jewelry in the form of multiples, the 1980s were dominated by individual exploration. Appenzeller's statement "This Ring is Me" identifies the new core of Dutch jewelry. The jewel was transformed from a neutral and formal object to wear into an individual document designed to emphasize personality. Visual qualities became steadily more important.

The use of expressive materials, such as papier-mâché, wood and metal wire was a logical development. The brakes were taken off in painting too, as in the "Wild Painting" coming out of Germany, while the Punk movement in Britain seemed to be pursuing an Umwertung aller Werte. The explosion was short but intense. It was rapidly followed by a renewed urge to see precious metals, as we find in the work of Philip Sajet and Annelies Planteijdt, which seems to call for the reestablishment of the goldsmith's craft. Gold, lapis lazuli, sapphires, and so forth were all permissible again by the latter half of the 1980s. Even Gijs Bakker began to use diamonds, albeit juxtaposed with everyday materials like laminated newspaper photographs of sporting figures.

The brooch, which had lain rather dormant since the late 1960s, when it had come to be seen as a little painting or object, mounted on a safety pin, now made a comeback. The development was illustrative of the desire for decoration and even for frills. It also proved to be an interesting vehicle for anecdotalism and symbolism – more so, for instance, than a bracelet can be. Lucy Sarneel has sought combinations of zinc and gold (and later the effect of corroded iron), while for

Marion Herbst, no material is taboo (wood, papier-mâché, gold leaf) when it comes to expressing herself within a small surface area. Even Onno Boekhoudt has produced small brooch objects.

Surveying the situation at the end of the 1980s, we find a dizzying range of expression and forms, in pinch rings, plaited necklaces, pendants with a Roman Catholic flavor and ingenious bracelets. The end of the 20th century in the Netherlands was a period of eclecticism. Society was ready to accept a greater element of aesthetics, decoration and exclusivity and this showed through in design, which experienced a boom, and also gradually in jewelry design.

TO WEAR OR NOT?

The Rietveld Academy has undoubtedly had a significant influence on this colorful flow of designs. Teachers like Onno Boekhoudt, Ruudt Peters, Marion Herbst and LAM de Wolf have all provided students with their artistic training. By the 1990s, decorative art and "Dutch Smooth" seemed a million miles away.

From around 1985, as social relevance and the "democratic ideal" steadily faded as goals to be pursued by jewelry, different aspects became more important. These included the designer's personal "signature", the ritual character of the jewel and its sensuality. To a designer like Sarneel, there is a story attached to her little boxes and cases, while for others – Robert Smit, for example, who returned to jewelry design at this point after a brief absence – brooches became collages with humorous references, like Smit's "Bello" series, each of which features a dog surrounded by gold and painted pearls.

Is a jewel still a jewel when it is not being worn? This was a question that gained in relevance in the 1990s, as jewelry continued to develop towards the status of an autonomous "thing". The body is both present and absent. In the 1960s, it was emphatically present as the servant for wearing, but two decades later, that link was sometimes entirely absent, as we find in the conceptual jewels of Dinie Besems, who views the body in a broader context – as a spatial being. This is a remarkable development, as the converse need has arisen in fine art to choose the body as an object for manipulations and transformations. Dutch jewelry designers have yet to go quite that far. Their designs could be autonomous art objects – a development that Marijke de Goey and LAM de Wolf, for instance, have been through – or almost classic additions to the body, as testified by the necklaces designed by Planteijdt, Sajet and Appenzeller. Nevertheless, they are entirely of their time, providing as they do an abstract transposition of the classic neckchain. In the case of other designers, the jewel cannot be seen in isolation from the body: this is so, for instance, in the

DUTCH

JEWELRY

DESIGN

1950
2000

case of Joke Brakman's canvases, which only take on their form when draped over the shoulder (p. 220-221), and that of Paul Derrez' enormous collar (p. 212-213), which bends and folds around the neck. Likewise, the huge, fabric-wrapped stick frameworks of LAM de Wolf can only be conceived of in relation to the body (p. 204). To put it more strongly, they require an attitude. The jewel that folds, slides and dances with every movement belongs to a trend that began in the 1960s and which has remained a constant in the final two decades of the 20th century. It is a symbol of dynamism in every respect.

Modernism and the principle of "less is more" are now played out. Jewelers never disappeared and designers – some of them at least – have all but joined their ranks. Romanticism has replaced formalism. The jewelry landscape differs entirely from that of the Dutch countryside – it undulates and varies between harsh and charming. It is all so unpredictable compared to what happened in the years after 1965.

THE BIRTH OF FASCINATION

There is a moment when it starts: at the age of four, perhaps, when your eye is caught by the sparkling of a stone, or for another, because you were fascinated as a child by something as mundane as a thread. Before you know it, you have become a jewelry designer and would-be buyers– museums or collectors – are knocking on your door. Your passport gives "designer" or "artist" as your profession.

After the war, Riet Neerincx went to London to study at the Central School of Arts. She remembers being "good with her hands" as a child, and was mad about handicrafts. Her talent as a goldsmith was quickly recognized when, in 1952, she entered a competition organized by the Netherlands Federation of Goldsmiths and Silversmiths to design a brooch. Neerincx won the contest with a prosaic-sounding design called Pea. It was an organically formed brooch, carefully documented and drawn with shadow lines (a technique she had picked up in London). The unusual feature of her design was that her jewel lacked a stone. "A stone ties you down so", she admitted. The winning design went into production, for which the designer was awarded a one-off payment of 125 guilders. "The finished product cost so much that I couldn't afford to buy one for myself. I searched the flea markets to see if I could find one of the brooches, but no. Sadly, I never had any luck". Neerincx' Pea got her into the newspapers, where, to her surprise, she was mentioned in virtually the same breath as Einstein. "Arnhem goldsmith wins prize", the headlines read. Neerincx' name was established. It was an orderly period, she recalls; a cosy little club. Not much went on – just Archibald Dumbar and Riet Neerincx regularly winning prizes.

JEWELS
of Mind and Mentality

She actually wanted to be an industrial designer and she studied to that end under Frans Zwollo, who was very successful at the time (as we said, there wasn't much going on just after the war...). After 1954, design was to play a less prominent part in her life. Having first taken a secretary's job at the Gemeentemuseum in Arnhem, she became its curator, catapulting her into a central position in terms of purchasing jewelry and decorative art.

MAKING MAGIC

"I started in this trade because I wanted to get away from intellectual things", explains Onno Boekhoudt, recalling the roots of his art. "I'm a tinkerer, I like to make things. Consequently, I was more attracted to setting stones than to drawing. It's an idea or a line from a book that gets me going. I look for several different things, I never head straight for my destination." He enrolled at the goldsmiths' college in Schoonhoven, because that's what you did in the early sixties, and began to train as a goldsmith. It was too dull for him, however, and so he switched to night school in Utrecht, where his creative bent could be better appreciated. Not that he had come to dislike gold and silver — on the contrary, the beauty of silver was later to charm him more and more — but at this stage, he was more taken with the expressive aspect of things. Things, he said, not jewels. "Making magic, that's what I want to do".

From Schoonhoven and Utrecht, he found his way to the Hoheschule in Pforzheim, where Robert Smit was the only Dutchman to have preceded him. In the 1960s, Pforzheim was just as famous for jewelry as the Fachhochschule in Ulm was for industrial design. This, Boekhoudt felt, was where it was all happening. It was an international meeting point for Norwegians, Britons and Italians, who were all attracted to the expressive aspect of jewelry making. "The image was important in Pforzheim. The material was paint, and gold is a pretty good paint. You could come up with an expensive blue, almost without trying."

The Netherlands, with its Constructivist tendencies and attraction to formal art, seemed a long way away in Germany. The first jewels they saw raised a smile — they found them amusing but not sufficiently attractive. Boekhoudt tinkered in the evenings, while mastering the classic skills in the day. "I remember making one thing, a necklace, which my teacher told me was straight off a fairground. Crap, I thought, what's he talking about? Everything had to be little for the Germans — they couldn't cope with the huge size of my necklace. When they saw it being worn, though, they were won over."

Boekhoudt remained a pioneer on returning to the Netherlands, where modern jewelry continued to be practiced on only a small scale. Ton Berends from the gallery

DUTCH

JEWELRY

DESIGN

1950
—
2000

Nouvelles Images in The Hague became his agent – "someone else with international interests". His first exhibition at the Kapelhuis in Amersfoort in 1970 was dismissed by the newspaper NRC as "pretty paintings, but too small"'. He laughs about it now. "I understood those reviews, but I felt I was above them. I had so much self-confidence at the time that I didn't care. I was strong. And I knew that my work was different from the usual Dutch standard."

BEADS AND WIRES

Gijs Bakker organized a parade in his home town of Amersfoort, for which he spent weeks working on the floats in a near trance. But when the parade happened, he wasn't at the front of the crowd watching it go past, but hidden and anonymous in the thick of it. "I enjoyed seeing people's reactions when the parade went by, but I was also very detached from it." He did not make an explicit decision to start designing jewelry. His father ran a garage in Amersfoort and couldn't do anything with the boy. In 1958, he let him enroll at the Rietveld Academy. "I remember hesitating between interior design, fashion and jewelry design. I don't know why I chose the latter. Probably because the department was friendlier." He learned the basics of the craft from Marinus Zwollo – how to work with copper, developing a physical sense of the material.

A photograph is all that remains of the first jewel that meant anything to him. For the first time, Bakker had a sense of escaping the tyranny of the ring and the ornament mounted on it by designing a trapezium-shaped jewel with a longitudinal stripe at the top of the finger but which, when turned around, was cross-shaped. "I've got something here", he thought excitedly, "I can get away from the classic form".

Emmy van Leersum (1930–1984) was the daughter of a coachwork builder. That brought her into indirect contact with the car industry, which retained its craft features at that time. The large steel sheets from which car doors and bonnets were molded probably sowed the seeds of the spatial constructions she would make in later life. He conversion to jewelry came relatively late – after she had escaped her first marriage in 1958. She enrolled at Amsterdam's Decorative Art Institute (the later Rietveld Academy), where she was seduced by "beads and wires". The foundations of what was to become "typical Van Leersum" were laid as she studied under Marinus Zwollo and met Gijs Bakker, who was initially just a friend. She developed an almost ascetic way of living, linked to perfectionism in her design of objects. Gijs Bakker remembers her 1966 Propeller Bracelet (p. 106-107) as a crucial step in her development, made as it was from aluminum and anodized to boot. "It could equally well have been made from silver, but Emmy did it in aluminum."

FASTENER

Hans Appenzeller originally wanted to be an interior designer. While studying at Amsterdam's Rietveld Academy, however, he realised that that meant designing houses that you never got to live in yourself. And that you had to deal with a client and a forest of building regulations. He was sold on the idea of jewelry making when he visited the designer Nicolaas van Beek at his farm in Bronkhorst some time around 1967. The idea of that kind of existence appealed to him: "He made things himself, he sold them himself and he could take off in any direction he wanted." The wonderful thing about jewelry, he discovered, was "its instant visual gratification".

In a former sitting room over his shop in Amsterdam, Appenzeller returns to his first jewels from 1972 – robust metal bracelets with an ingenious rubber fastener that you had to slide up your wrist. The bracelet immediately became a museum piece, not least because of the art collector Benno Premsela, who recognized the power of the design. The piece takes the fastener as its point of departure. "I was always fascinated by those hidden little locks on chains. The way they were incorporated. I just thought I'd turn the thing around. The fastener became the jewel."

Paul Derrez' father was a watchmaker and his grandfather a goldsmith, so it was quite natural for him to become a jeweler. There was, however, something of a detour along the way. This took him to Eindhoven's Academy of Industrial Design, where he finally got fed up designing yet another Philips-style toaster and switched one day to the Academy of Word and Gesture in Utrecht, where he thought he would study movement and dance. The director of studies soon changed his mind – "We provide professional training," he told Derrez, "not therapy". This was the beginning of the 1970s, at which point the future designer realised he would be better off doing the things he was good at.

Having trained at Schoonhoven and completed an internship at Lous Martin and Hans Appenzeller's Galerie Sieraad, he concluded that jewelry was his strong point: "Everything comes together – presentation, making and the thing itself". He was actually more interested in "that thing" than in people. Or rather, he is better at it than at using "the person as material". He takes his first jewel from the cupboard. What to him was initially a statement has since become a classic. The Swap Ring proved its value as a good entry-level design for the up-and-coming jewelry fan, in that it is striking without being too conspicuous. The system is simple – the user can swap the colored perspex ornament, while the actual ring – a double golden circle – remains as the basis. Although it is a serial product, the buyer feels that it is unique, as it always has to be adapted to the finger.

The ring, which dates from 1975, was influenced by what he saw and learned at

Galerie Sieraad. It was a geometrical period, with triangles, cylinders and squares as shaping elements, the trail for which had already been blazed by Appenzeller, Bakker and Van Leersum. "I came later. I realized that I'd made a detour by the mere fact of coming from Sittard. Until I made my real choice in Amsterdam and said 'here I stay – this is where I will become a jewelry designer'." His late arrival did not prove to be a problem for the Swap Ring. On the contrary, his first design proved a lasting product at his gallery.

BUTTONS AND THREAD

Marion Herbst, who died in 1994, had her roots in fine art. In a letter to Galerie Sier(r)aad, in late 1973, she answered the question of how she came to be a jewelry designer: "After training as a sculptor, I began to work with jewelry because it was easier to handle. It actually seemed to happen by itself."

We know that Françoise van den Bosch (1944–1977) had already developed a fascination for pure geometric form – as embodied in the triangle and circle – during her study period. Goldsmithing, which she learned at Arnhem's Academy of Applied Art in 1964, was a logical step for Van den Bosch, who came from a well-off family. She found herself in the company of other genteel young women and the goldsmith's art gave her the opportunity to study a trade while also being creative. Her early attraction to decorative art was apparent when she designed her own stationery – something she was to repeat in 1977 when she designed the lettering for a medal for the Dutch Post Office.

While her friends were playing with their dolls, LAM de Wolf preferred her mother's sewing box. "I later realised that what I liked were the simple things you could use to make something. I've always been interested in textiles. I used buttons and thread to make a bracelet, where other children would have used beads." She got her name from a pool manager who presented her with a swimming certificate. She was actually called Loes – short for Louise Antonia Maria. "You should call yourself Lam", the pool manager said. "Lam de Wolf – then you'll be famous one day." Without realizing it, it was then that she took her first steps on the road to becoming an artist, with a name – literally "Lamb the Wolf" – that embodied a contradiction and a constant – things that can be stroked. De Wolf had been converted to textiles, which she would raise to the level of jewelry.

Lucy Sarneel's earliest memory of her fascination for jewelry is of a ring that she wore when she was four years old. It had a polished stone that glittered in the sun when she moved it around. It lasted until the day that it slipped off her finger and disappeared into the bushes. The Sarneels moved house a year later. "I drew a lot as a child. I started at a very early age and it was encouraged in the family, because my father used to paint. I remember drawing branches in a gold and silver pen that I adored – branches with seeds on. That was a kind of jewel already."

She decided that becoming an artist was too obvious and that she'd rather work with children. She enrolled at a College of Social Studies. "I can see now that I was just trying to break away from my father." But breeding will out, and she ended up at the Municipal Academy of Art in Maastricht, which taught "classic" goldsmithing, and then at the Rietveld Academy in Amsterdam. "I remember a classic goldsmith who displayed his work in niches in the wall. I thought it was magical, the way the welds were concealed in the ring. It was like sorcery, being able to do that. That you could make things that you couldn't see." This feeling was to determine Sarneel's career. Seeing and not being seen – and all measured in square centimetres.

Dinie Besems began by making earrings. Her ambition, however, was not to be a jeweler at all. At the age of ten, she fell under the spell of Jackson Pollock's abstract art, which freed her imagination, and Mondrian, whose white rectangles, she could fill in herself. "I was doing technical and vocational education and I wanted to be an artist. My dream was shattered when I found out you needed to be in higher general education to do that." She then thought of becoming a goldsmith, which took her along the route followed by many a Dutch artist – the "Schoonhoven route". She began at the college in Schoonhoven, moved to the one in Arnhem, where she never quite settled, and then ended up at the Rietveld Academy in Amsterdam.

Her first piece, if we don't count the little chain she made at nursery school from an old margarine tub, forgetting to go to the toilet in the process, was the square ring she made at Schoonhoven. This was the ring that, for a few seconds, had her floating on air, the one that made her realize that she was an artist. The piece ran away with her for a moment. "I made a square ring and I was so proud of the way I had sawed the joints. I dripped gold onto it and then painted it black, to create a panther pattern. This will remain, I thought, just like the Night Watch remains."

TECHNIQUE AND MATERIALS

In the years after the Second World War, Riet Neerincx continued to work in sawn-out copper, which she attached in the manner of stained-glass windows using drips of enamel. She also produced gold and silver cigarette-holders and jewel-boxes in those early years. The jewelry world in the 1950s Netherlands was a straightforward place. The first thing people bought or were given was a watch. Then came the wedding ring and finally the brooch. Neerincx designed brooches, brooches and more brooches. It is a jewel, she says, with a handicap, "Because it has to be worn

on something. It has to be attached to the fabric. It is not a thing in its own right."

When she was appointed decorative art curator at Arnhem Municipal Museum in 1952, she witnessed the development of a conservative and restrictive discipline into a rich and valued strand of Dutch art. Silver, gold and precious stones were joined by stainless steel, plastic, fabric, wood and who knows what other materials. "Looking back, I sometimes think that artists sought refuge in those other materials because they didn't need a maker's mark. Plus the fact that gold was expensive." As a curator, meanwhile, she was well aware of the fact that silver invariably tarnishes and attracts dirt, even when kept in a sealed container. "You're always having to clean it." All the same, one of her favorite rings is made of silver. It has an abstract diamond shape on the band. "You can stand on it and nothing would happen."

The older Boekhoudt gets, he admits, the more he is attracted to silver. Throughout his career, however, he has turned to all kinds of materials to convey his ideas. Wood, stones, rusty steel – it doesn't matter. "I don't really focus on the outside." He can spend weeks and even months working on a design, scratching out his ideas on paper with a draftsman's pen – ideas like how to turn a pair of swimming trunks into a ring. Figuratively, that is. Finally, he has the design executed on a lathe or using a mould. "One idea isn't enough for me. A piece of jewelry has to have several layers, so that it can constantly be reinterpreted. It has to have more than one meaning. Then I don't have to worry so much about anyone copying it, as it will be strong enough." No one can steal that kind of idea.

Yet the final result is not Boekhoudt's principal concern – a fact that he impresses on his students at London's RCA and previously on those at the Rietveld Academy in Amsterdam. "The making of the piece is virtually everything. It's about what you discover in the process." That's how he works himself. From time to time, he leaves an unfinished piece in his workshop, suddenly returning to it when it demands his attention again.

Boekhoudt acknowledges that his way of working has changed. Twenty years ago, he couldn't do what he wanted. Now he can, "and that's damned hard". The pressure increases, as does the amount of reflection about your work, because you can't just rely on the technique you crammed in during your training. "I spend more time on my jewelry nowadays. I like to compare myself with the Japanese, who think that you don't become a true craftsman until you're 60."

Van Leersum and Bakker made their breakthrough in the 1960s with materials not previously associated with jewelry – stainless steel, aluminum and, later, plastics. It was jewelry as a social and democratic mode of expression, rooted in the Constructivist Art of which Bob Bonies, Ad Dekkers and Peter Struycken were the embodiment. The group met and stimulated one another at Riekje Swart's gallery in

Amsterdam – the epicenter of a new artistic movement around 1968.

Bakker: "We had a positive view of the future, even before the moon landing. There was a belief that you could make design anonymous, that you could leave out the personal signature. It might seem naïve now, but that's what we believed at the time." It lasted until the mid-1970s. According to Bakker, the turning point came with his shadow jewelry, which left its imprint on the arm after it was removed. The era of "Dutch Smooth" was over. It was all right for jewelry to be expensive again – objects of desire – and Bakker began to experiment with the confrontation of extremes, such as laminated newspaper photographs and diamonds. What he sought to create was something everyday and something precious on the same level and in the same image. It was a challenge that could be tremendously exciting when it worked. "First and foremost, it was a challenge to myself. That's why I consider making jewelry to be the core of my work. It contains everything. For me, design has always been a derivative of jewelry and by making jewels, I am in the vanguard. In other disciplines, I often feel like a spectator, but not with jewelry."

Françoise van den Bosch worked in parallel with Bakker and Van Leersum, and certainly not in their shadow. She specialized in industrial-looking jewelry, such as her famous 1971 bracelet consisting of two aluminum semi-circles that grip one another (p. 140). Van den Bosch pursued a calm, simple and geometric design consisting of clear lines and honest materials. Her modest body of work displays an urge towards spatiality – enlarged versions of her jewelry could almost be sculpture. They were not necessarily linked to the body, but were objective and autonomous objects, as befitted the period 1969–75. Still, they remained objects to wear.

REVOLUTIONARY

The neutrality of Dutch Smooth prompted a reaction. Neerincx remembers how Marion Herbst turned up one day in 1969 at the Kapelhuis gallery in Amersfoort, which was a leading center of jewelry design at the time. She asked if she could take part in the Jewelry 69 exhibition and was promptly placed on the cover of the catalogue with a highly personal and expressive necklace. It had to come, Neerincx thought. Van Leersum and Bakker's monopoly was crying out for a reaction. "What Herbst did was revolutionary. She threw a real spanner in the works." Herbst could be fascinated by an everyday object – a shower hose, say, or a salad basket – which she magically transformed into a bracelet or necklace (p. 138-139). She hung a piece of weaving from a stick (p. 187) and painted a sheet of iron in a lyrical abstract style. Herbst's miniature sculptures were the product of prior research. She was particularly interested in questioning the essence of existing things. She said in a 1993

interview that "Knowing is pleasant but passive. Not knowing is disturbing but active. Activity invites a reaction, it invites you to take a stance. And that stance can then be undermined, and so on and so forth." In the early years – round about 1970 – Herbst's research focused on the combination of precious metals with plastics – gold and silver with perspex, for instance. She began to experiment in 1981 with steel wire, which she wrapped in paper, and with the painting of little pieces of wood.

Marion Herbst shares her plastic artist's gaze with LAM de Wolf. De Wolf, however, who began to make her presence felt in the early 1980s, sees herself as more experimental than Herbst. She describes her way of working in the following terms: "I'm seized by a material, a word, a text or an image and go to work like one possessed. It grows in my hands. The work itself only arises through doing." A word is all it takes to get De Wolf going: "Bitter", for instance, or "Eensaam" – an invented word with all sorts of connotations, from "one" and "together" to "once" and "lonely". She arrived almost automatically at textiles, strips and pieces of wire, which she paints and winds around satay sticks to create almost architectural structures (p. 199). "I need the stick to fix the shape, because you can't do that with fabric on its own. The textiles then hold the whole thing together. I once tried it with iron, but that rusts when you put glue on it."

PLEATS AND FOLDS

Around 1974, Hans Appenzeller had second thoughts about offering the public big plastic bracelets, which were on sale at the Bijenkorf department store (p. 144/147). They were made of multicolored transparent plastic and cost an affordable 15 guilders. And no one wanted them. Appenzeller realised that jewelry had to be desirable and not a democratic mass product. His favorite material is metal, because you can polish, flatten, hammer, emboss and cast it. "I can get effects with it that are impossible with other materials. That's why I could never be a sculptor: I can work this way." As his career progressed, he added precious stones, having realised that it took a certain amount of nerve to wear a piece of jewelry. "I opened a shop in New York's Madison Avenue, where I was a total nobody. I noticed that American women were totally uninterested in the ideas that dominated the Netherlands at the time. Jewelry really did mean jewels – it demanded a gesture on the wearer's part."

That did not, however, prevent Appenzeller from returning to plastics in the latter half of the 1980s. He opted on this occasion for Corian – an expensive plastic, through which he inserted rubber strings. These were 350 guilder bracelets that had evidently taken a lot of hard work to produce. They had a lot more appeal than the cheap versions of a decade earlier.

Making jewelry is a slow process – much slower than fashion, which lives by the pulse of the moment. Derrez begins by drawing and then performs lots of trials, which allow him to continue improving the object. A constant element in his work is the folding and pleating of thin silver plate or PVC – a highly skilful process. "I think I have become a master in the folding of wire and metal sheets. It takes brains and precision, that's all." Like Gijs Bakker, he seeks applications of the Moebius circle – the figure eight that, twisted, can be hung around part of the body. A successful example of the Moebius shape is the pleated collar in colored PVC – a 1982 design – that fans out around the neck (p. 212-213).

Derrez' work consists almost exclusively of serial products, in which he is happiest combining metal with plastic – silver, steel, aluminum and perspex. "I don't consider my things to be unique. Uniqueness is not a quality in itself."

Lucy Sarneel was intrigued by the way steel assumes its rusty skin. She used rusty steel to make brooches and earrings that look like little tree trunks, camouflaging the welds with drops of molten gold (p. 297). She is most interested in metal that reacts, which naturally drew her in her early career towards zinc and steel, and to boxwood too. "Materials that have no value, to which you add meaning – the same kind of meaning, perhaps, as gold. It comes from the energy that you yourself invest in the material. What really fascinates me is that all those metals, the iron, the zinc, are in our bodies. Wearing them makes them visible."

Sarneel's trademark is her boxes or cases. No matter how small they are, they seem to contain a secret. After all, boxes are for putting things in, a part of yourself perhaps – a treasury of the soul. She wanders round with a vague image fixed in her mind, which has to be turned into jewelry. But before getting to that stage, the image first has to be broken apart again and checked and counterchecked to make sure that it's right. And then it turns out to be a box again. "I started getting despondent at one point. It just kept on coming back, even though I didn't want to repeat myself. I didn't want to be hobbled by it, but I still found myself cramped. It started to prey on my mind. I went into my workshop with a heavy heart. My confidence was restored when it occurred to me that these boxes were a part of me. So let them come."

MIMICRY

"I don't see myself as a jewelry maker", Dinie Besems announces So what is she then? She thinks for a long time and eventually says "a conceptual artist". That makes it a lot more difficult to describe her raw material – an idea. Through that idea, she tries to deviate from reality, to give it a spin, so that even as she seeks she

DUTCH

JEWELRY

DESIGN

1950
–
2000

finds the essence. What making conceptual art means to Besems is that a burgeoning thought prompts an exploration. She immerses herself in libraries and books and tries things out. This is apparent in her Mimicry jewel, which she made in 1993. It consists of a small piece of cloth that is almost lost against the wearer's clothes. "You read about how animals in nature assume facial expressions that seem to imitate their surroundings. How do you achieve that effect in a piece of jewelry? You explore, you hone your idea and you eventually reach a conclusion: this is how it has to be."

Besems' goal is to create jewelry that is part of space or which marks space. The result, from a piece of woven cloth, the color, texture and type of which correspond almost exactly with its background thus becomes the only logical result that Besems can conceive. She is all meaning – her material is a thought, not something tangible. "The form is not important, the brooch you make is actually a bit surreptitious. It's the way of thinking in itself that gives me space. When an idea like that comes, because the time is plainly right, I get really obsessive. I have to know all there is to know about it and I read voraciously."

BODY AND AESTHETICS

First comes the object, then the body. Gijs Bakker thinks there are dangers in this approach, because some jewels only assume their meaning from the body. He has in mind those aluminum collars that adapt themselves to the wearer's neck (p. 113). The cage affair (Profile Jewel) that he designed in 1974 especially for his wife Emmy van Leersum cannot be conceived without Emmy's profile.

Until falling victim to tuberculosis in the 1940s, Van Leersum was totally in thrall to ballet. In an indirect way, she later returned to its movement by having her jewelry respond to the softness and vulnerability of the body. Her own body was her yardstick, with its white page-boy bob and the knitted clothes she wore – all this made her the perfect backdrop for her own mathematical jewelry.

To wear or not to wear, that is the question. In the museum, Neerincx says, there is only one answer. Those jewels will never be shown on the human body, just as you never see flowers in the museum's collection of vases. Viewers are seemingly able to cope with this abstraction – they can imagine the arm in the bracelet or the neck beneath the necklace. Neerincx' principle was that the museum should only buy things that could be worn: "it also had to have quality". She did not shrink from acting as an ambassador of Dutch jewelry. She wore it, for instance, to a curators' conference in Trondheim, Norway. "I was the odd one out – the only person wearing anything contemporary."

DUTCH

JEWELRY

DESIGN

1950
2000

JEWELS
of Mind and Mentality

Françoise van den Bosch called on dancers and models to wear her jewelry – in the dance composition Movement-Object, for instance, on 14 November 1969. Her motto was playful: the object had to be a challenge that induced movement. Stronger than that, it had to *be* movement. She seemed to view the body as a sculpture, of which the jewel was either an extension or an accentuation. The way Van den Bosch sought out points of connection with dance, fine art and decorative art made her a child of her time, and it was this aspect of her work that drew a lot of comment at the time of her death in 1977. Its roots in De Stijl and even earlier were recalled, as were the similarities she displayed with the 17th-century Dutch painter Saenredam.

EMBARRASSMENT

Bakker's primary focus is not the body but the object he feels compelled to make. "I want to come up with something new every time. For me, the challenge of thinking something up for a small surface is not even the most important thing. Communication is – conveying and provoking a message. It's great if women wear my jewels, provided I don't have to see them. I find that embarrassing. Even if I see someone wearing one of my big pieces – which happens to me in the States – I just feel like I'd rather go and sit on the other side of the room."

Appenzeller takes the completely opposite view. For him, wearing is everything – "Show it" is his motto. The designer's job is to make the wearer more beautiful. Consequently, aesthetics has a different meaning for Appenzeller than it does for Bakker, who considers aesthetics to be useless and boring. "An object only becomes aesthetic when it is familiar, when the image fits into a particular category. As soon as it refers to something, I cease to find it interesting. In the early days, for instance, people viewed aluminum bracelets as machine parts, which they found totally ugly. A few years go by and they suddenly start to say, 'ah, how interesting', because aesthetic appreciation has finally arrived." By the time that happens, the designer needs to be one step further down the line, working on a new object – preferably one that stirs the emotions.

Rings are a physical experience. Onno Boekhoudt is fascinated by the little jewel on the finger that you hardly see, but can feel all the more. Ears, by contrast, offer him little in the way of a challenge. "You might just as well decorate your ears with a felt-tip pen." Boekhoudt does not believe in a direct relationship between object and body. "The body – what is it exactly? What is a chair? Those are big questions. But I gradually came to the conclusion that I had to say something about the body. I've been pussyfooting around it."

JEWELS
of Mind and Mentality

Boekhoudt would never deny that the wearer is the most important factor for jewelry. All the same, his jewelry could just as well be considered as abstract sculpture – he sometimes refers to his work as "collections" – which have no direct relationship with the body. They are separate from it. Boekhoudt's work is similar in this respect to that of Herbst, who is also led first and foremost by the story she wishes to convey and the associations that she incorporates in her collages. Around 1970, Herbst had her perspex necklaces with "cap-rings" photographed around a man's neck – 20 years later, her designs have become autonomous. They can be worn or exhibited.

Like Bakker, Boekhoudt feels embarrassed when he sees people wearing his "things". "Jewelry to me is not intended as a public exhibition. You don't have to wear them to parties or as Sunday best." Boekhoudt does not, therefore, see jewelry as something necessarily made to beautify people – he would rather that it was something tangible for the wearer, that the object's aura was directed inwardly rather than outwardly. "How it actually looks is less and less important to me."

GEMS

Wearability does not come at the top of Lucy Sarneel's list. She is equally happy for her jewelry to be put down somewhere and admired. She has no preference for any specific part of the body. Away from their wearer, her brooches and earrings take on the character of still lifes through the contrasts that she seeks to evoke in this tiny space. "When you see a brooch inspired by nature, you think 'is that a leaf? What kind of leaf is it?'" Sarneel's jewelry momentarily confuses the eye.

When people wear jewelry, it means they are paying attention to their body. LAM de Wolf takes that idea considerably further: "If you pay attention to your body, you also have to pay attention to your posture. With my objects, there's no escaping that. Around 1981, they were big, square fabric hoops that you had to pull over your head and place round your body. You couldn't just sit down in them – you were forced to adjust your posture (p. 204)." You certainly stood out with a De Wolf round your neck. London architects loved them, because the jewelry seemed to perform structural interventions on the body.

The body was not the first thing that De Wolf had in mind when she turned to jewelry. "I began by producing autonomous art and went from there to the wearable object. Not the other way round. The autonomous element remained and actually established such a hold on my work that I eventually outgrew the Ra gallery."

Because he began as a formal jewelry designer, Paul Derrez was not too concerned at first with the body as a platform. But there was no escaping it – his

JEWELS
of Mind and Mentality

pieces were hung on that body and so it was interesting to study what effect they had there. "A new aspect has occurred to me in recent years – the fact that jewelry is a fitting element within the total picture. That it supports an image. I think it's great that jewelry is worn, but it doesn't affect the form of the thing." He was once asked specially to design a jewel for the male body – an accessory. He was surprised by the request, because he does not categorize his work by gender. The commission resulted in two pendants, with the eloquent names "Face" and "Dick". Face was a pierced penis with two balls, while Dick was an erect penis. Both were made of stainless steel and belonged to Derrez' "Erotic Tools" series.

He drew inspiration from the signals emanating from gay subculture by fastening a cock-ring to an epaulet. These are both, he feels, cliched modes of expression – "because you can spot a leather queen from a mile off anyway". The logic for jewels of this kind was lacking, as he found in his investigations: why would a man want to wear a dick when he has one already? "I then started to look for things that were male and macho, but which could also put those things into perspective. Face is, of course, a pierced penis, but it is also a smiling face." The nicest thing, Derrez muses, is that they were not bought and worn by a gay man, but by a 60 year-old woman. Preferably on the train. "Things always turn out differently to how you expect."

Body or no body, design for Dinie Besems is a constant battle. Ideally, there isn't a body, or there ought not to be one, because she views space itself as a body. "You have an idea, but as soon as you transfer it to the body, you find yourself in a vulnerable world. You and your body are vulnerable. Given that that's so, it is good to place the art there, in that area of tension." Before the jewel is linked to the body, however, it first has to be tried and tested spatially.

When she decided in 1996 to part with her gallery owner and to expand her artistry, she got the frightening feeling of being totally alone in the world, unnoticed and without support. "I felt like I was trapped in the circuit. I wanted to get out and the first thing that I did was to open my house." She ran a chain around and through her house, and called the project "No More Naked". "The idea was that you could take your house with you as an amulet and that you were naked without it. The people entered semi-naked, as it were, and left dressed". The chain, as the elaboration of a conceptual idea, defined the space. Besems sadly had to acknowledge that the project did not take off. The time was clearly not ripe – three years later, her friends suddenly got it.

That body again. She'd be happier if it didn't figure, if she only had space to work with. But if, in spite of all her efforts and maneuvers, the body is still there, then it has to be right.

JEWELS
of Mind and Mentality

DESIGNERS AND CUSTOMERS

According to LAM de Wolf, the jewelry collector buys, the art collector looks. There is a clear divide between lovers of modern jewelry and collectors of modern art. It is probably a question of perspective. Wearers don't see their own jewels. They are observed by the other, who gets a total picture: facial expression, body, posture, clothes and jewelry. It is the difference between looking and being seen. The modern art that someone buys ends up almost automatically against a neutral wall, where it can be viewed more or less objectively. Jewelry is always part of a personality, sometimes even strengthening it. Yet even that isn't entirely true, Gijs Bakker corrects: "My collectors also buy art. There is a lady in America who lives in a Richard Meier house and has had her bathroom fitted out with lots of square display cases in which she places my jewels. She wears them once." Bakker does not acknowledge any difference between the types of collector. "They want both – art and jewelry." Art, then, as a complement of jewelry. Or vice versa.

"If buyers are drawn to a piece, I don't insist that they have to wear it – I'm happy for them to put it somewhere", Herbst said in late 1973, indicating that to her, the relationship between jewelry and the consumer is not a direct one. It is, in the time-honored way, an object to wear. Yet Herbst is anything but absolutist when she says that it is people that prompt her to make jewelry, with the aim on occasion of actually provoking them.

Paul Derrez is more likely to tell customers that a piece of jewelry suits them than that it looks good. What looks good is, after all, relative. "You might have a dumpy figure, but put on a big necklace and you look fantastic, simply because you're the perfect person for that jewel."

The public he has seen coming into the gallery over the past 25 years has changed and broadened. Attitudes have changed too. "Around 1980, there was a difference in education between men and women. There was still a division between their respective roles, with the men going out into the world. The man would come in and pick out a piece of jewelry for his wife. He knew what he was buying and who it belonged to. It sometimes happened that the woman would bring it back the next day because she needed to buy shoes for the kid. Men picked up on the latest developments in design – women followed later. All that changed in the 1990s. Men and women now buy jewelry for themselves with money that they have earned themselves."

Although there is evidence of emancipation, the discipline has not widened. The public may have expanded, but it has also been diluted. According to Derrez: "There is less intensity, which reflects the fact that the supply is broader, while a lot of

people stay on the fringes and don't get to the core." It is as if the customers are less concerned about the content. They are interested in the maker's name, in prestige and in the place where it was bought, more than in the meaning of the object.

RED STICKER
Derrez first noticed it happening in ceramics, where collectors became so important that makers began to view vases and dishes purely as collector's items. "They were queuing up to have galleries slap their red stickers on their work." The upshot is that designers no longer work for the market, but for a fixed customer or group of customers. "You can see it in the jewelry world, even among students fresh out college. They make things for a public that already exists and which buys purely on the basis of the designer's name." Jewelry has "arrived", which does nothing for its freshness or its development. Derrez is jealous of the worlds of fashion and music, which appeal to young people and to the ethnic minorities. Attempts to link jewelry and fashion have had little success.

Lucy Sarneel had a problem with jewelry's elite status, which made it inaccessible to a wider public. It then occurred to her that you didn't have to own the jewelry. "That was very liberating, the idea that you could also enjoy the knowledge that it was somewhere, in a museum, for instance, where everyone can see it." It is almost a precondition for Sarneel that her jewelry should be shown, because that is how the artist maintains contact with people. "I still think it's wild that a jewel of mine should be in a museum."

When Bakker and Van Leersum took jewelry off its pedestal and christened it "objects to wear", it seemed as if it would henceforth be available to everyone. The whole of the Netherlands would be decked out in stainless steel and aluminum. That's not how it turned out. The jewelry world may have earned international prestige, but it has remained a limited activity, similar in scale to ceramics or glass-making. Fear of standing out, is how Riet Neerincx explains it. "You can't derive any status from it, which makes it unattractive to up-and-coming designers."

Did the ambitions go unfulfilled? Was the great breakthrough a failure? What is failure, Bakker asks. "Take Constant's New Babylon. That also remained an utopia. Even Le Corbusier's city of the future never came to pass. It would be terrible if people were still walking around wearing those collars from the 1960s – I'd be horribly embarrassed." Bakker belonged to a little group that formed at Riekje Swart's gallery, where artists from a variety of disciplines came together. That interdisciplinary factor has gone now. Specialist galleries draw a selective public. "There's no more and there's no less. It's very strange, however, that the

Netherlands has three prominent galleries. That's not something you find abroad."

It is true that the galleries have broadened their horizons, looking abroad in a way that has given the Netherlands a special place in the international jewelry world. When Derrez joined the Sieraad gallery as an intern in the early 1970s, its sphere of influence was strictly national. By the time the Ra gallery was set up in 1976, he was convinced that an international approach was needed. It proved beneficial to the qualitative and quantitative scope of Dutch jewelry.

There are, however, several clouds on the horizon. Industry has failed to take up jewelry design, as has fashion. Boekhoudt, who now teaches at the Royal College of Arts in London, is well placed to make a comparison with the situation in other countries, and he concludes that the links with other branches of culture are lacking. "Designers in Germany and Britain have more baggage, simply because of the history they carry with them, which is full of stories and mysticism. The Netherlands remains stuck in minimalism – in a kind of deconstructivism." Costume jewelry is taught in college, but people invariably pull a face whenever it is mentioned. Because the galleries have concentrated on their specialist areas and have not been involved, modern jewelry has ended up isolated. And in elite isolation, at that.

EVERYTHING CAN BE USED

Dinie Besems did not leave the gallery and start up on her own lightly. She wanted to create space, both literally and figuratively. "I have a wide orientation. Everything can be used: biology, music, philosophy and psychology". This attitude, combined with the fact that she does not insist on a link between her art and the human body, helps explain why she has ended up on the fringes of jewelry design. She wonders whether she is actually a designer at all. "I'm more of an ideas person, I'm a kind of pioneer. What I've brought to the discipline is to develop a free way of thinking that has not destroyed what already exists. I've added a way, without condemning the old one."

LAM de Wolf had already run up against the clearly delineated character of the jewelry world when she decided to take her autonomous art in a more applied direction. She was more interested in the British designers who had brought color and material experimentation around 1980. "Jewelry in Holland was all about Dutch Smooth. Everything was intended to hang in a museum for years, whereas I thought it should be used." De Wolf opted for a different approach – jewelry was not to be a value added to clothing, as it had always been before, but was to take precedence, with the clothing as the derivative. "If you're actually going to wear an 'object to wear', you have to show it too."

DUTCH

JEWELRY

DESIGN

1950
–
2000

The tempestuous sixties and seventies were followed, as Hans Appenzeller discovered, by a hangover. People in New York were not remotely interested in conceptual jewelry. In the Netherlands, meanwhile, the sides had been drawn up: art and business were poles apart and there was a strict divide between fine jewelry, costume jewelry, industrial jewelry and objects. Appenzeller was forced to acknowledge that the commercial aspect of modern jewelry was viewed skeptically, even in his own circles. Suddenly, museums were no longer interested in his designs. "And you don't count in the Netherlands unless your work is exhibited."

THE POINT OF JEWELRY

You can get by perfectly well without body decoration, just as you can without an electric toothbrush or an ice-cream maker. On the other hand, African cultures demonstrate that the urge for decoration is deep-seated, simply to challenge the opposite sex and to convey signals. Jewelry is the perfect way to do this, possibly because it comes it comes even closer to the person than clothing does. For a man, deciding to wear jewelry is a sign of daring, Derrez says. When Emmy van Leersum began to design, "emancipation" was one of her motives. Reinforcing women's self-awareness could be an ideal and this lent jewelry a social charge.

Jewelry has no direct utility, although it can, Derrez thinks, be an icon and can reflect the spirit of the age. Decoration alone is not sufficient, nor is aesthetics, as it is not a constant concept. If the jewel is set aside and not worn, it wastes away, while wearing it can make it a symbol of a period or an idea. In his gallery, Derrez prefers makers who "put down a marker". Provocation is probably putting it too strongly, but they have to take a stance. If the maker does so, this can then stimulate the buyer. Think, make, buy and wear, in that order,

PENIS AND PEARL

Making jewelry is a form of communication for Gijs Bakker and Dinie Besems, although the two designers have different interpretations of that idea. Besems: "I see jewelry as a medium. Communication is an important idea for me. That a brooch says something about someone's personality doesn't count for me. I want the viewer to see it as part of a larger space. Bakker, by contrast, offers a highly personal view: "I only make jewelry when I have something to say." Since the middle of the 1980s, the story he has been telling has been about the intertwining of the banal and the precious — laminated newspaper photos sprinkled with diamonds. "It's a mix of ingredients."

DUTCH

JEWELRY

DESIGN

1950
2000

Since 1997, Bakker has added Johnny Awakes to the "Jewelry as Communication" series. It is a necklace modeled on Elvis Presley, who was the subject of an exhibition at the time. The idea stayed at the back of his mind, until it woke him up one night. How about a collection of penises moving from flaccid to full arousal? Laminated and held together by silver links. "I am fascinated by the way women wear strings of pearls. The custom is to have the biggest pearl at the front and the smallest ones behind the neck. There's absolutely no way I can reach women like that. 'Johnny Awakes' is a reaction against that kind of thing. The biggest pearl is at the front. And when it has shriveled up again, it becomes a little pearl." That was Bakker's message circa 1997 and it is one that he could not have conveyed ten years earlier, nor, in all probability, ten years hence. For that reason, "Johnny Awakes" tells us as much about the "pornographic" nineties as the "emancipatory" stovepipe did about 1967.

Genitalia as the subject of a necklace popped up in the 1990s – a period in which ideas about pornography were in motion, in which ethical ideals like morality and decency returned and art seemingly regained its ability to shock, despite the earlier demolition of pretty well all the remaining barriers. Besems designed a testicle chain in 1994. It was basically a conceptual object, she says, as the form was the principal focus. Her necklace was a response to her fellow artists. She hated the trend whereby everything had to be erotic, and which simply succeeded in making everything vulgar and impoverished. She felt the need to strike back, though without shouting. "For me, it was a provocation, but it was not received that way. I bought a piece of iron wire and began to free-associate. I used the wire to make circles, which eventually turned into the ball chain. The word itself is more important – it's probably the key strand in my work." The purpose of making jewelry for Besems is that it functions as a platform for conceptual art.

De Wolf is inclined to stretch the definition of jewelry. She saw her work more as clothing than jewelry and she turned large objects into small, derivative things, like a little ball or block that you could sew into a pocket to give wearers something to play with when they were embarrassed. "What do you call that? An amulet maybe? It isn't intended to make you more beautiful but to give you strength. All that the outside world could see was a thread hanging out of your trouser pocket. Like an iceberg, part of the jewel is invisible. I make a distinction between large and small objects. The large ones are like pieces of clothing, which you use to distinguish yourself and to emphasize your personality. If you wore my stuff, your body had to adapt (p. 198-199-204)."

ESSENCE

Jewelry for Marion Herbst fulfilled the same function for fine art that the projection screen does for a movie. Within that small surface area and that free form, she could display her humor, her attitudes and her expression. In this way, she represented a significant strand of Dutch design for which jewelry was an autonomous art object, and in which she reflected the ideas that she had picked up in Italy or Africa.

What does a piece of jewelry have to achieve? It needs an essence, because, Lucy Sarneel believes, a jewel without a soul is a jewel without meaning. LAM de Wolf, meanwhile, thinks that just wearing a jewel without being conscious of it is pointless. De Wolf views jewelry as clothing that demands an attitude from the wearer. A slightly uncomfortable posture does no harm. You either wear a LAM de Wolf or you don't.

Sarneel gradually shifted from her little boxes towards collages, which seem at first sight to have been inspired by nature, but which contain a small, disruptive element – alien tree trunks or artificial leaves. Making jewelry for her is a technical quest – how do you weld silver? How does corrosion work? – in which meaning arises as soon as it is instilled. Viewed in this light, jewelry becomes the embodiment of love. "And love to me is the most important thing in life. What I make is something that I long for myself, a little place of my own."

FINE OR DECORATIVE ART?

The multiplicity of Dutch jewelry design makes it difficult to pigeonhole individual practitioners. Are they industrial designers or fine artists, are they autonomous or do they owe something to society? Are they a new kind of jeweler or small manufacturers? Modern jewelry basically cannot be placed under a single common denominator. It refers to a group of individuals, each of whom has left his or her stamp on the discipline, although some of them, like Onno Boekhoudt, like to think of themselves more as artists than others, like Hans Appenzeller, do.

In Appenzeller's view, by unilaterally opting to ally itself with modern art, modern jewelry in the Netherlands has missed the opportunity to renew itself, because fine artists focus entirely on their own expression and not on the manufacture of a serial product.

Derrez looks back to the old ideal of the 1970s, when jewelry was liberated from its classic, elitist label and was simply permitted to be a product, without a romantic charge. A personal signature was not required – reproduction was vital. "We got our feet back on the ground." Derrez too found that mass-produced plastic bracelets came in for little applause and even fewer sales – only museums wanted to buy

DUTCH

JEWELRY

DESIGN

1950
–
2000

JEWELS
of Mind and Mentality

them. When he began, he believed that in due course, there wouldn't be any jewelers any more, that everyone would buy from galleries. The reality turned out to be more complex – galleries have to take care, these days, not to turn into jewelers' shops.

Modern jewelry developed in a fairly one-side way in the direction of modern art, with the number of one-off products outnumbering the serial ones. The occasional industrial designer, like Bruno Ninaber van Eyben, gave up after a couple of bracelets or watches, while, with the odd exception, the marriage with fashion designers never really got off the ground. Everything changed when Emmy van Leersum appeared on the scene. Although she worked in an emphatically autonomous way, taking herself as her point of reference, she continually sought points of contact with fashion, modern dance and formal art. One of the final designs before her death was a geometrical drawing for a sweater. In a 1970 interview, she described her objects to wear as industrial designs. In retrospect, they have an undeniably sculptural character: Van Leersum's miniature objects are spatially and conceptually comparable with the sculpture of Bob Bonies or Andre Volten.

DOLLS

Gijs Bakker is the most flexible of the jewelry designers. If industrial design and architecture are art forms, then so is jewelry design. Each is, after all, a variant of spatial design, with the jewel as the smallest product. The various colleges, however, have imposed a restriction by failing to give costume jewelry, industrial jewelry and art jewelry an equal status in their training. As a result, industrial designers often decline the invitation to design a piece of jewelry. Serial production, wearability and price range can all be particular headaches. Let alone the idea that the designer is expected to deliver expression by the square millimeter. This, to Bakker's mind, is the reason why jewelry has never caught on among industrial designers. It is why he and Marijke Vallanzasca set up the foundation Chi ha paura...? to produce and distribute jewelry by well-known designers.

Dinie Besems is, first and foremost, a conceptual artist, for whom jewelry is one potential subject. The next day, it could equally well be an Internet chat room or a book about the magic square. It is understandable, therefore, that she aligns herself with fine art. LAM de Wolf has also gradually maneuvred herself away from the discipline of jewelry, as demonstrated by the dolls she hangs up every week in the Ra gallery and onto which she projects words or texts. The dolls are made of paper and pins, and are dressed in baby clothes from Waterlooplein or her own stuff. She calls them personalities. They are dolls with character – one sad, the other happy. "I've always said that I wanted to be an artist, and to do that, you need a wide

orientation. That's what I teach my students, too. Experiment. Look beyond the boundaries of your craft. Jewelry on its own just seems too limited. I see it as a component of all art. What is art all about? It is about learning to see. That is one of the most important qualities – that you teach people in a relaxed way how to see things differently."

In this way, De Wolf has picked up the baton from Marion Herbst, whose work evolved in the 1980s in the direction of fine art. She occupied a special position in Dutch jewelry, which was recognized in 1982, when she received the Françoise van den Bosch Prize. Herbst allowed herself to be led by loose ideas – elusive influences that surprised her as much as anybody. Her relationship with sculpture was always essential – "It was within that discipline that I learned how to see."

Appenzeller got to see the other side of the coin during his time in New York, where he experienced the difference between fine jewelry, costume jewelry and art jewelry. Fine is the kind supplied by jewelers and is made of precious metals and stones, while costume jewelry can be anything it wants, and is thus frequently linked to fashion. Art jewelry is the article offered by art galleries. He didn't see much point in making costume jewelry in the Netherlands, because of the limited size of the market and the large numbers that would have to be produced. Meanwhile, he did not fit in among the jewelers, with his non-precious materials, such as plastic and aluminum. "As far as New York was concerned, it was all so confusing that I opted to make fine jewelry, which obliged me to work with stones and gold." But what about the Netherlands? No way would Appenzeller take the art route – he thinks jewelry is far too intimately linked to the wearer for that to be justified. It is almost impossible for something tailored to the body to be placed in a museum. "In other words, I don't fit into any of the pigeonholes."

THE JEWEL OF JEWELS

Riet Neerincx cherishes her ring with the diagonal bump, which, 30 years on, has proved literally and figuratively indestructible. If she had to choose something by another designer – which, as curator of Arnhem's Gemeentemuseum, she has been able to do – her favorite piece is a chain that she bought from a Swiss amateur at a flea market. Among the Dutch designers, she particularly likes Herman Hermsen, the former assistant of Emmy van Leersum, who, following in Emmy's footsteps, has produced the most balanced designs.

Your most recent jewelry need not be your best, although this is the case with Dinie Besems. The work in question is a little book with letters and words that form an investigation of the magic square. Although it does not look literally like a jewel,

DUTCH

JEWELRY

DESIGN

1950
–
2000

Besems feels that it is one.

For other designers, the most recent work can embody so much research, and trial and error, that the sharp edges of the original idea have already been worn smooth. That's why Paul Derrez still looks back to his first piece – the Swap Ring – as his most important. It is followed by a necklace he made in cork in 1985, when he realised that you couldn't go on with the same theme forever and that you had to allow the spirit of the age into your work. The necklace with cork eggs (p. 235) and the pleated PVC collar (p. 212-213) are explorations of volume. "I thought I'd try turning it around. A traditional jewel is supposed to be small. If I make a ring that I already made 20 years earlier, then I'm doing something wrong." Boekhoudt too prefers not to pick a single piece that sums up all of his work. He does, however, have favorites from each period – Room for the Finger (p. 277) in 1993, Flower (silver and brilliant) for the Chi ha paura...? project, a brooch with an eccentrically positioned triangle, which in turn contains a small protuberance (silver, 1992) and his very first necklace, which he made during his training in Germany. Not to mention all the things he has made from lead, which do not feature in a single museum collection. Boekhoudt's enchantment with lead – the most inert of the metals and the opposite of gold – was also shared by the critics, who homed in on this aspect of his work during his retrospective at the Groninger Museum in 1998.

ON THE WALL OR ROUND YOUR NECK

LAM de Wolf believes that all her ideas are embodied in a voluminous collar (p. 198) that she made in 1981 from sticks wrapped in fabric. There is, however, a jewel from each period to which she is attached. "My best work consists of the things that give the public the greatest scope for experimentation – that you hang on the wall or round your neck." She recalls with pleasure a project consisting of lengths of fabric that lay like packages on the floor of the Ra gallery. You could pick them up and drape them around yourself. As bits of cloth, they formed attractive, Mondrian-style compositions, while as decoration, you could do anything with them. When visitors walked out with them, she took a polaroid to show them how they looked. Jewelry that encourages interaction between maker and user is vital for De Wolf.

Like De Wolf, Gijs Bakker identifies periods in his work, and is able to pick out a highlight from each one. The spot-welded bracelet (p. 105) is his favorite early piece, followed by his shadow jewelry, his "Chrysantium" – dried flower petals frozen in laminated PVC – from the late 1970s, the sports stars (p. 257) from the newspaper, tumbling or jumping over a diamond, from the 1980s, and Johnny Awakes, his "penis necklace" as the most recent. "That one is still fresh, though, and the

freshest ones are the most difficult to place in your work as a whole."

In the early 1990s, Lucy Sarneel made jewels inspired by tools, with visible traces of workmanship, rusty looking material and sharp sawteeth (p. 273). It marked a break with her previous work, which gave her a kick. "These are tools for a disturbed world, you can arm yourself with them. For me, they are a turning point in my work, because I was able to make a social statement. My time at Social Studies College suddenly came in useful."

THE BEAD

What is jewelry, and within that, what is Dutch jewelry? Is it the "object to wear" – a term that seeks to be neutral – or is it the thing that lends the wearer glamour and reflects the artist's personal expression? It is all things to all people – gold and wood, nylon and steel wire. Or it can be an idea. In the second half of the 20th century, a fringe grew up around the country's jeweler's shops (2,500 in 1980), sustained by specialist galleries, a fixed group of collectors and museum collections.

The endless series of exhibitions abroad – beginning with Objects to Wear in 1969 – testifies to the fact that jewelry design has become a mature branch of decorative art. The training provided by the art colleges has borne fruit, ensuring that Neerincx, Van den Bosch, Boekhoudt and Van Leersum now have their successors – people who view themselves as conceptualists, decorative artists, pure designers or postmodernists.

They are all looking for the ultimate jewel. In one case, this took the form of a thread running through a room, while in another it is the thread tied around a satay stick. In all probability, however, the primordial jewel, the mother of all jewels, is the bead – a ball with a hole through the middle or through one edge. Or maybe vice versa – who knows? Onno Boekhoudt saw large beads on his travels around the Pacific – beads that were almost too big for the eye to take in. To his mind, in spite of their size, these are the least obtrusive jewels. Just as the designer Otto Künzli performed an important act in the 1970s by placing a golden sphere in a black, rubber cover, so that only the wearer knew the value of what he or she was wearing. Obtrusive, unobtrusive.

A jewel that manifests itself emphatically by hardly being there – perhaps this is the essence of modern jewelry in the 20th century. A pin by Emmy van Leersum, most of which is concealed beneath the fabric, the ideas of Dinie Besems, the sealed newspaper photos of Gijs Bakker and the ball and thread in the trouser pocket by LAM de Wolf – presence through absence. No longer a question, but a fact.

DUTCH

JEWELRY

DESIGN

1950
2000

JEWELS
of Mind and Mentality

JEWELS
of Mind and Mentality

DUTCH JEWELRY DESIGN

1950 — 2000

Unless stated otherwise, all illustrated works come from the Museum Het Kruithuis collection.

All works cited are in actual size including details.
Exceptions exist when fullviews of details of works are documented.

circa

1950

ARCHIBALD DUMBAR

brooch
white gold, pearl

RIET NEERINCX

Little golden pea
brooch
gold
private collection

1
9
5
2

circa

ARCHIBALD DUMBAR

necklace
yellow, red and white gold
private collection

circa

ARCHIBALD DUMBAR

bracelet
gold
private collection

circa

1954

CHRIS STEENBERGEN

necklace
gold

CHRIS STEENBERGEN

brooch
gold, silver
private collection

1956

CHRIS STEENBERGEN

necklace
silver, gold
private collection

1956

1957

brooch
silver, gold
collection J.J.G. Martinus, Amsterdam

circa

1957

CHRIS STEENBERGEN

brooch
silver, gold
private collection

CHRIS STEENBERGEN

bracelet
silver, gold
private collection

1958

circa

1958

ARCHIBALD DUMBAR

bracelet
gold
private collection

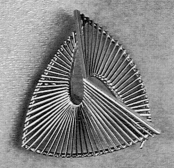

circa

ARCHIBALD DUMBAR

brooch
gold
private collection

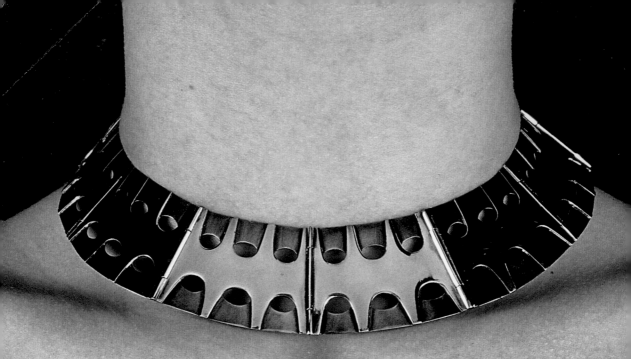

NICOLAAS VAN BEEK

collar
silver
private collection

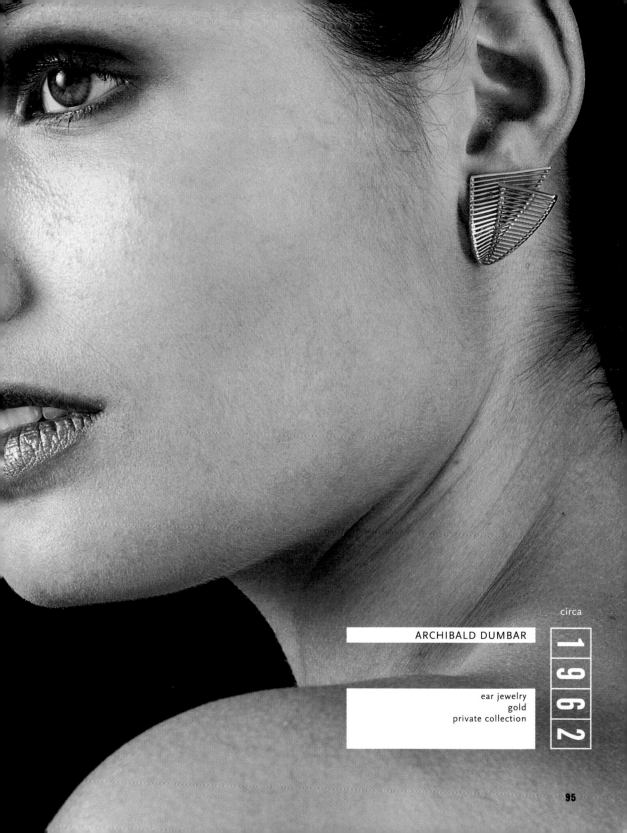

circa

ARCHIBALD DUMBAR

1
9
6
2

ear jewelry
gold
private collection

1963

ARCHIBALD DUMBAR

brooch
gold, citrine
private collection

CHRIS STEENBERGEN

necklace
gold
private collection

1963

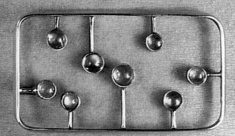

RIET NEERINCX

brooch
gold, moonstones
private collection

RIET NEERINCX

Motto 229107
brooch
gold
collection Museum voor Moderne Kunst
Arnhem

1 9 6 4

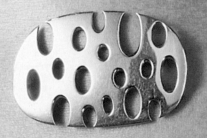

RIET NEERINCX

Motto 993388
brooch
gold
property E. van der Hoek- van Eijk

necklace
gold
private collection

1
9
6
5

RIET NEERINCX

brooch
gold, malachite
private collection

1965

CHRIS STEENBERGEN

necklace
silver

1965

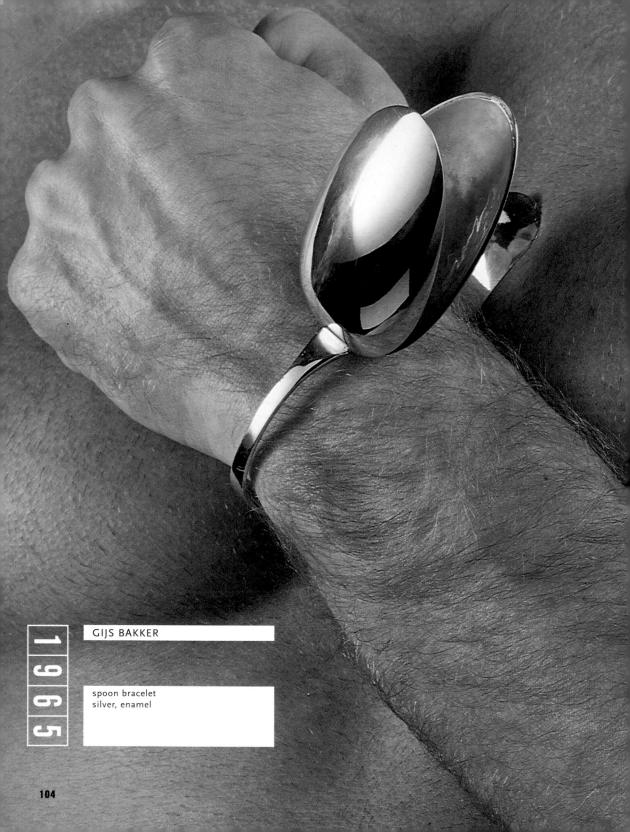

1965

GIJS BAKKER

spoon bracelet
silver, enamel

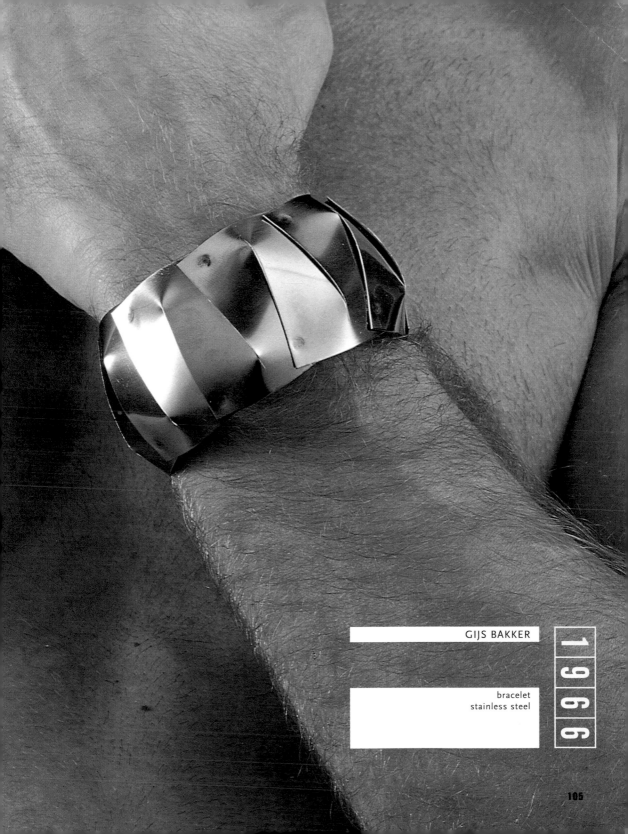

GIJS BAKKER

bracelet
stainless steel

1966

1966

EMMY VAN LEERSUM

bracelet
aluminum

106

EMMY VAN LEERSUM

bracelet
aluminum

1966

EMMY VAN LEERSUM

1967

collar with fastening and dress
aluminum, textile

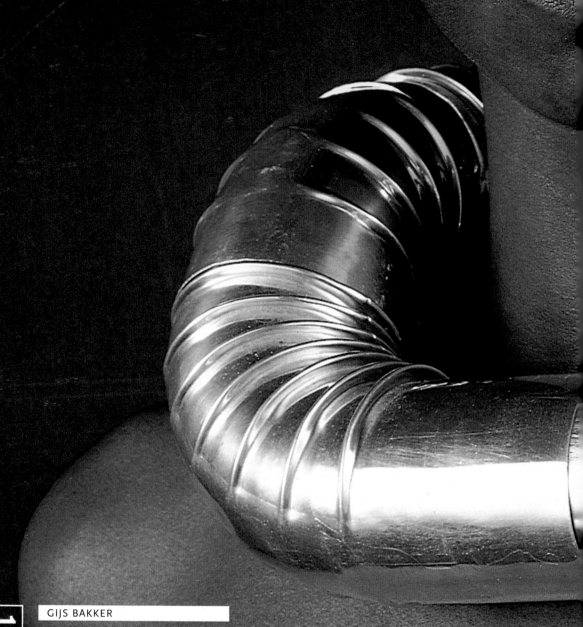

GIJS BAKKER

1967

Stovepipe
neckpiece
aluminum

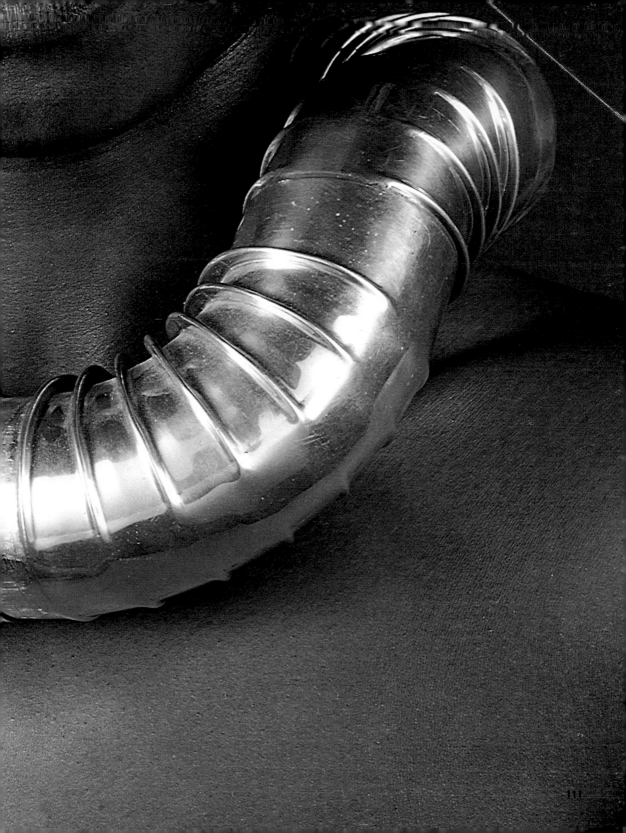

1967

GIJS BAKKER

Stovepipe
bracelet
aluminum

GIJS BAKKER

neckpiece
aluminum

1
9
6
7

GIJS BAKKER

1
9
6
7

neckpiece
aluminum
detail

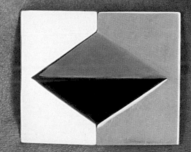

circa

1967

CHRIS STEENBERGEN

brooch
gold
collection J.J.G. Martinus, Amsterdam

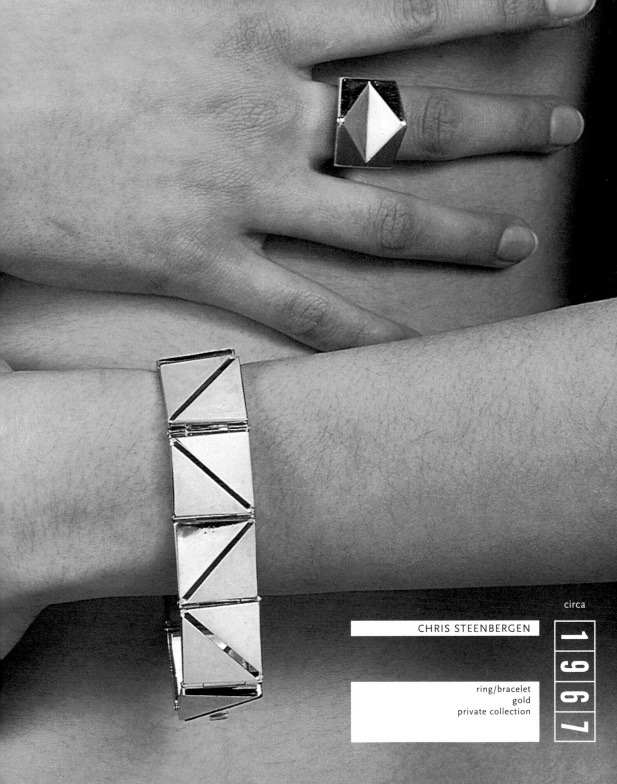

circa

CHRIS STEENBERGEN

1
9
6
7

ring/bracelet
gold
private collection

EMMY VAN LEERSUM

collar with fastening and dress
aluminum, textile

EMMY VAN LEERSUM

bracelet with fastening
gold

FRANÇOISE VAN DEN BOSCH

1968

bracelet
alpaca
collection Van Reekum Museum
Apeldoorn

FRANÇOISE VAN DEN BOSCH

bracelet
alpaca
collection Van Reekum Museum
Apeldoorn

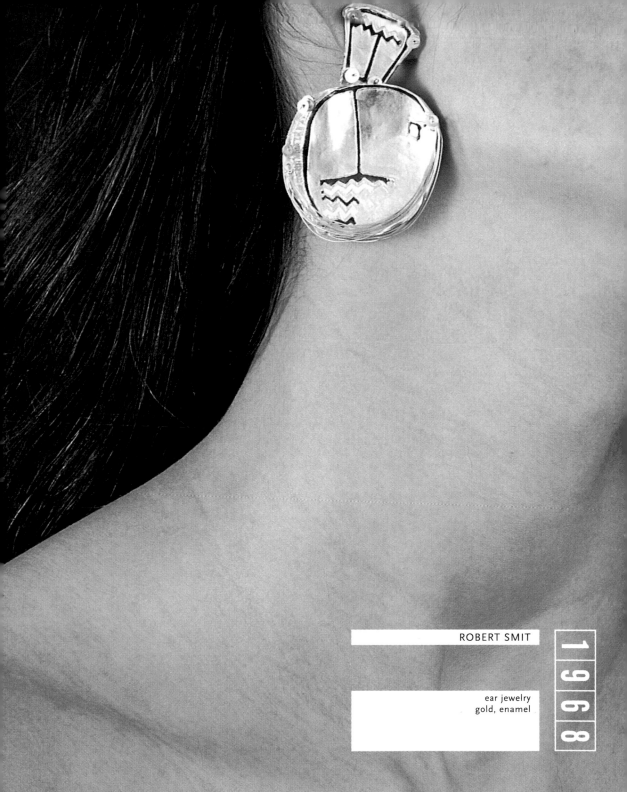

ROBERT SMIT

1968

ear jewelry
gold, enamel

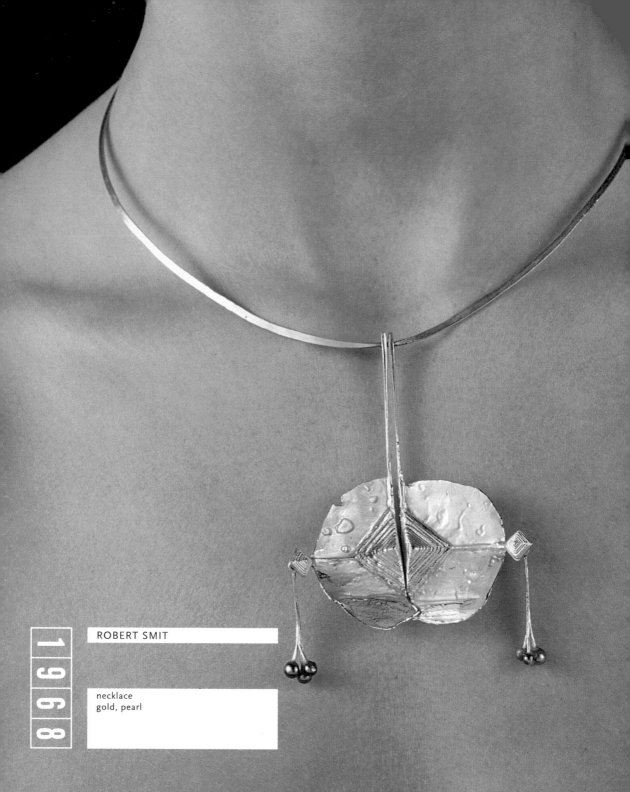

1 9 6 8

ROBERT SMIT

necklace
gold, pearl

124

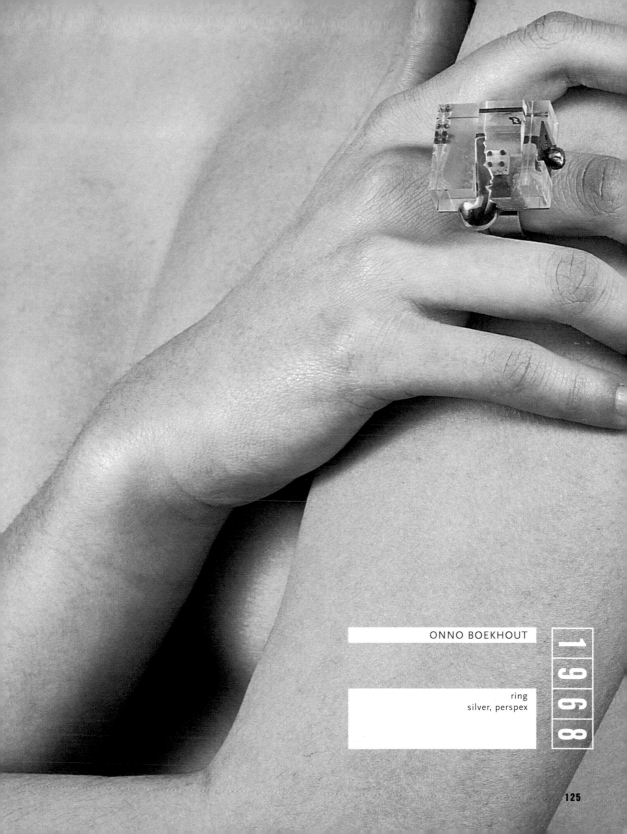

ONNO BOEKHOUT

ring
silver, perspex

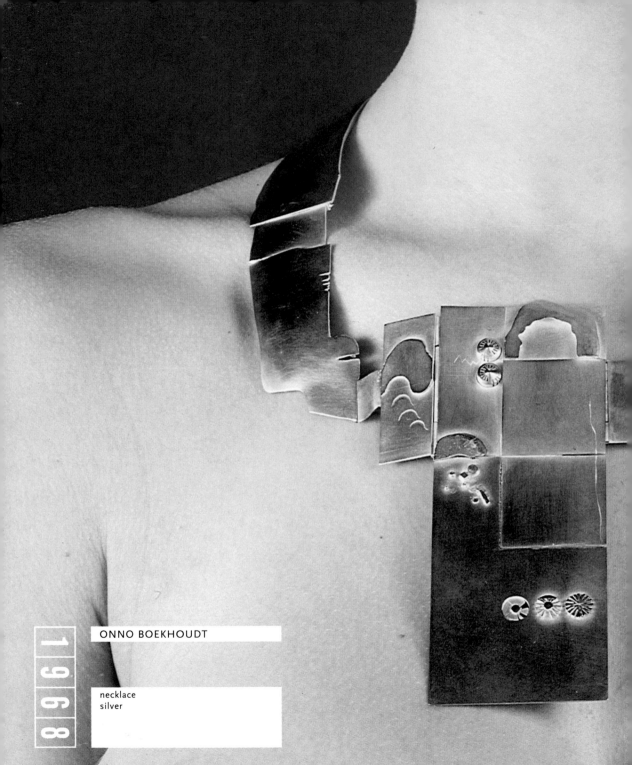

1968

ONNO BOEKHOUDT

necklace
silver

126

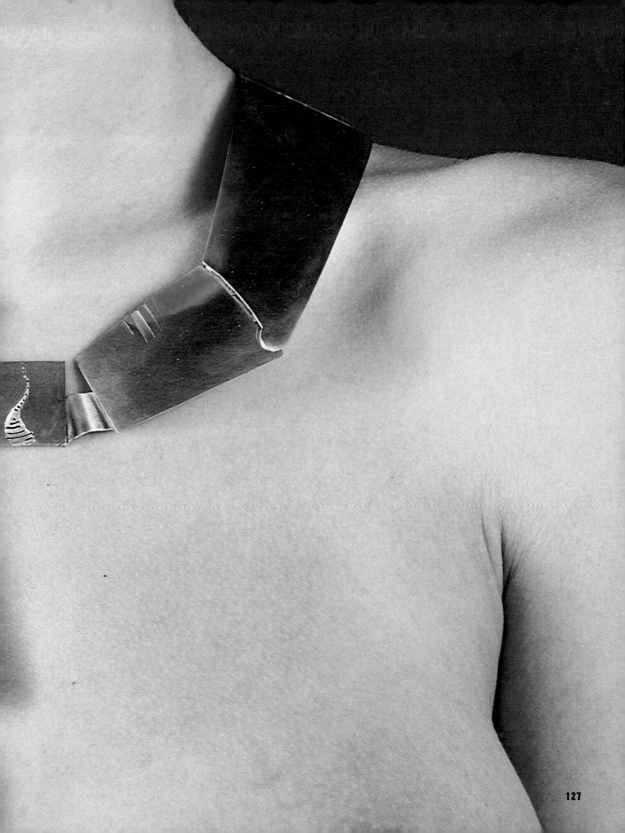

NICOLAAS VAN BEEK

head cap
stainless steel
detail
private collection

1
9
6
8

NICOLAAS VAN BEEK

1968

head cap
stainless steel
detail
private collection

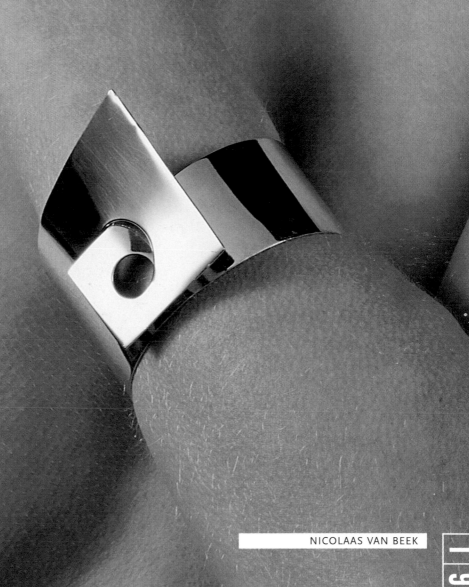

NICOLAAS VAN BEEK

bracelet
silver

CHRIS STEENBERGEN

1969

bracelet
gold

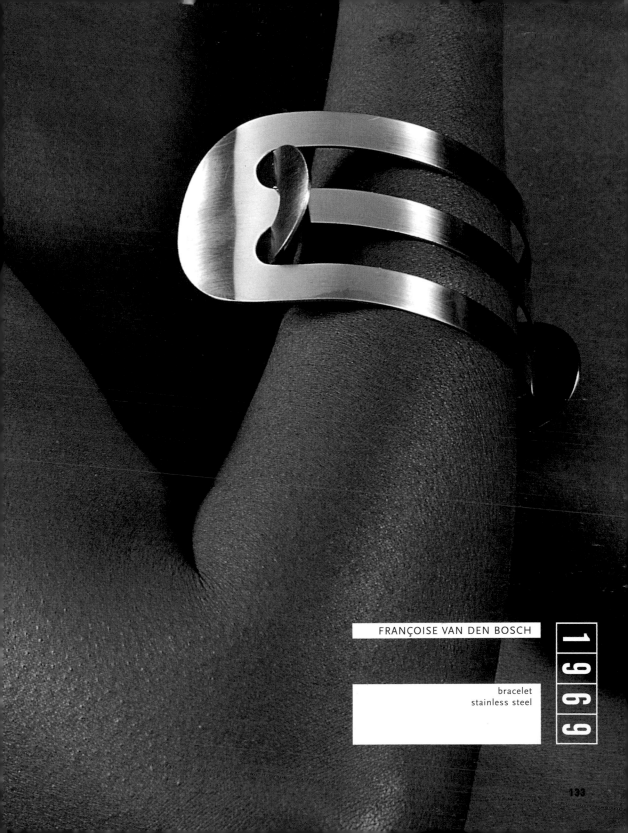

FRANÇOISE VAN DEN BOSCH

1 9 6 9

bracelet
stainless steel

FRANÇOISE VAN DEN BOSCH

bracelet
alpaca
collection Van Reekum Museum
Apeldoorn

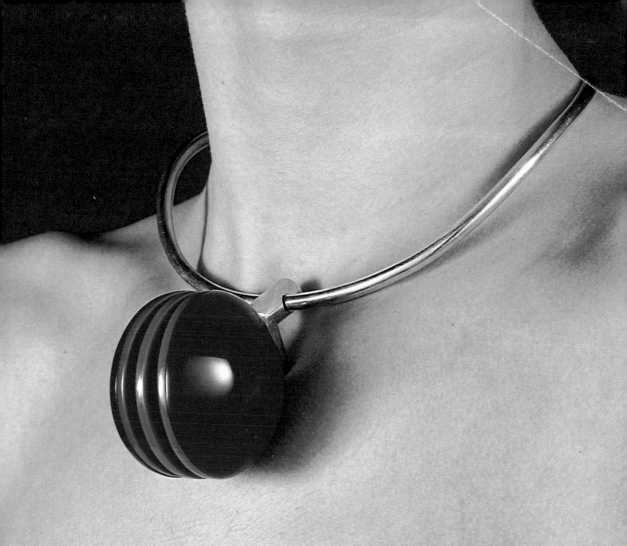

MARION HERBST

necklace
silver, perspex

circa

NICOLAAS VAN BEEK

head cap
chromium-plated aluminum
collection Adelheid/Huub Kortekaas

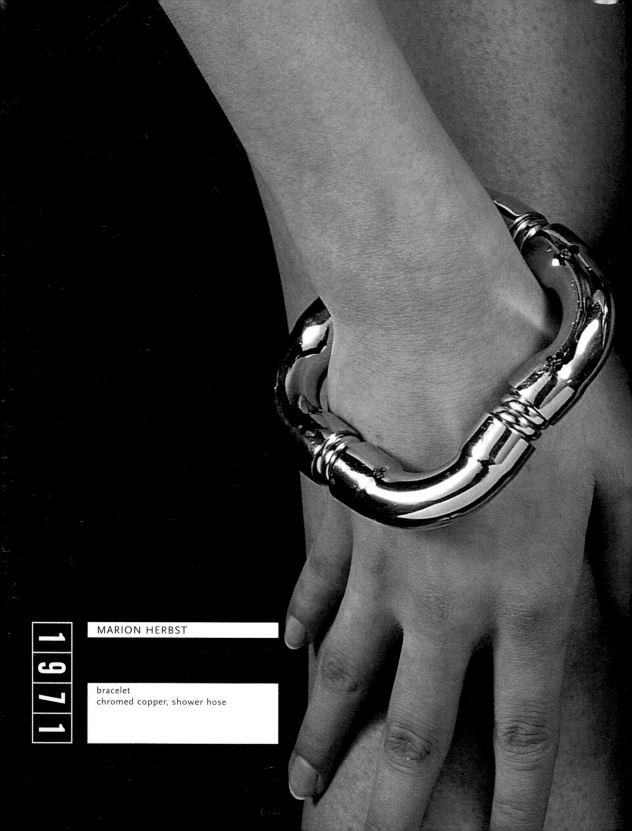

1
9
7
1

MARION HERBST

bracelet
chromed copper, shower hose

MARION HERBST

bracelet
chromed copper, shower hose

1971

FRANÇOISE VAN DEN BOSCH

1971

bracelet
aluminum

140

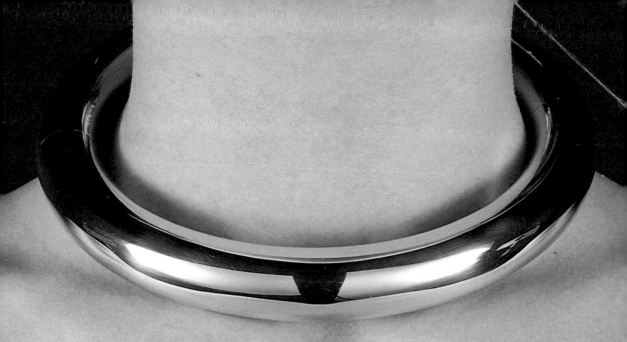

FRANS VAN NIEUWENBORG

MARTIJN WEGMAN

necktube
chromium-plated aluminum

1 9 7 2

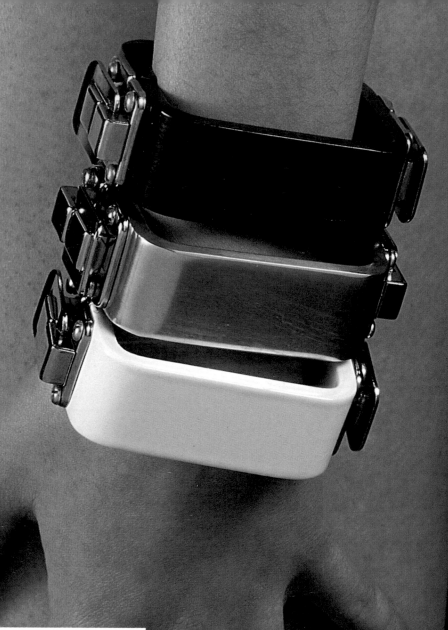

1 9 7 2

CHARLOTTE VAN DER WAALS

bracelets
aluminum

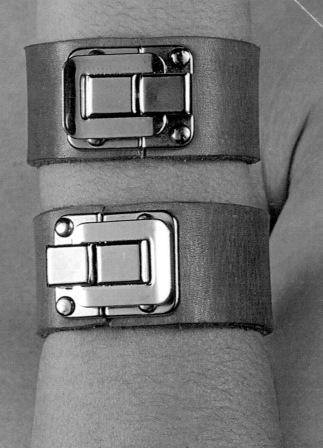

CHARLOTTE VAN DER WAALS

1972

bracelets
tack leather

143

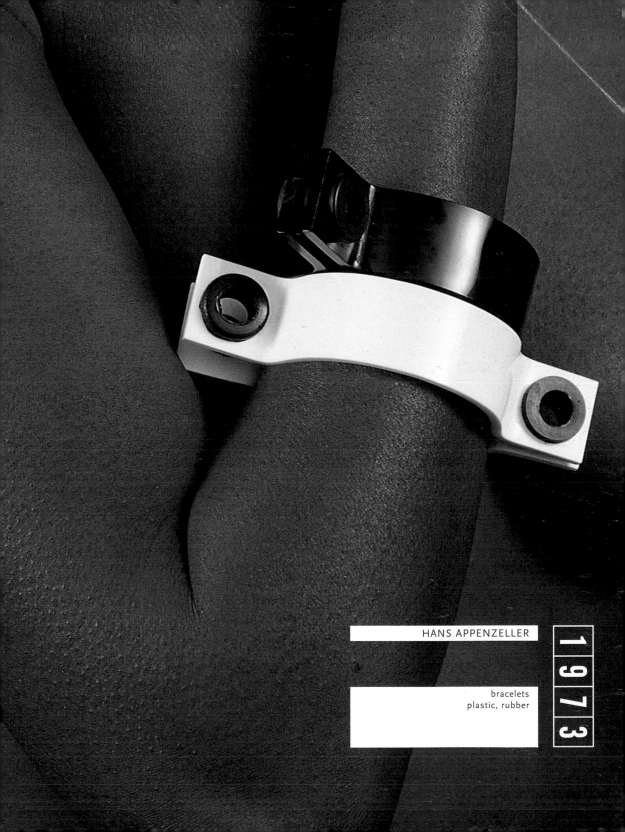

HANS APPENZELLER

1973

bracelets
plastic, rubber

HANS APPENZELLER

1 9 7 3

bracelets
plastic, rubber

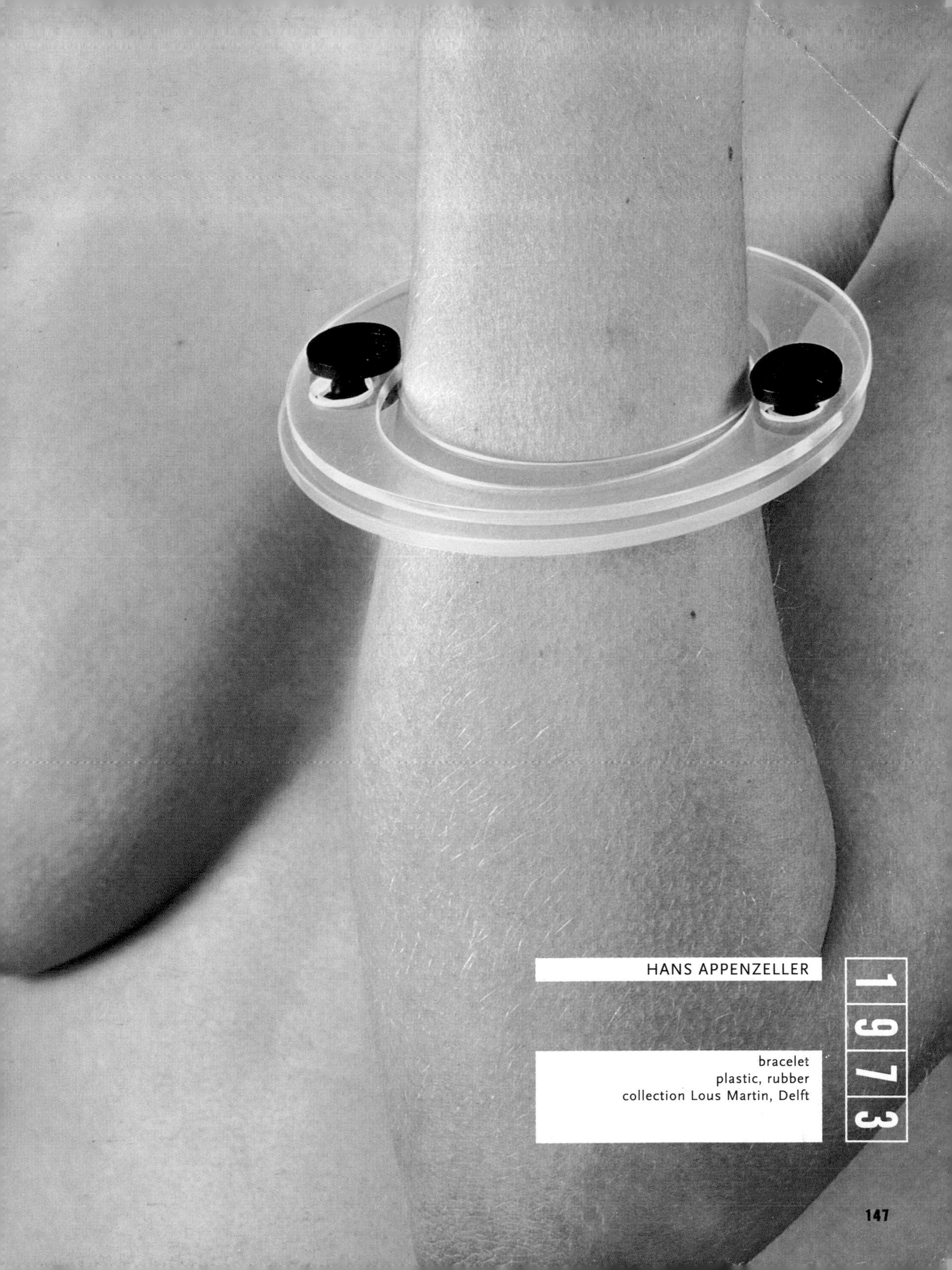

HANS APPENZELLER

bracelet
plastic, rubber
collection Lous Martin, Delft

1
9
7
3

circa

1
9
7
3

RUUDT PETERS

bracelet
aluminum, rubber

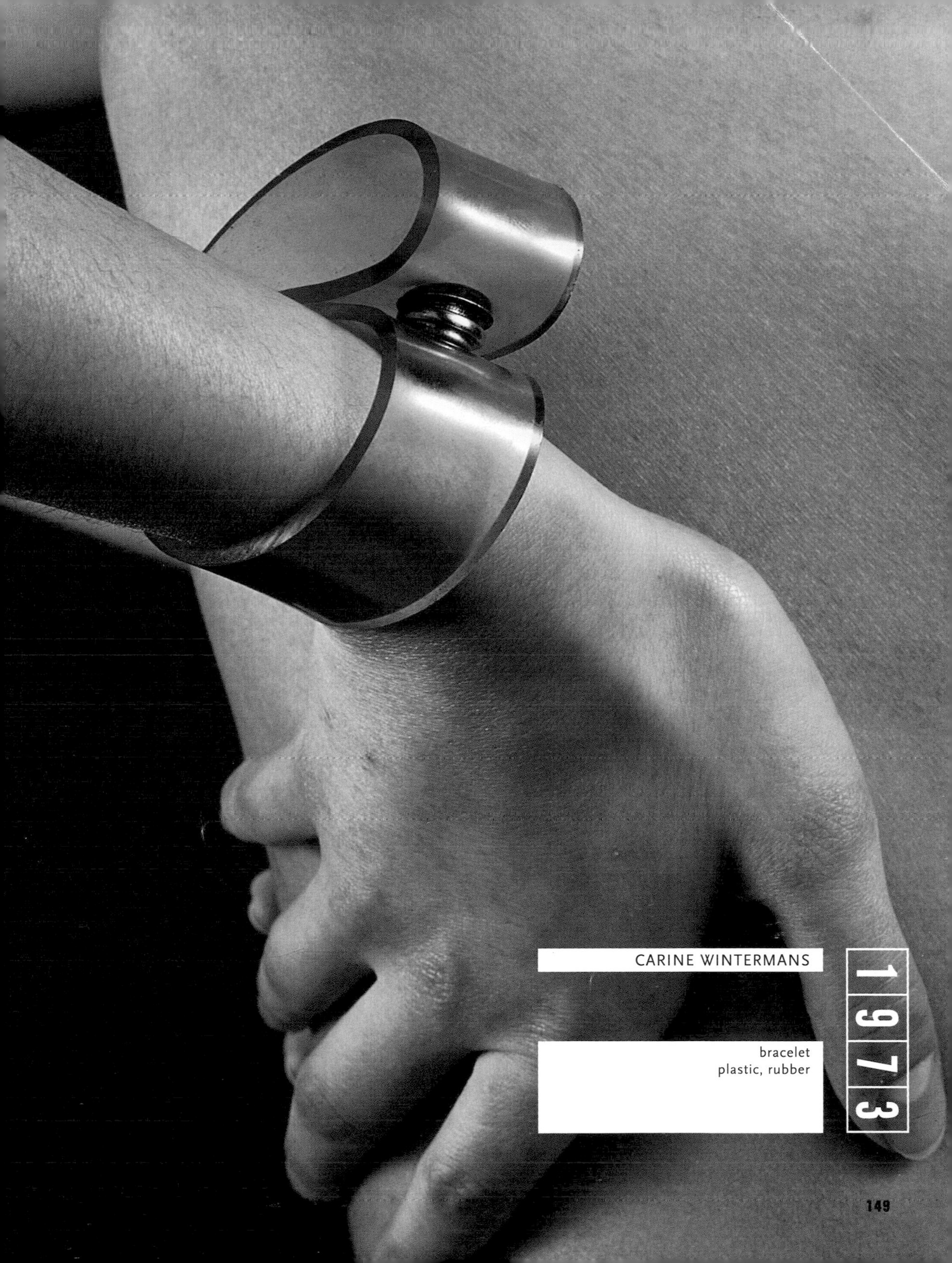

CARINE WINTERMANS

1
9
7
3

bracelet
plastic, rubber

circa

1974

LOUS MARTIN

Do it yourself kit
necklace & bracelet
aluminum, pipe cleaner

„doe het zelf sieraad":

armband/collier. ontwerp: faus martin.

model a: ▮▮▮▮▮ zie tekening

model b: ▨▨▨▨▨

model c,1,2: aenb, in twee kleuren.

```
      9   7   5   3   1
    ┌─────────────────┐
    │ o   o   o   o   o │
    │ o   o   o   o   o │
    └─────────────────┘
     10   8   6   4   2
```

alle modellen: schuur de scherpe randjes en de buitenkant van de alumin.
band, maak hem verder schoon met een lapje met ...
een brillo schuurspons ... buig de pijpen... dubbel...
lusuiteinde ... open uiteind...

model a: steek ... buitenkant af, het open uiteind... door gat ...
... de door gat 2. haal het open uiteind... door het lu...
... en trek voorzichtig aan ✳ steek nu aan de binn...
... t het open uiteinde door 3, dan via de buitenk...
naar 4: op dezelfde manier van 5 naar 6, 7 naar ... tot h...
eind. het overgebleven stuk pijpenrager steek u o...
de binnenkant terug, onder de laatste 3 lussen ...
het geheel met los ... aan. de rest knipt u af.

steek, van ... ...teinde door gat...
het open ...
steek ... voor de lus en ... voorzichtig aan
... naar ... de binnenkant her... en uiteinde o...
naar ... en door gat 4 weer naar ... innen. zo ook
... 5 naar 8, tot het eind. afwerking als mo...

werk... model ✳ ho ... al dit ... de an... eur
voor ... 3 en a. ri... de kleu... en ... verde... het
ei... afwerking ...odel a.

c₂ ...s model b ... her... ... a... kleu...
... het openuit... in de ...
... at 3 ...

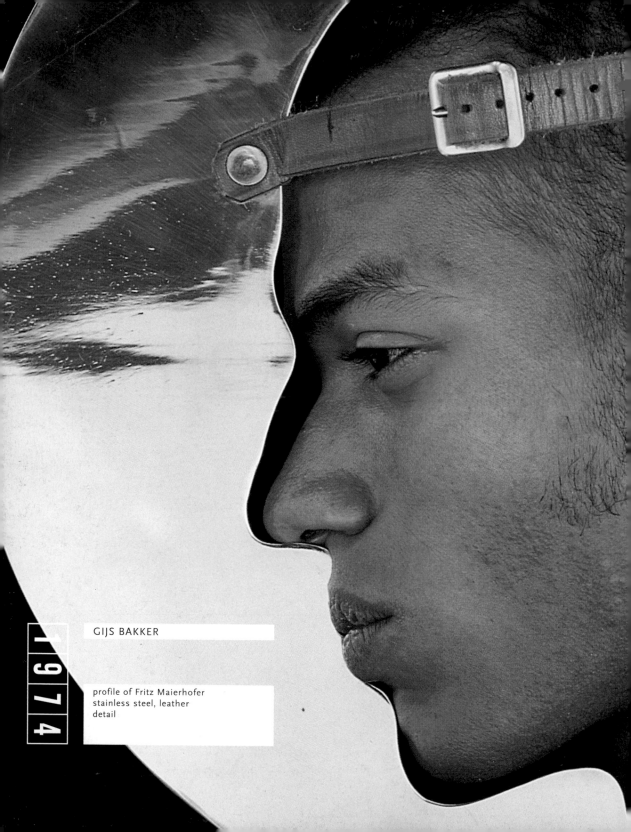

GIJS BAKKER

1974

profile of Fritz Maierhofer
stainless steel, leather
detail

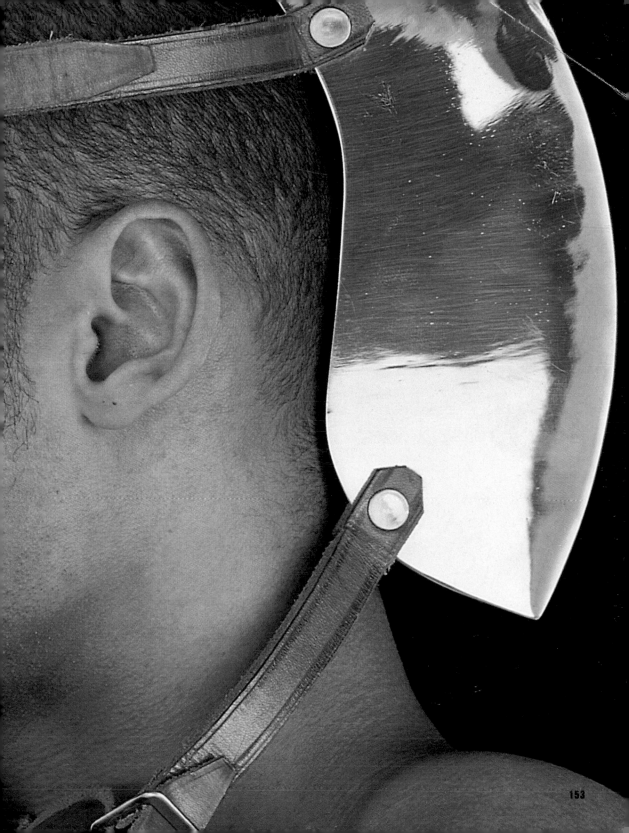

1974

GIJS BAKKER

profile of Fritz Maierhofer
stainless steel, leather

EMMY VAN LEERSUM

bracelet
series: vertical sawcuts
stainless steel

1974

1 9 7 4

EMMY VAN LEERSUM

bracelet
series: vertical sawcuts
stainless steel

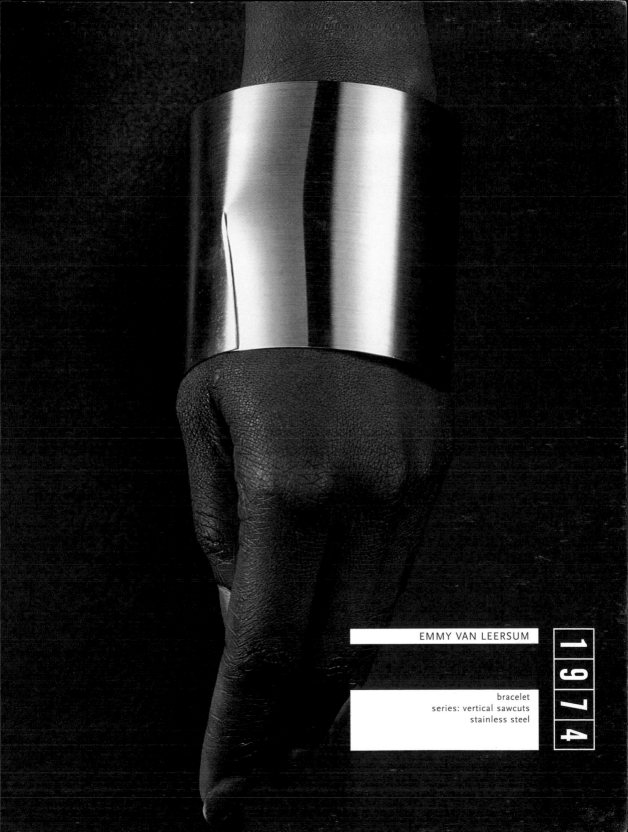

EMMY VAN LEERSUM

1974

bracelet
series: vertical sawcuts
stainless steel

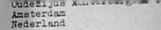
Oude~~zijds~~ Amsterdam
Nederland

Marion Herbst 4/100

MARION HERBST

Boe box
various materials
in collaboration with Onno Boekhoudt,
Françoise van den Bosch, Karel Niehorster
and Berend Peter (detail)

Françoise van den Bosch

1
9
7
4

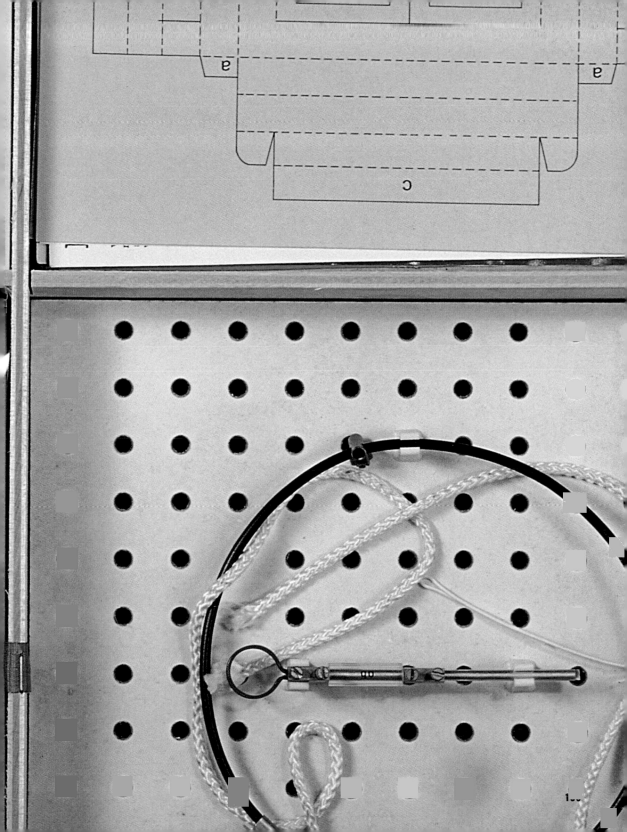

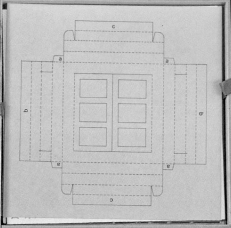

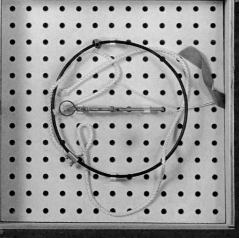

MARION HERBST

Boe box
various materials
in collaboration with Onno Boekhoudt,
Françoise van den Bosch, Karel Niehorster
and Berend Peter

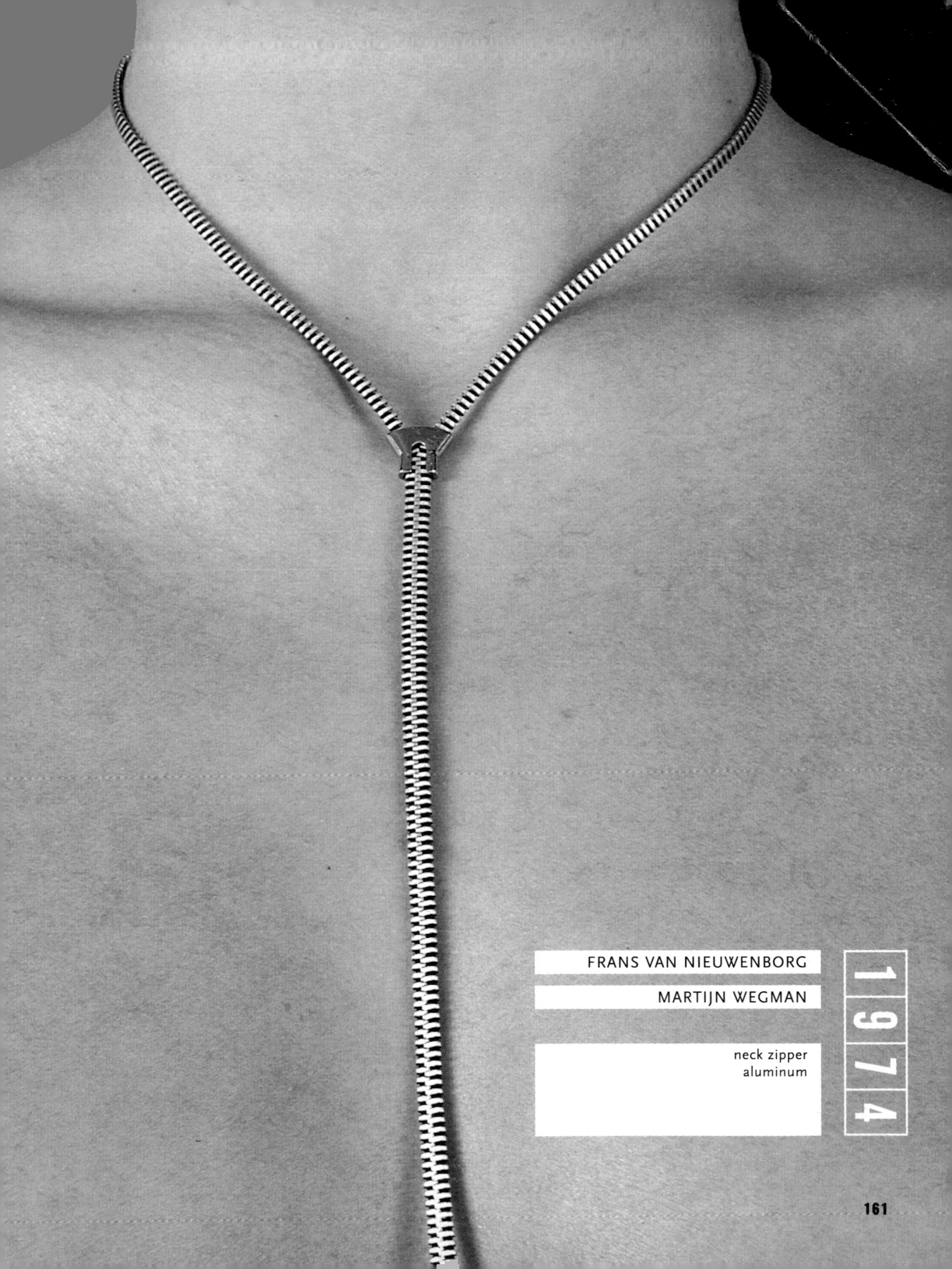

FRANS VAN NIEUWENBORG

MARTIJN WEGMAN

neck zipper
aluminum

1974

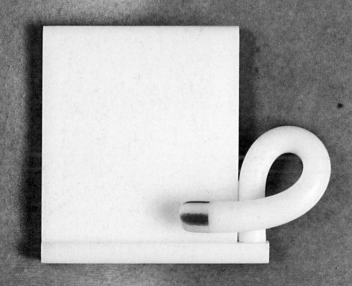

1974

MARION HERBST

brooch
perspex

152

MARION HERBST

brooch
perspex

1974

1974

FRANS VAN NIEUWENBORG

MARTIJN WEGMAN

necklaces
aluminum

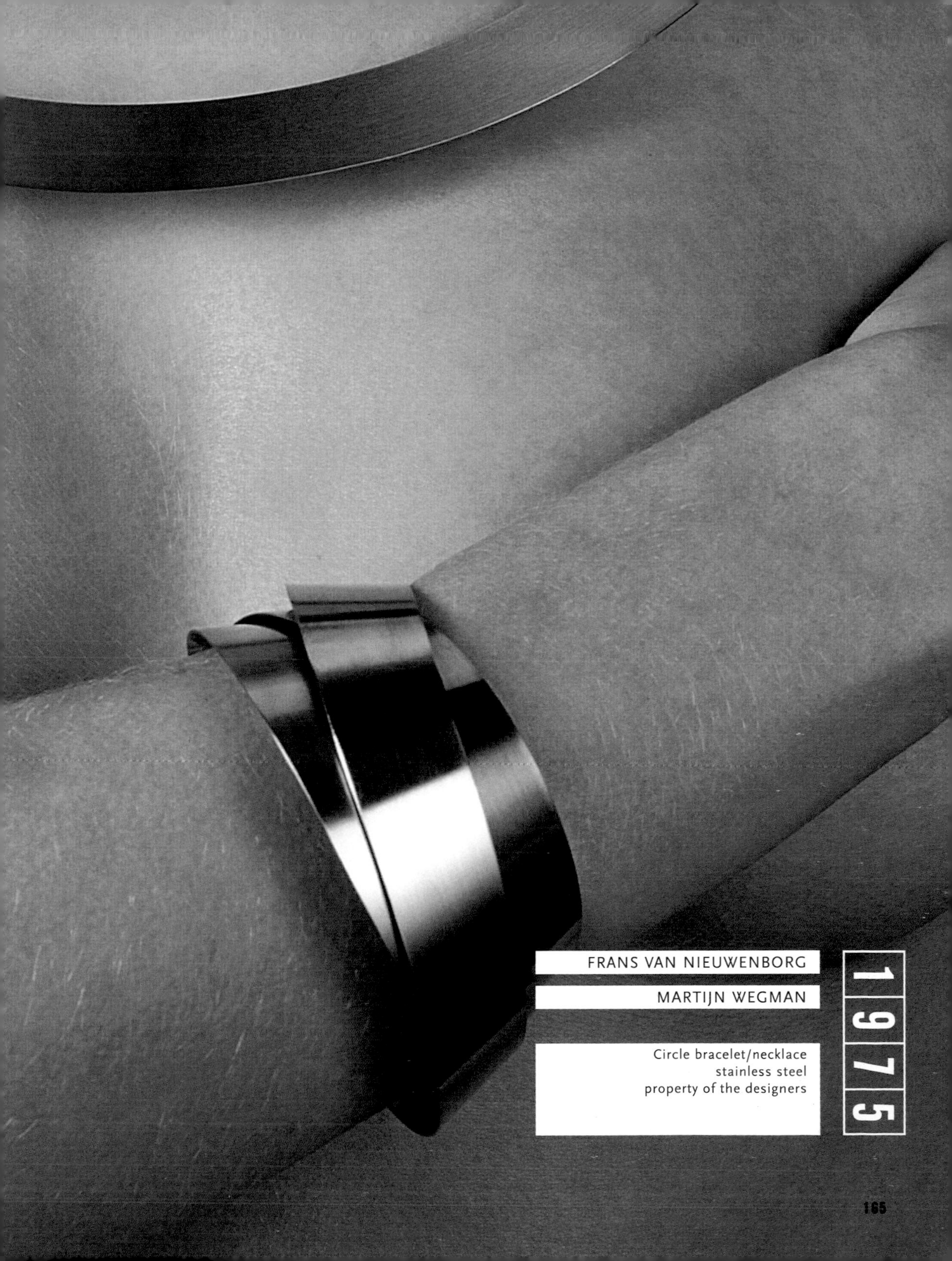

FRANS VAN NIEUWENBORG

MARTIJN WEGMAN

Circle bracelet/necklace
stainless steel
property of the designers

1975

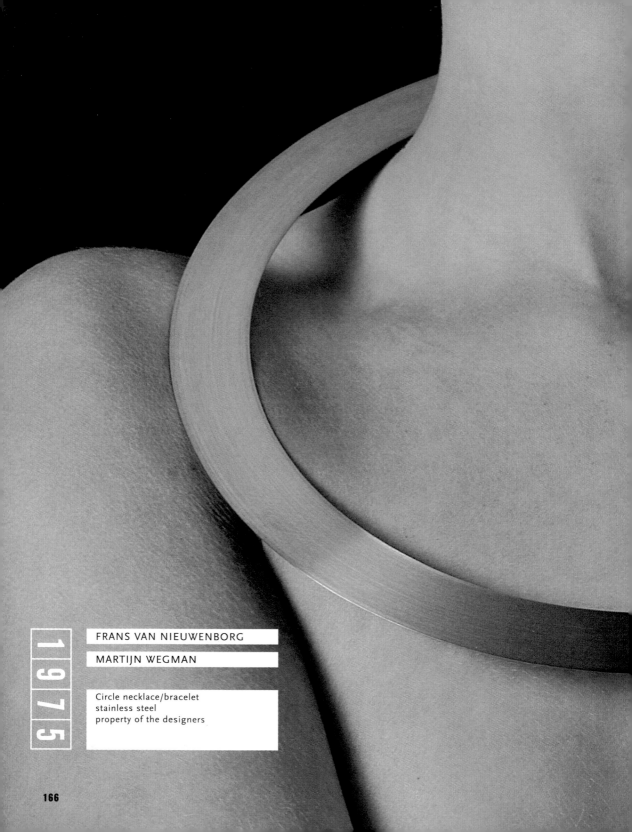

1975

FRANS VAN NIEUWENBORG

MARTIJN WEGMAN

Circle necklace/bracelet
stainless steel
property of the designers

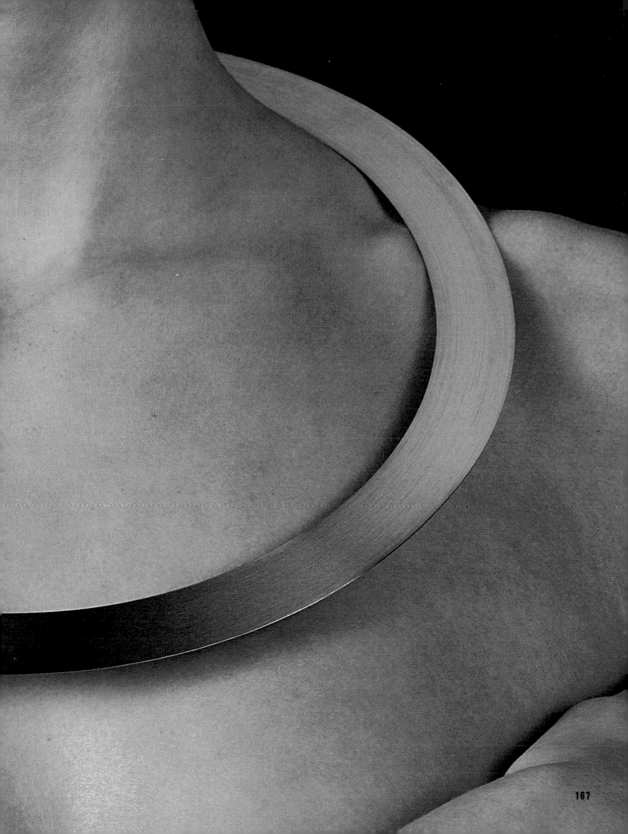

BRUNO NINABER VAN EYBEN

bracelet
stainless steel, perspex

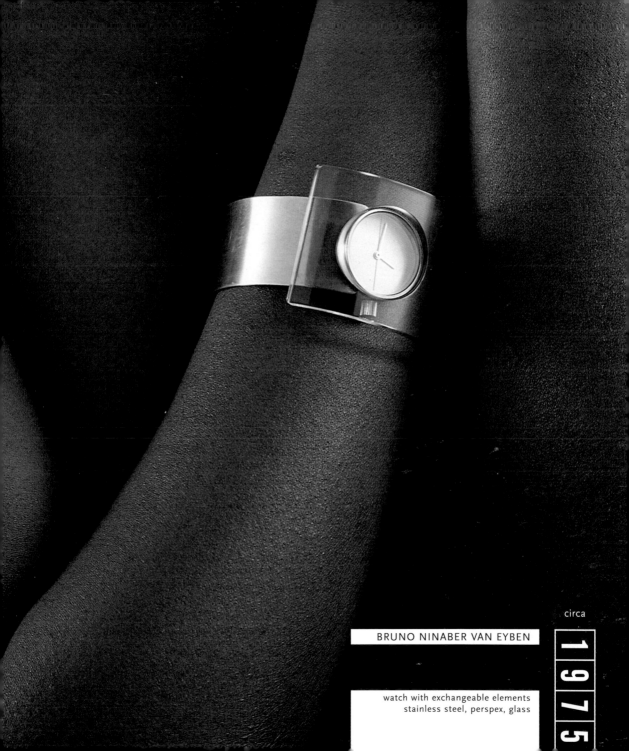

BRUNO NINABER VAN EYBEN

circa

1975

watch with exchangeable elements
stainless steel, perspex, glass

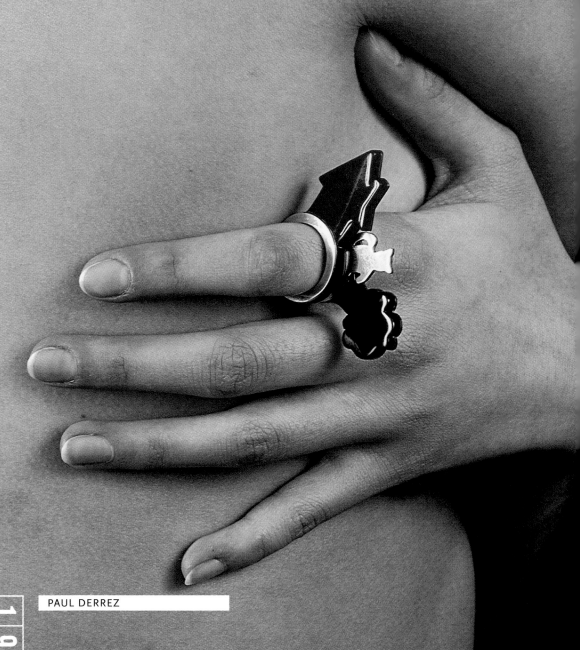

1 9 7 5

PAUL DERREZ

Suburban bliss
ring
silver, acrylic

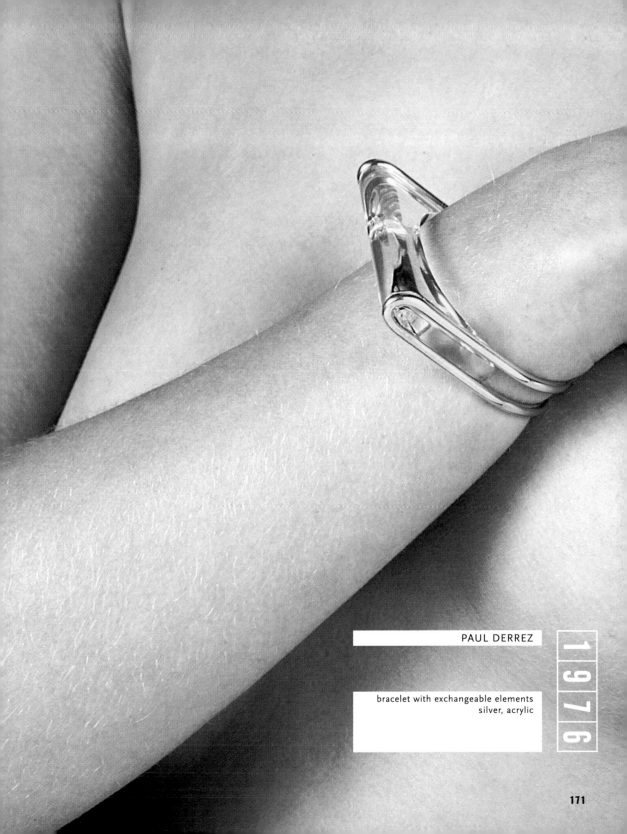

PAUL DERREZ

bracelet with exchangeable elements
silver, acrylic

1976

BRUNO NINABER VAN EYBEN

1
9
7
6

bracelet
wood, rubber

172

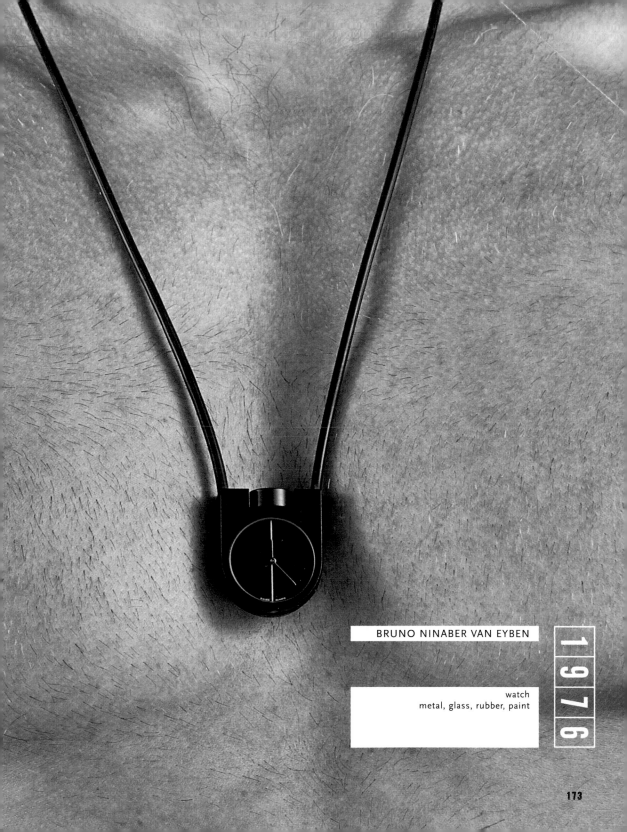

BRUNO NINABER VAN EYBEN

watch
metal, glass, rubber, paint

FRANÇOISE VAN DEN BOSCH

Pillow brooch
aluminum

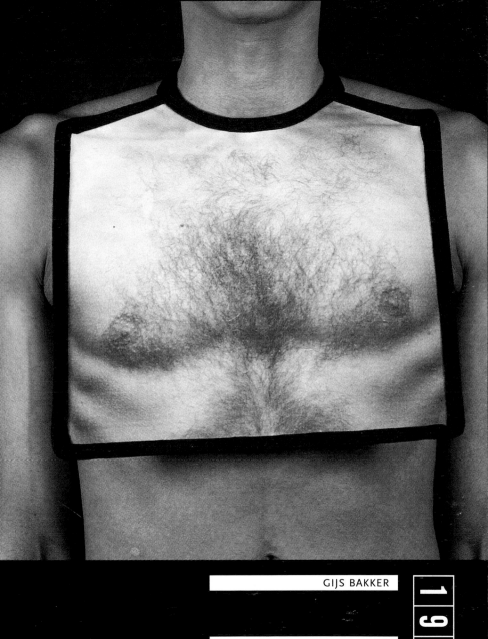

GIJS BAKKER

Bib
neckpiece
photograph on linen

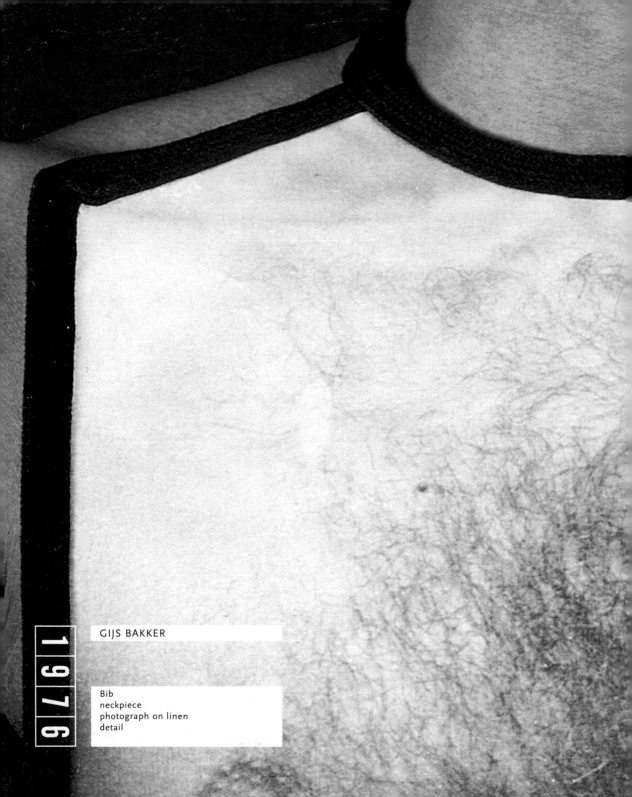

GIJS BAKKER

1976

Bib
neckpiece
photograph on linen
detail

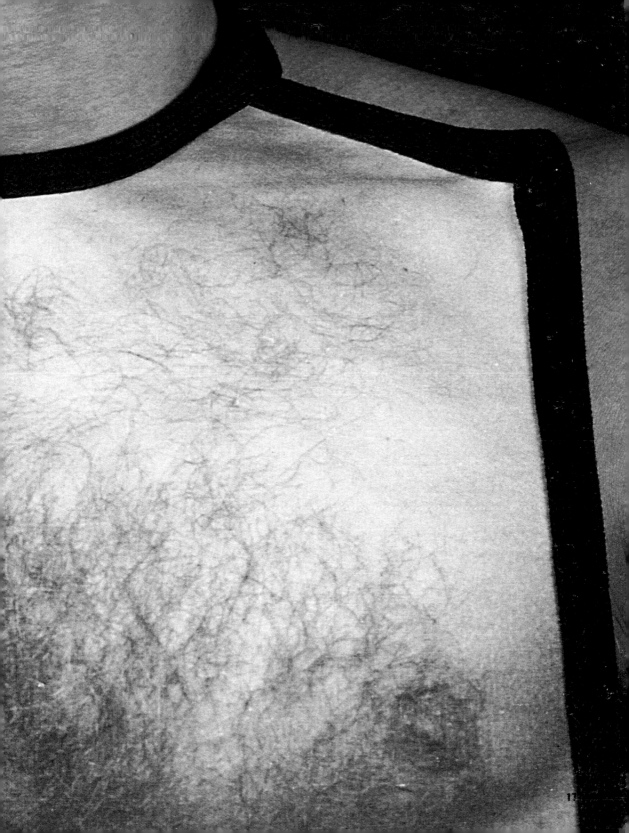

179

1 9 7 8

MARIA HEES

garden hose bracelets
pvc garden hose

MARIA HEES

1
9
7
8

brush brooches
plastic hairbrush

1 9 7 8

MARGA STAARTJES

bracelets
plastic scouring pad

MARGA STAARTJES

bracelets
pipe cleaner in plastic tube

1 9 7 9

EMMY VAN LEERSUM

bracelet
series: cutting the square
gold

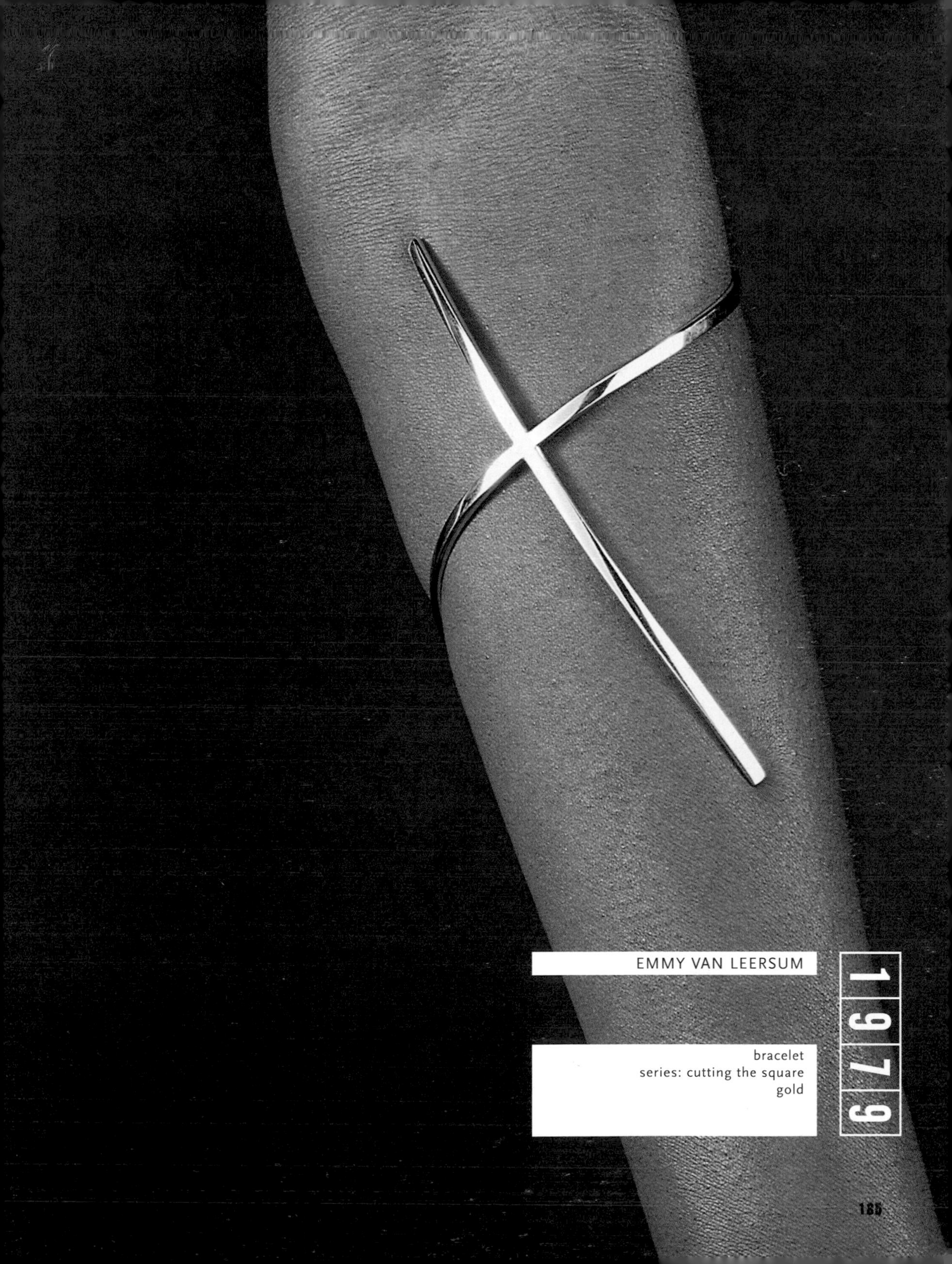

EMMY VAN LEERSUM

bracelet
series: cutting the square
gold

1979

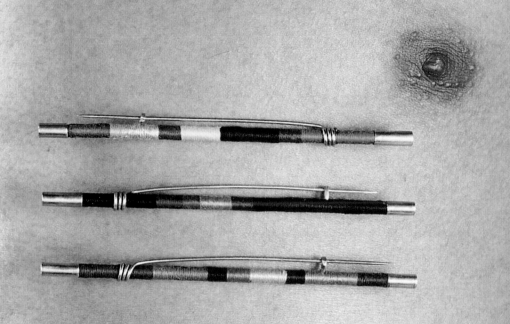

1 9 7 9

MARION HERBST

Stick
brooches
silver, brass, embroidery thread

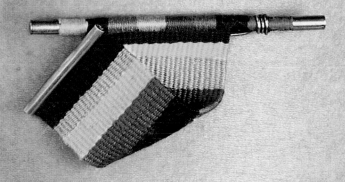

MARION HERBST

HENRIËTTE WIESSING

Turnover decoration
brooch
woven embroidery thread, silver

1979

ONNO BOEKHOUDT

1979

brooch
silver

circa

ONNO BOEKHOUDT

1980

brooch
silver

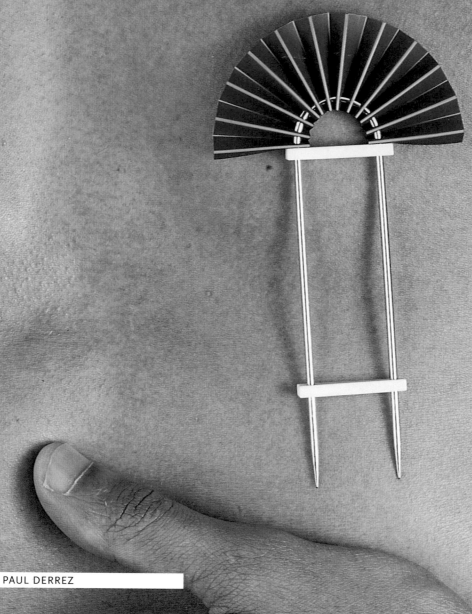

1980

PAUL DERREZ

Fan pin
aluminum, plastic, acrylic

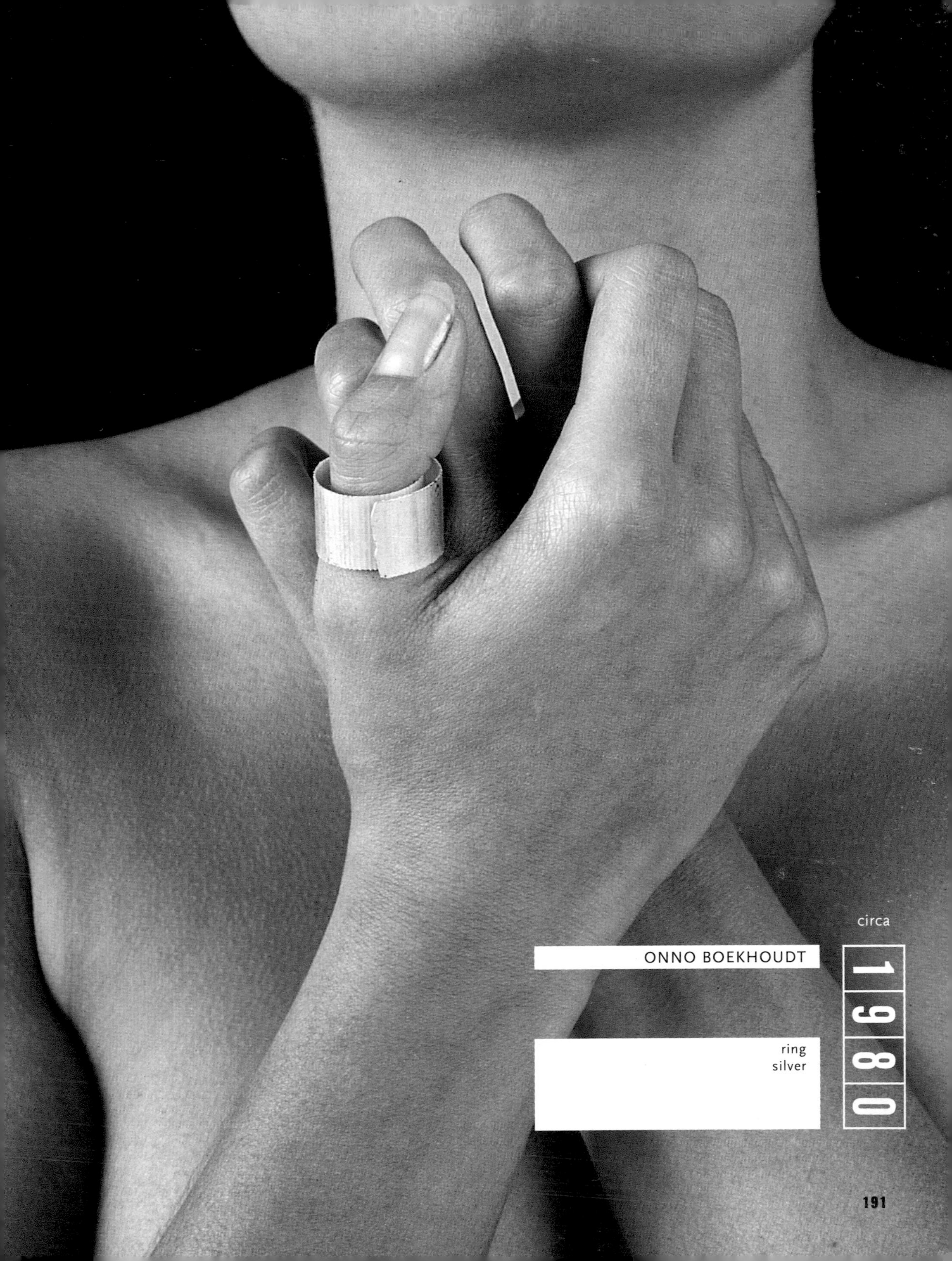

circa 1980

ONNO BOEKHOUDT

ring
silver

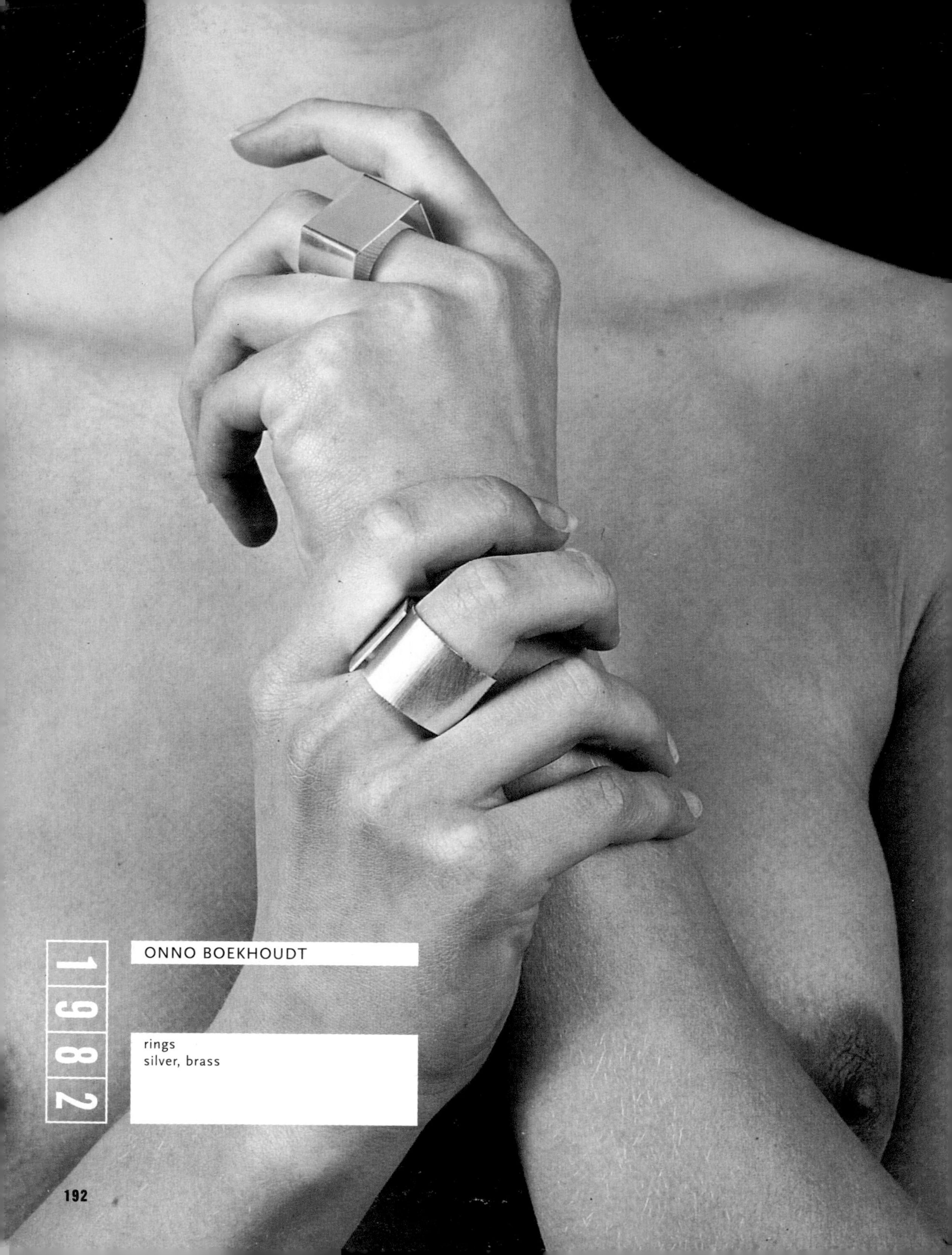

ONNO BOEKHOUDT

rings
silver, brass

ANNELIES PLANTEIJDT

necklace
cardboard
detail

1982

1982

ANNELIES PLANTEIJDT

necklace
cardboard

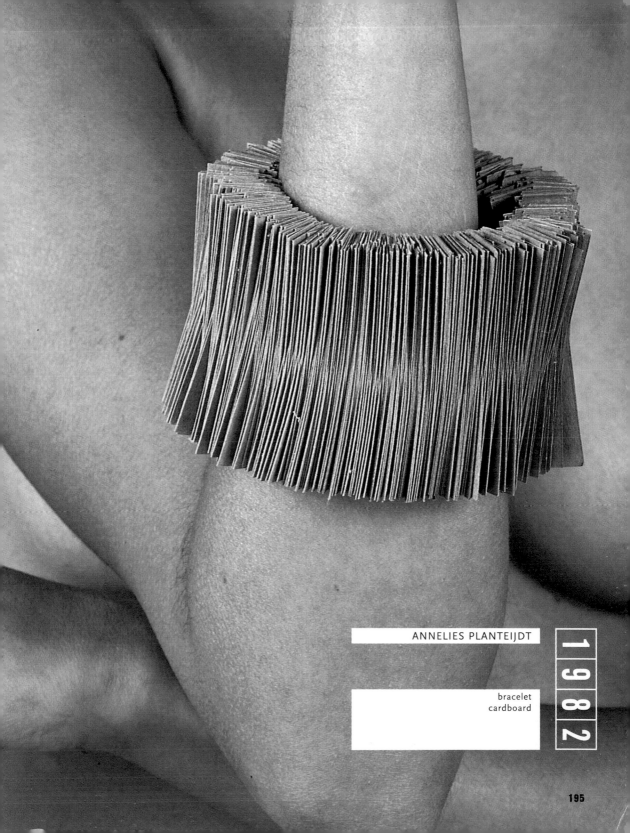

LAM DE WOLF

1981

object to wear
textile, paint, wood
detail

LAM DE WOLF

object to wear
textile, paint, wood

1 9 8 1

LAM DE WOLF

object to wear
textile, paint
private collection

1982

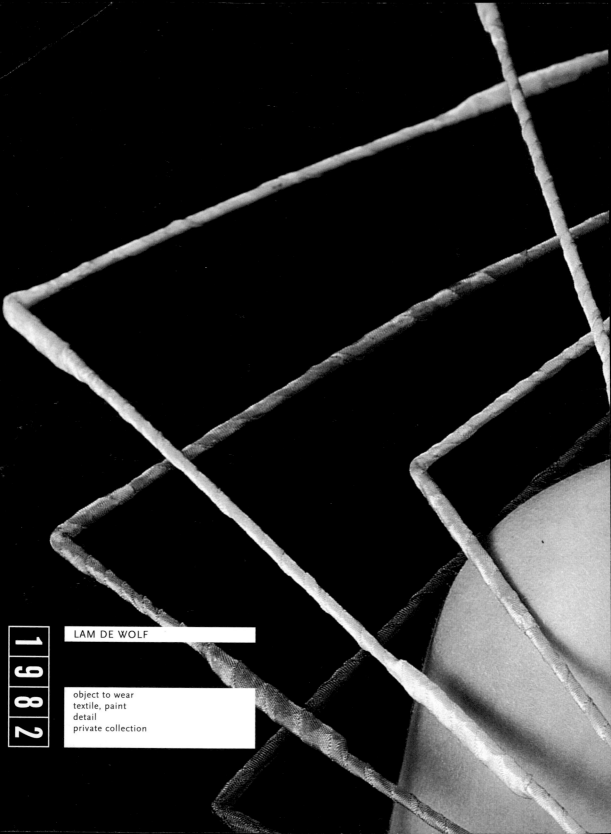

LAM DE WOLF

object to wear
textile, paint
detail
private collection

1982

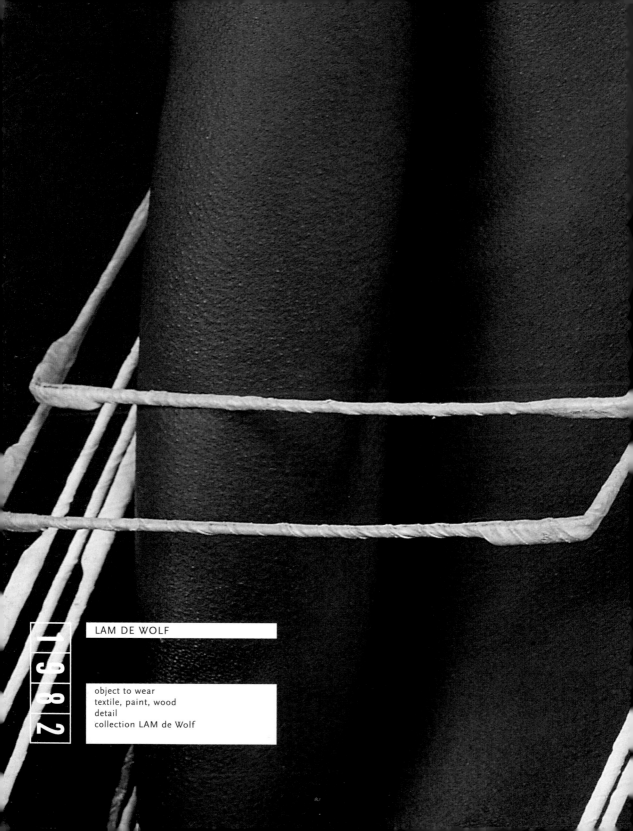

LAM DE WOLF

1 9 8 2

object to wear
textile, paint, wood
detail
collection LAM de Wolf

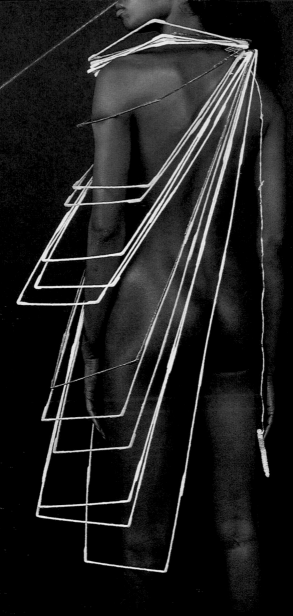

1982

LAM DE WOLF

object to wear
textile, paint, wood
collection LAM de Wolf

GIJS BAKKER

1
9
8
2

Dew drop
neckpiece
pvc laminated photograph

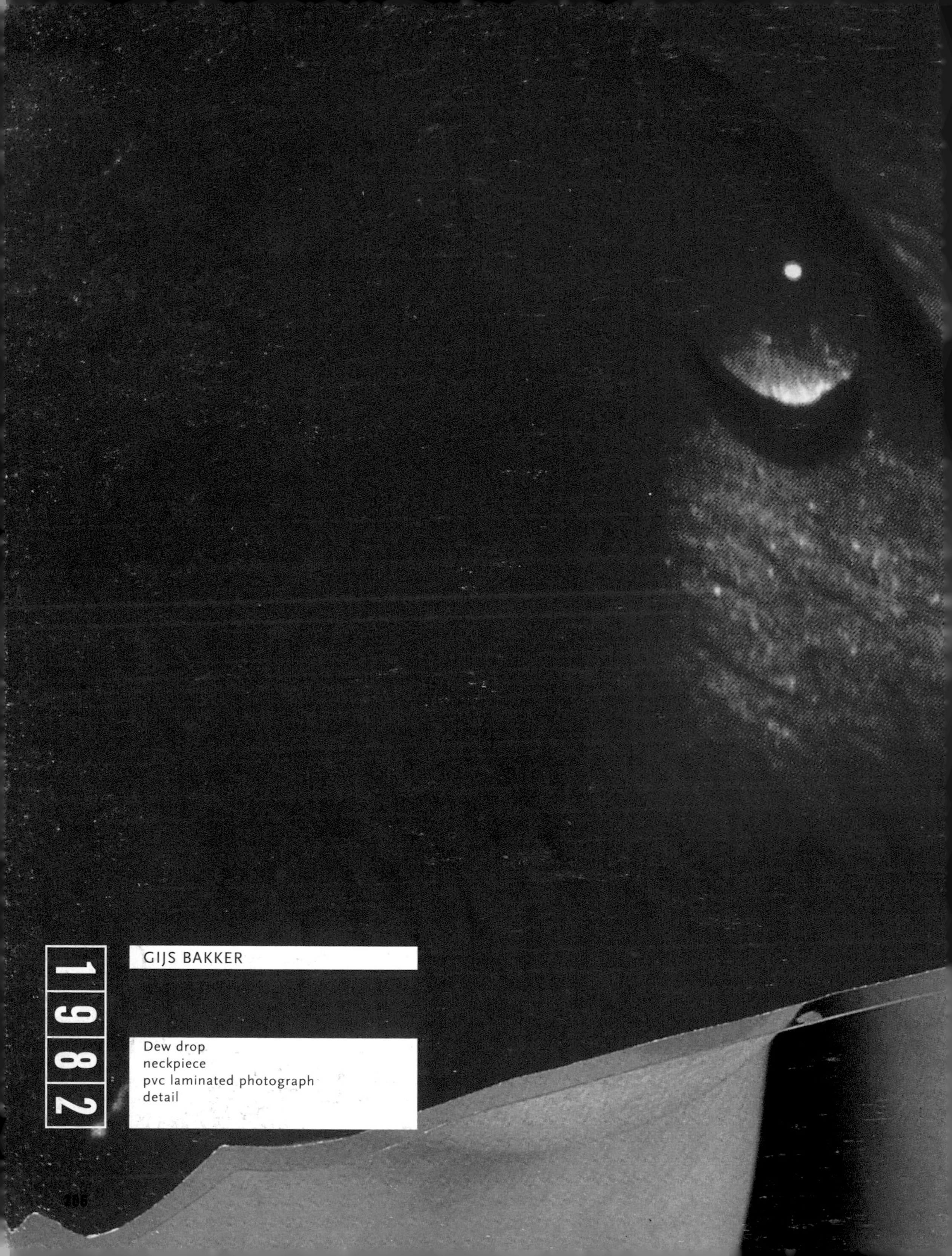

GIJS BAKKER

Dew drop
neckpiece
pvc laminated photograph
detail

1982

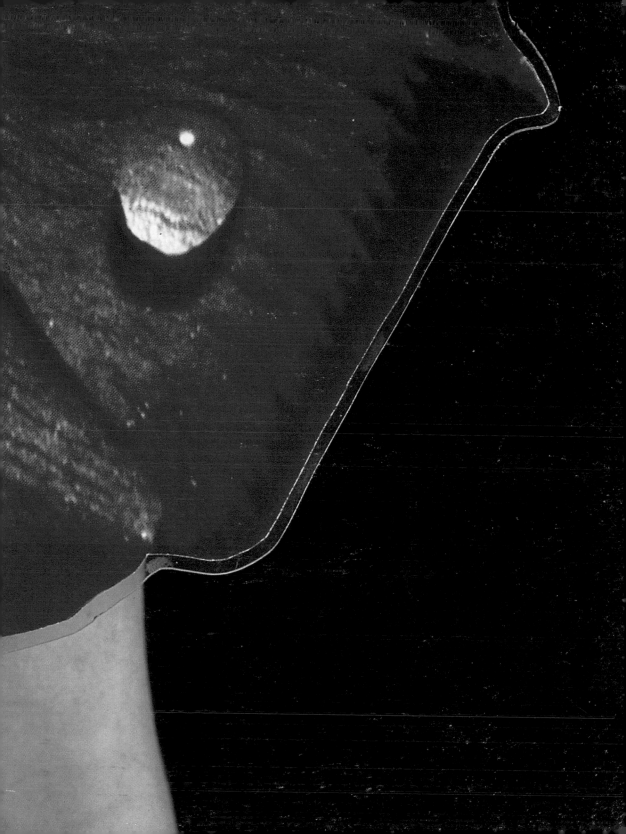

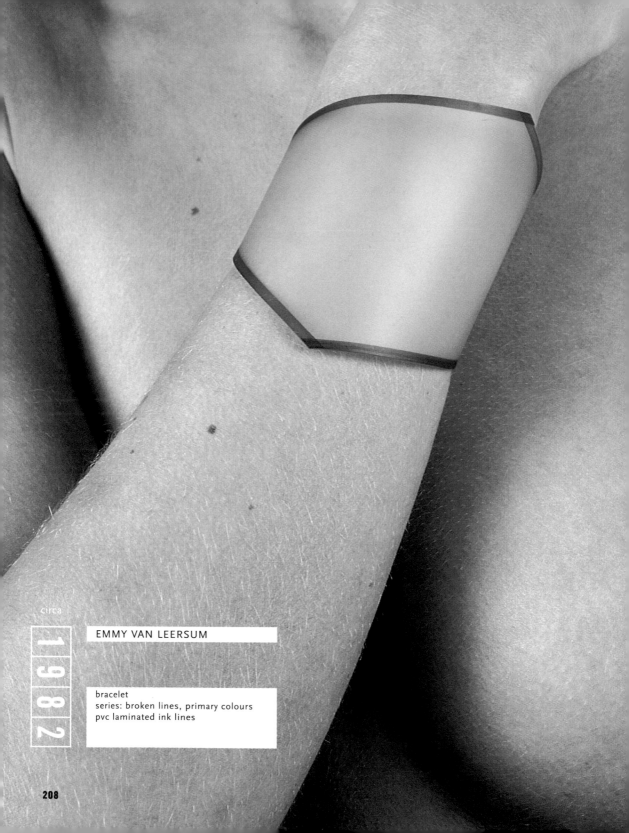

1
9
8
2

EMMY VAN LEERSUM

bracelet
series: broken lines, primary colours
pvc laminated ink lines

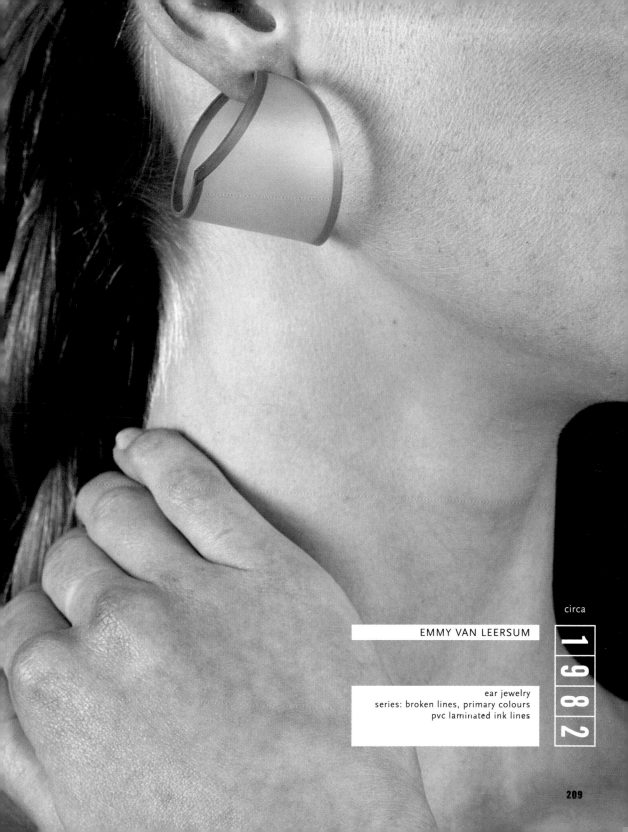

circa

1
9
8
2

EMMY VAN LEERSUM

ear jewelry
series: broken lines, primary colours
pvc laminated ink lines

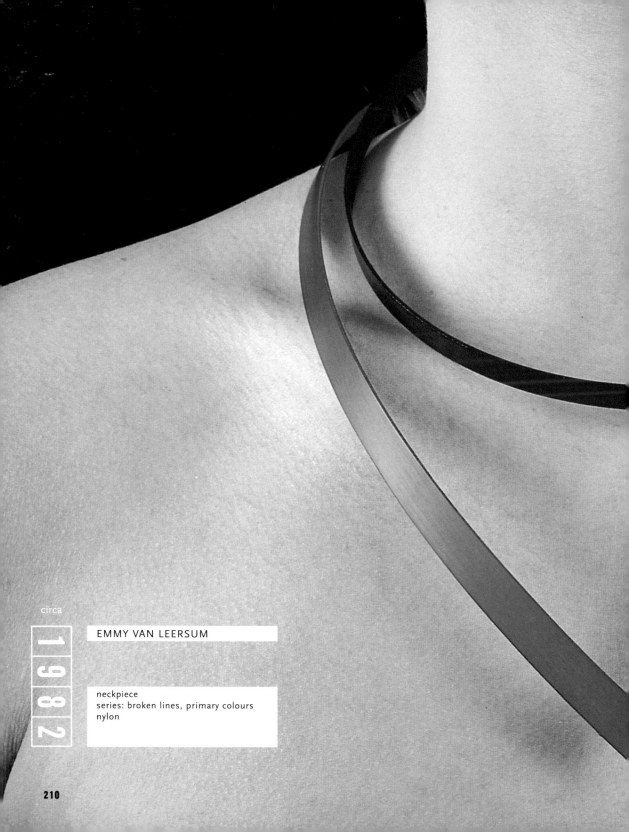

circa

1 9 8 2

EMMY VAN LEERSUM

neckpiece
series: broken lines, primary colours
nylon

211

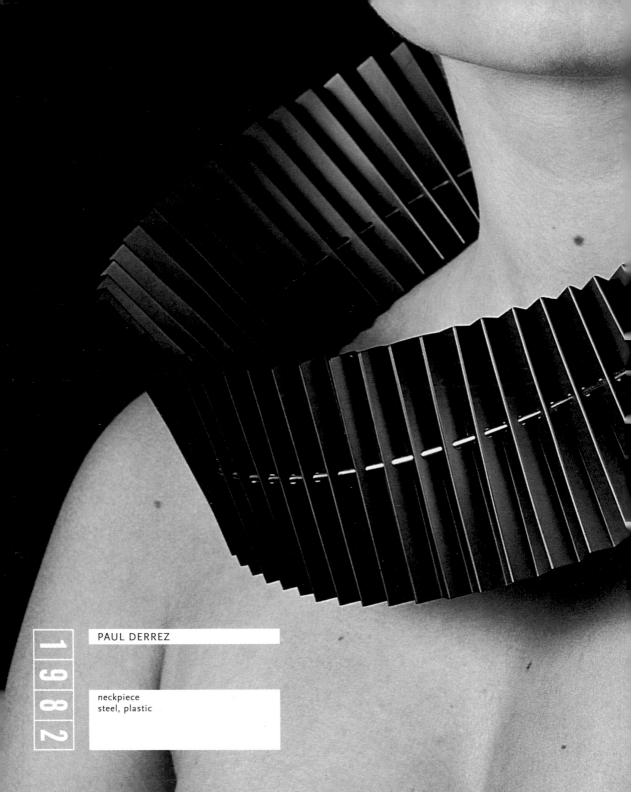

PAUL DERREZ

1982

neckpiece
steel, plastic

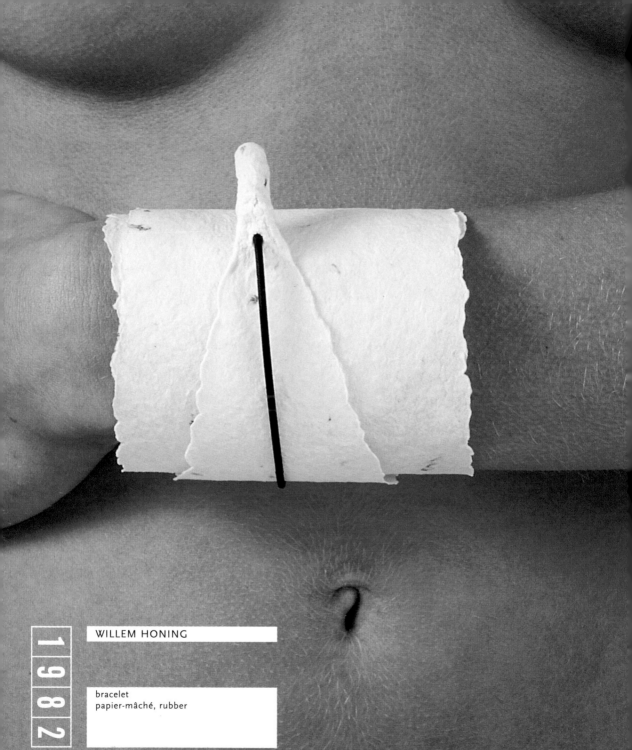

WILLEM HONING

bracelet
papier-mâché, rubber

214

LAM DE WOLF

object to wear
textile, paint
collection LAM de Wolf
detail

1 9 8 3

1983

LAM DE WOLF

object to wear
textile, paint
collection LAM de Wolf

object to wear
textile, paint
collection Centraal Museum Utrecht
dress: Heidi de Raad & Marlies Kwade

1983

LAM DE WOLF

1983

object to wear
textile, paint
detail
collection Centraal Museum Utrecht
dress: Heidi de Raad & Marlies Kwade

1983

JOKE BRAKMAN

CLAUDIE BERBÉE

Overall no. 5a
shoulder piece
cotton, paint

1 9 8 4

JOKE BRAKMAN

CLAUDIE BERBÉE

Overall no. 10b
shoulder piece
cotton, paint

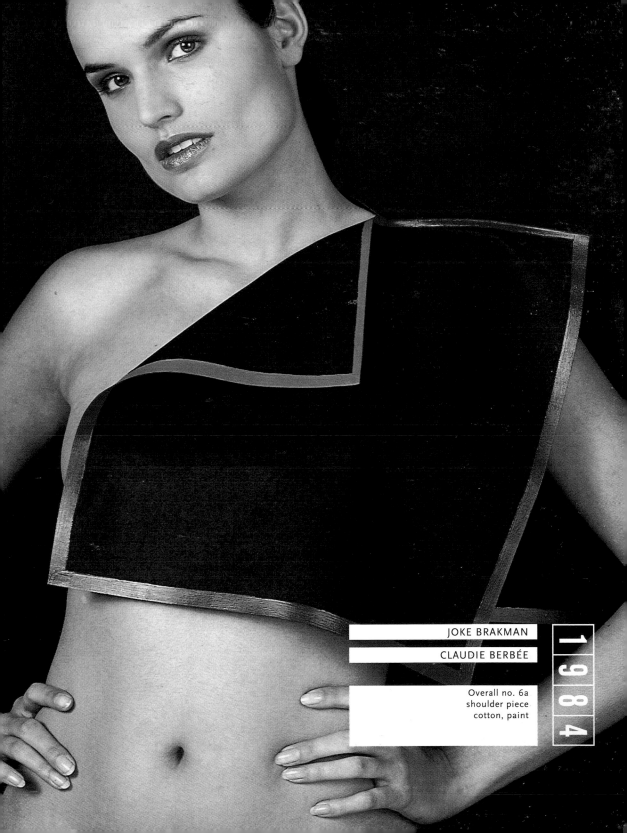

JOKE BRAKMAN

CLAUDIE BERBÉE

Overall no. 6a
shoulder piece
cotton, paint

1984

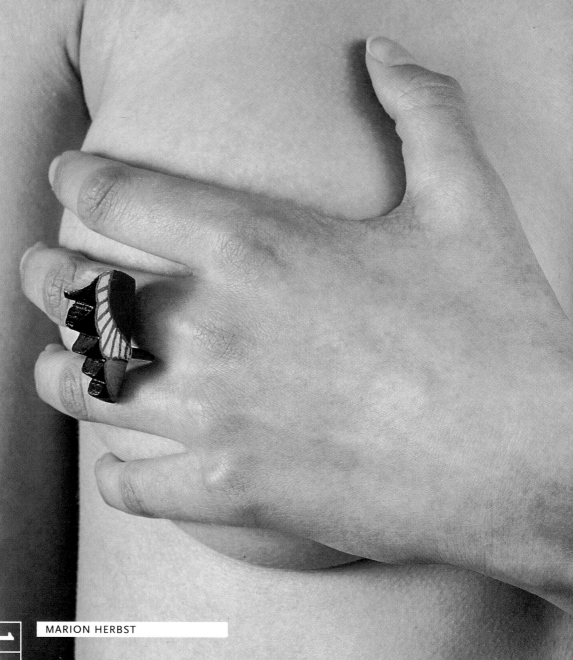

MARION HERBST

ring
silver, painted wood

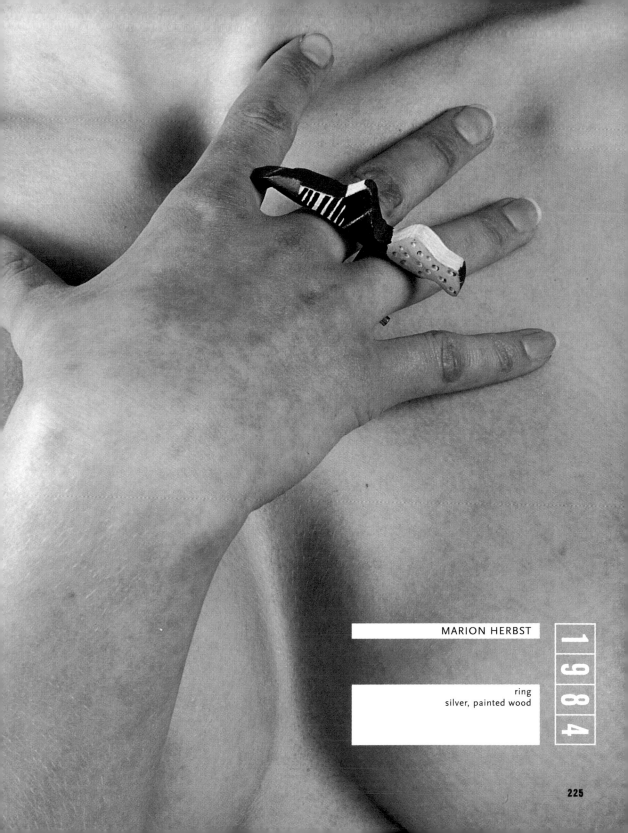

MARION HERBST

1984

ring
silver, painted wood

225

1984

EMMY VAN LEERSUM

brooch
series: cutting the square
gold

WILLEM HONING

necklace
paper
detail

1984

1982

WILLEM HONING

necklace
paper

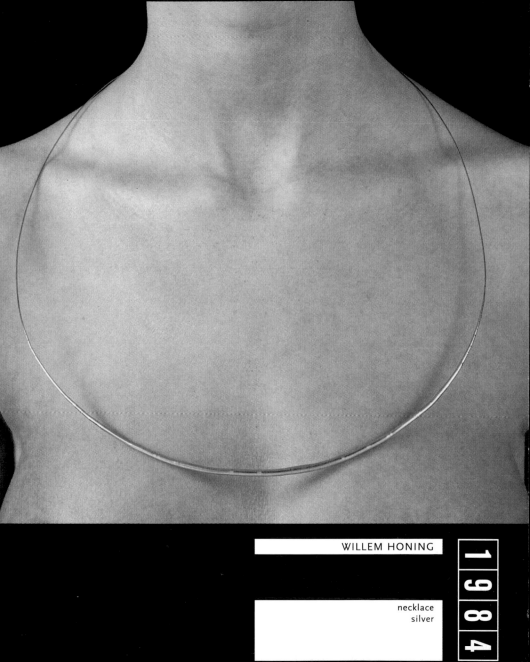

WILLEM HONING

necklace
silver

1984

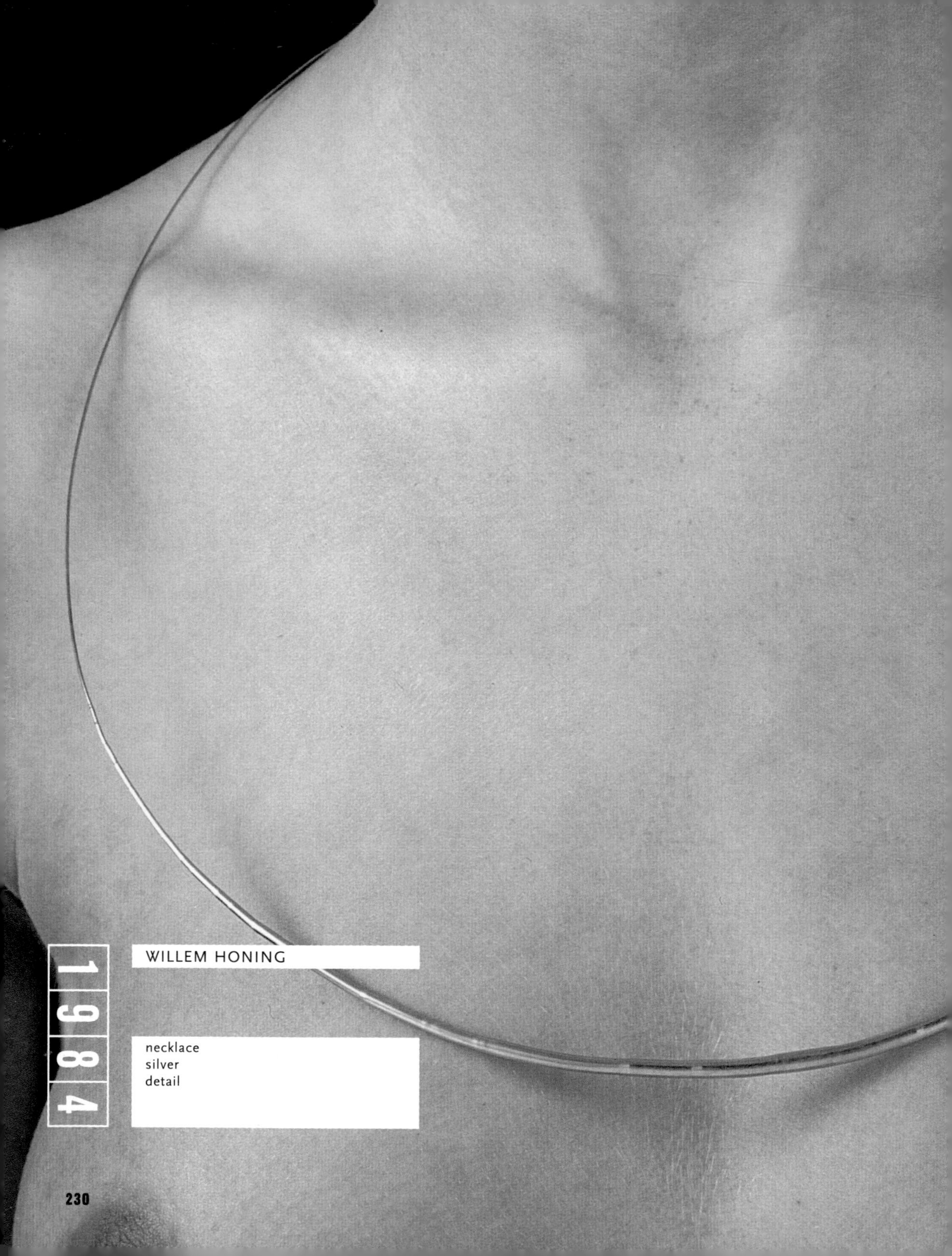

WILLEM HONING

1984

necklace
silver
detail

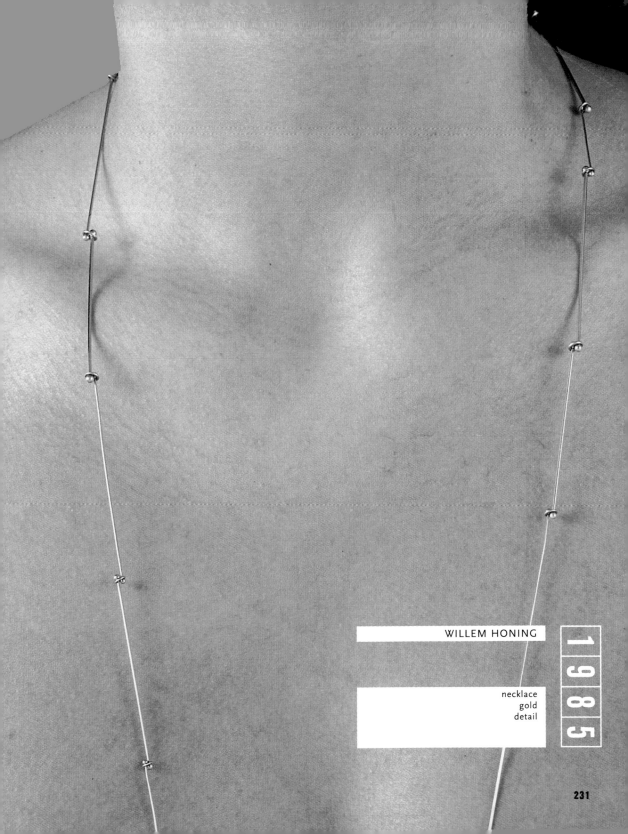

WILLEM HONING

necklace
gold
detail

1985

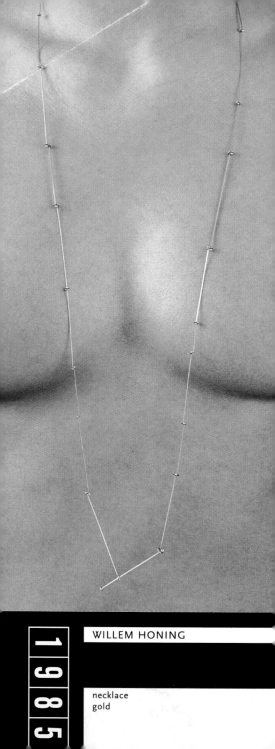

1 9 8 5

WILLEM HONING

necklace
gold

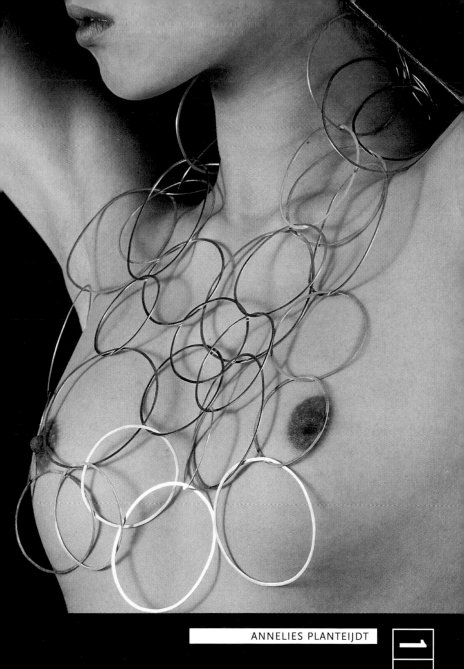

ANNELIES PLANTEIJDT

necklace
gold

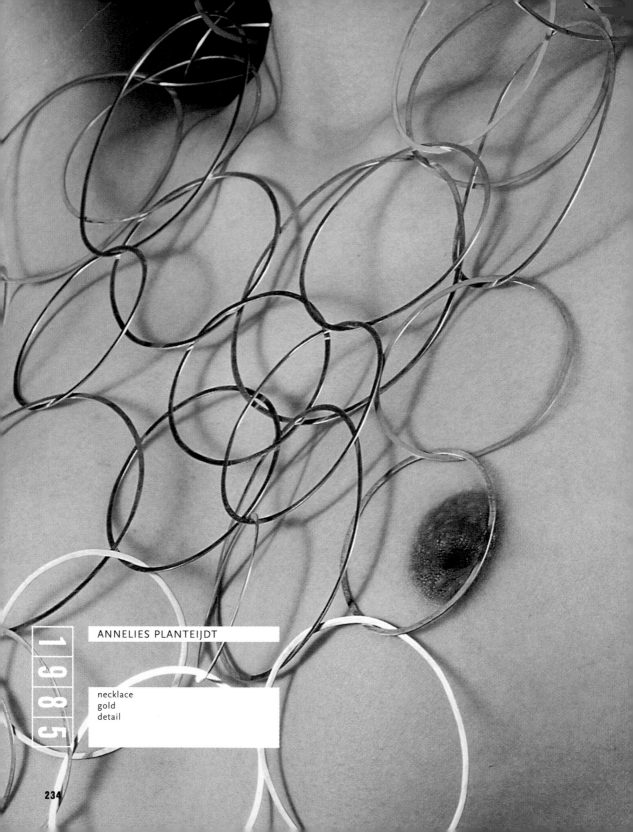

ANNELIES PLANTEIJDT

necklace
gold
detail

PAUL DERREZ

cobble collar
cork, pigment

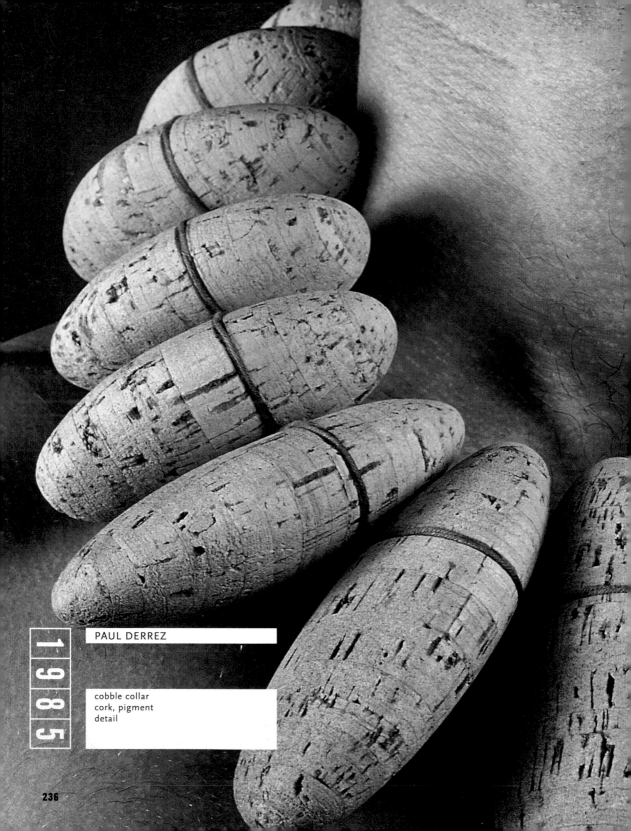

PAUL DERREZ

1985

cobble collar
cork, pigment
detail

1985

ONNO BOEKHOUDT

Studies for rings
wood, metal, paint
collection Paul Derrez/Willem Hoogstede

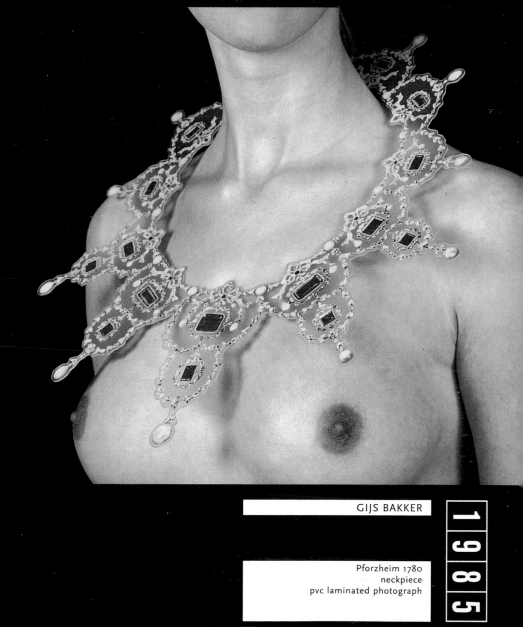

GIJS BAKKER

1985

Pforzheim 1780
neckpiece
pvc laminated photograph

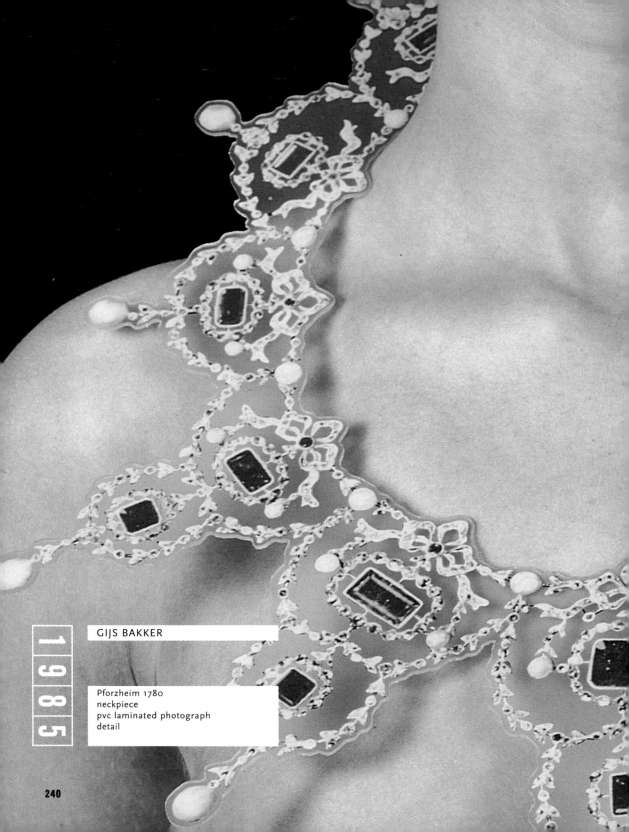

GIJS BAKKER

Pforzheim 1780
neckpiece
pvc laminated photograph
detail

1985

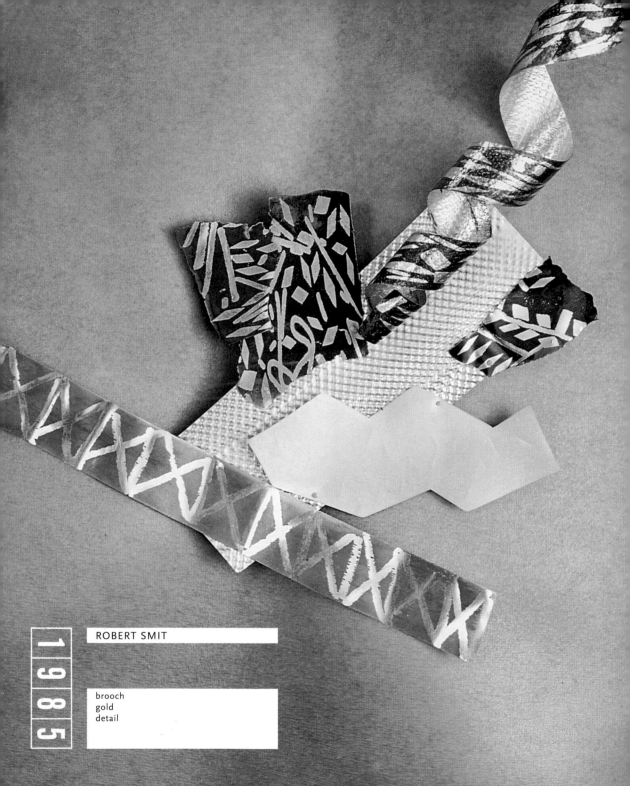

1 9 8 5

ROBERT SMIT

brooch
gold
detail

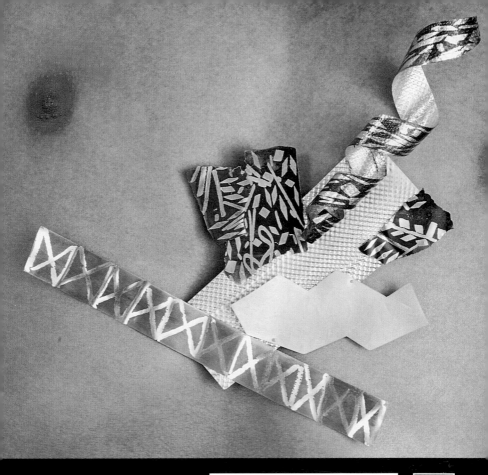

ROBERT SMIT

brooch
gold

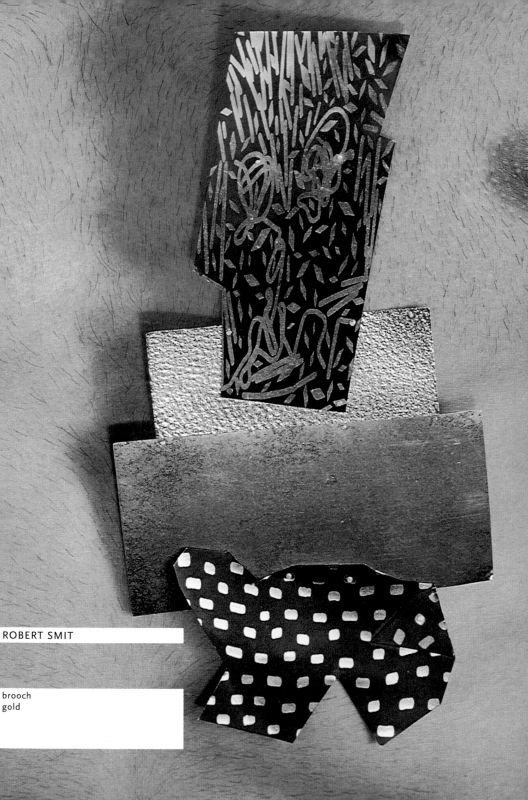

ROBERT SMIT

brooch
gold

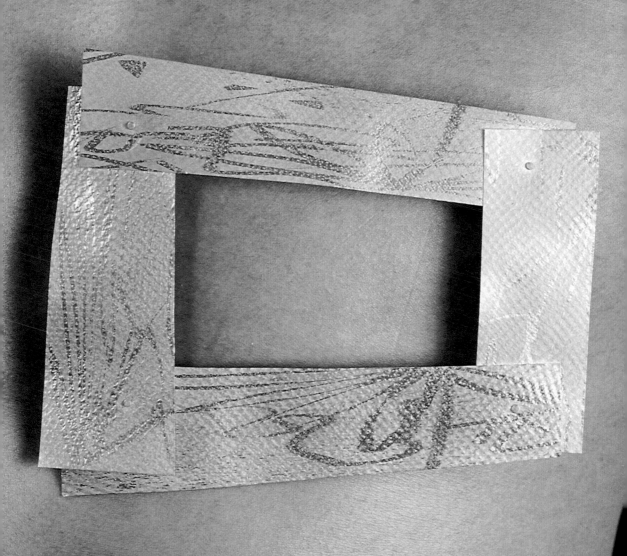

ROBERT SMIT

brooch
gold

1985

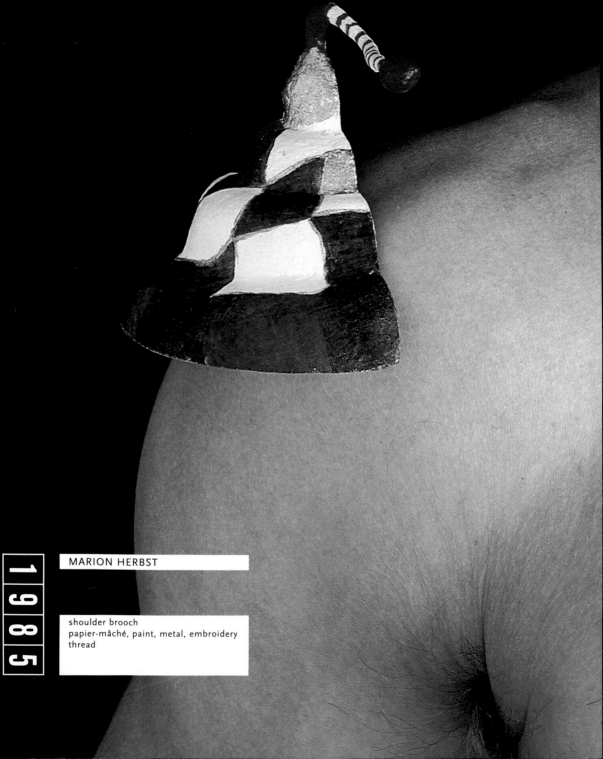

1985

MARION HERBST

shoulder brooch
papier-mâché, paint, metal, embroidery
thread

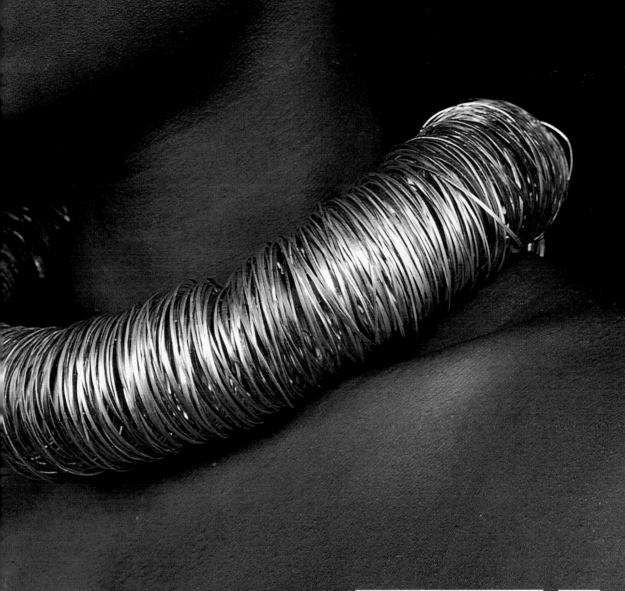

WILLEM HONING

necklace
brass
detail

1986

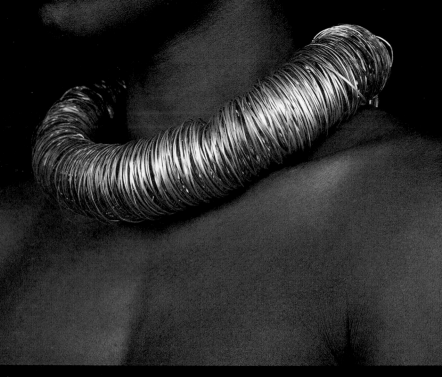

1986

WILLEM HONING

necklace
brass

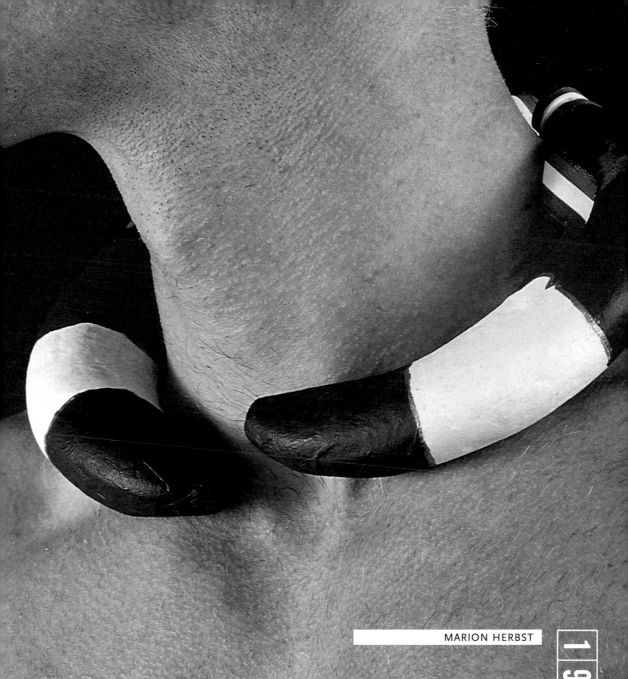

MARION HERBST

necklace
papier-mâché, paint, ribbon

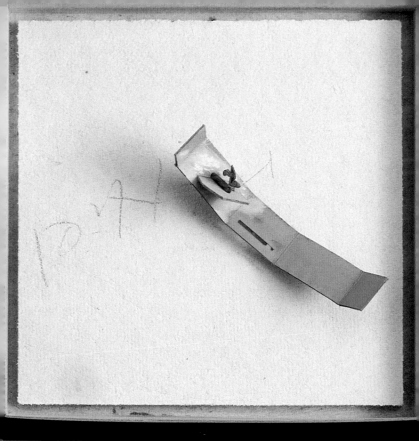

ONNO BOEKHOUDT

brooch in box
card board, wood, metal, paint
collection H.J. v.d. Valk/T. Woudstra

1987

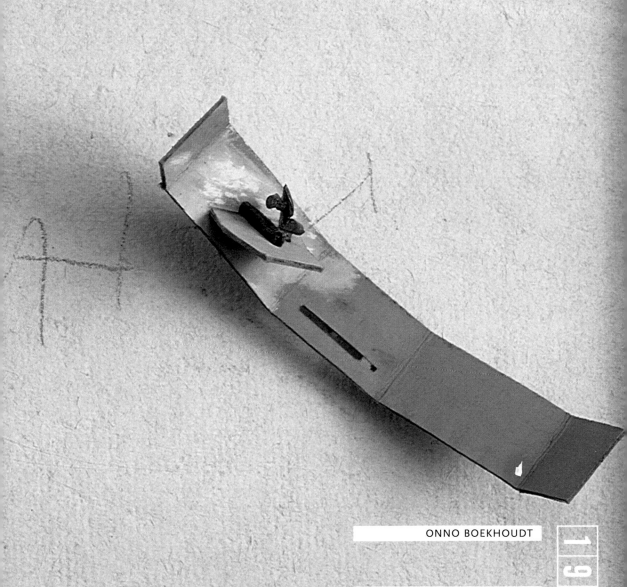

brooch in box
card board, wood, metal, paint
detail
collection H.J. v.d. Valk/T. Woudstra

1 9 8 7

1988

box with bench pin and brooch
wood, stainless steel, silver
collection Paul Derrez/Willem Hoogstede

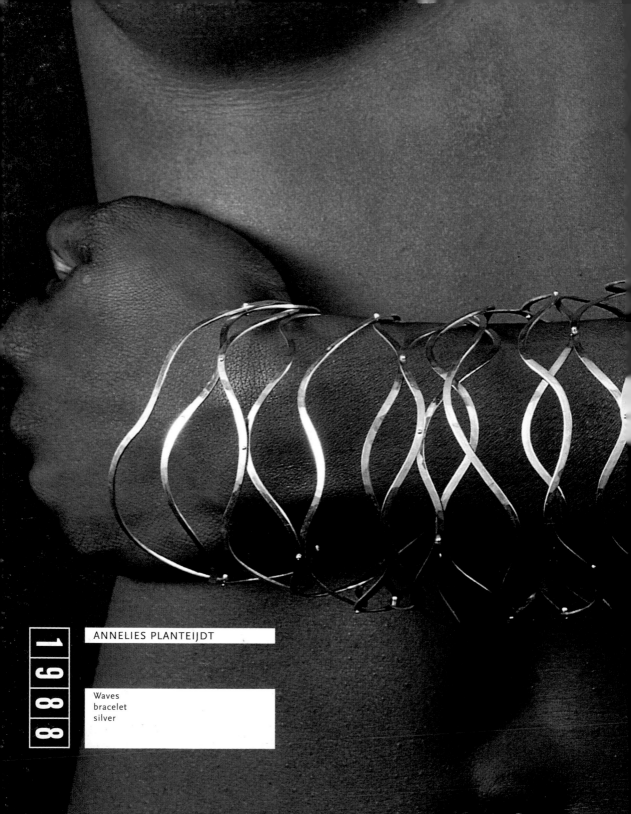

ANNELIES PLANTEIJDT

1988

Waves
bracelet
silver

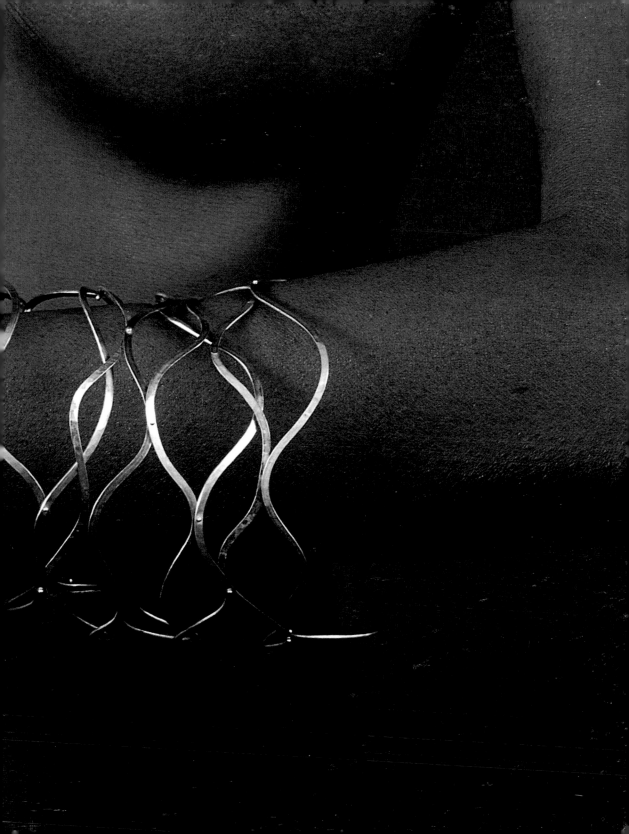

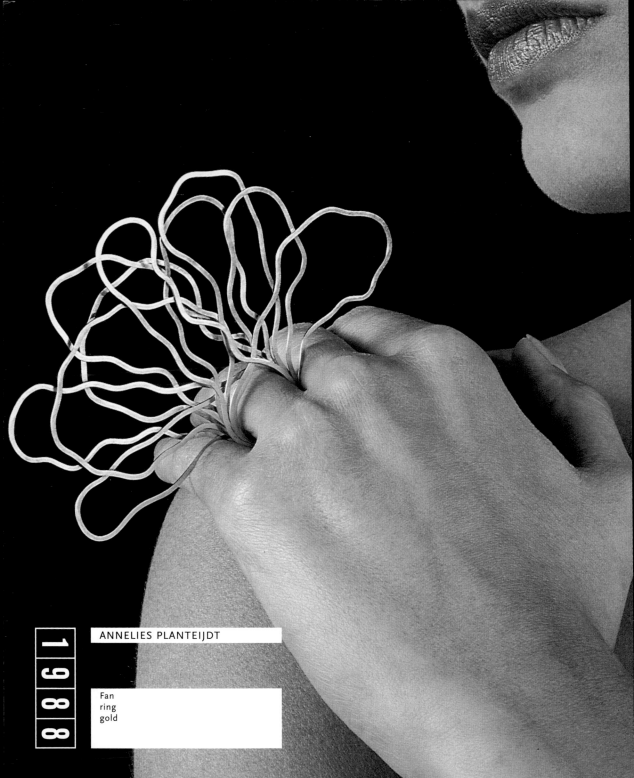

ANNELIES PLANTEIJDT

Fan
ring
gold

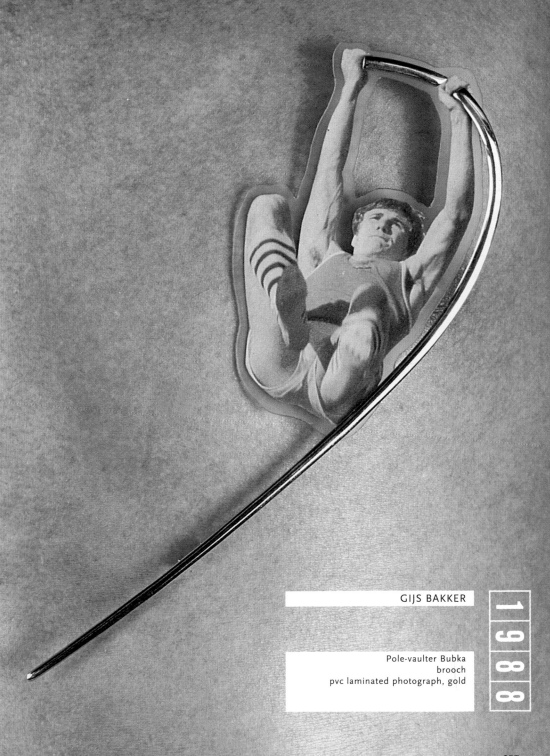

GIJS BAKKER

Pole-vaulter Bubka
brooch
pvc laminated photograph, gold

1988

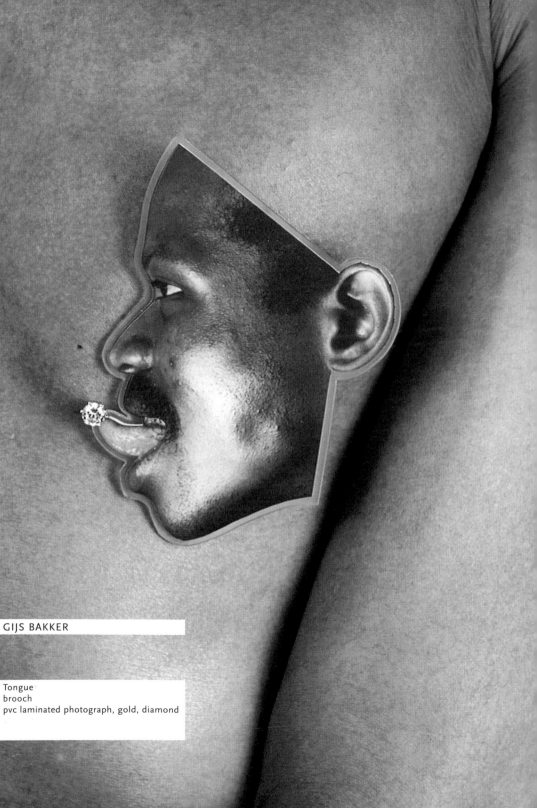

1989

GIJS BAKKER

Tongue
brooch
pvc laminated photograph, gold, diamond

GIJS BAKKER

Bouquet
brooch
pvc laminated photograph, diamond,
citrine, gold

1989

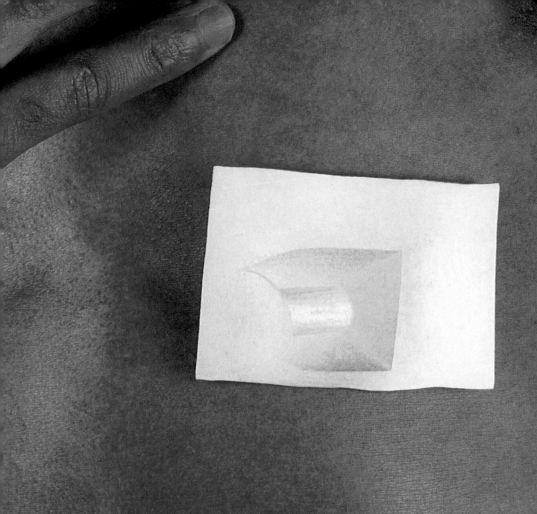

1989

ONNO BOEKHOUDT

brooch
silver

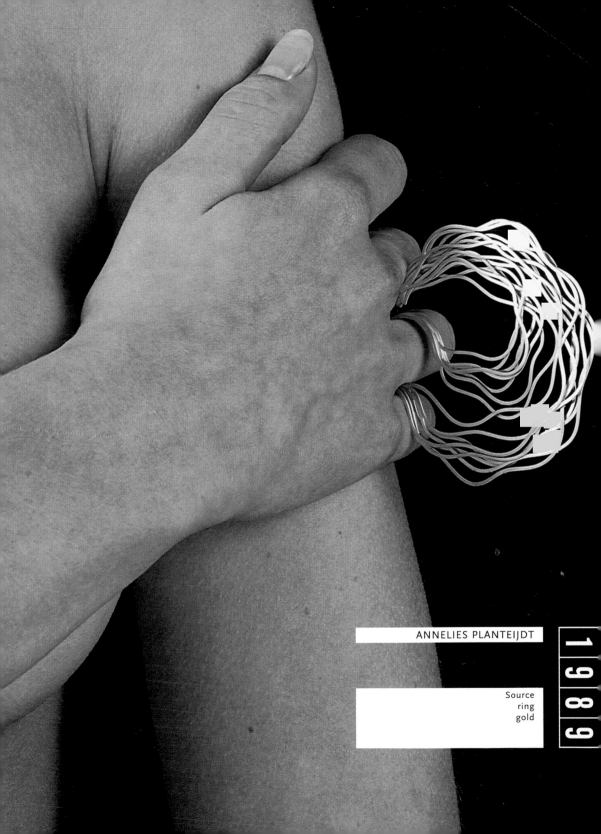

ANNELIES PLANTEIJDT

1989

Source
ring
gold

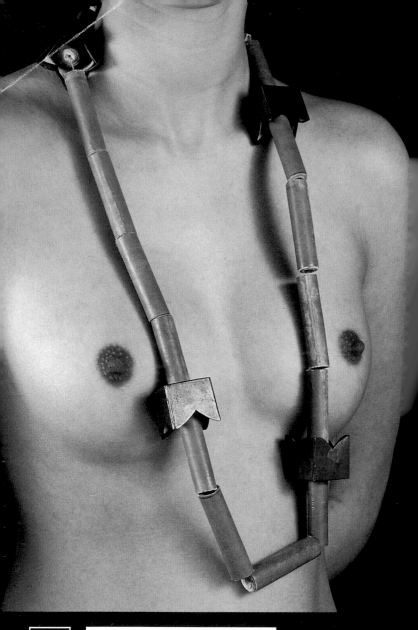

LUCY SARNEEL

necklace
paper, steel

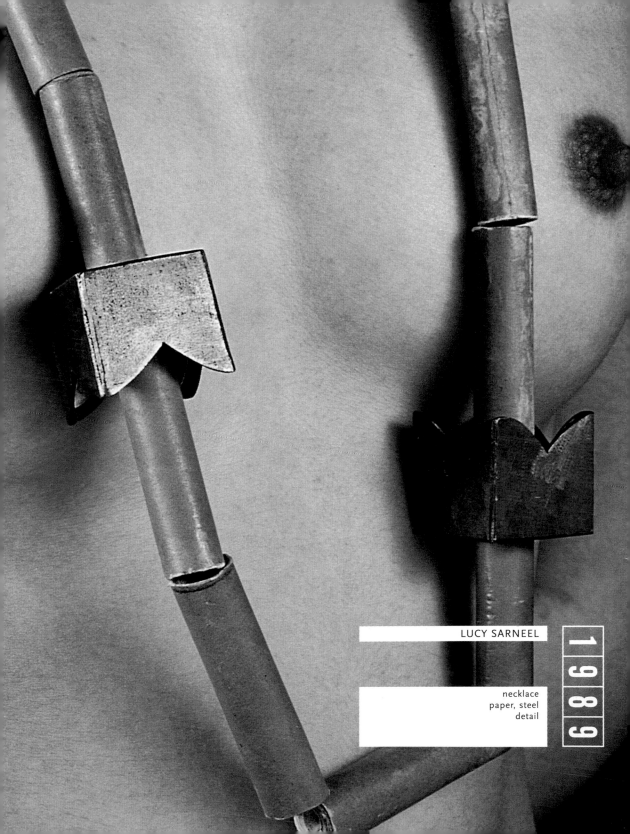

LUCY SARNEEL

1 9 8 9

necklace
paper, steel
detail

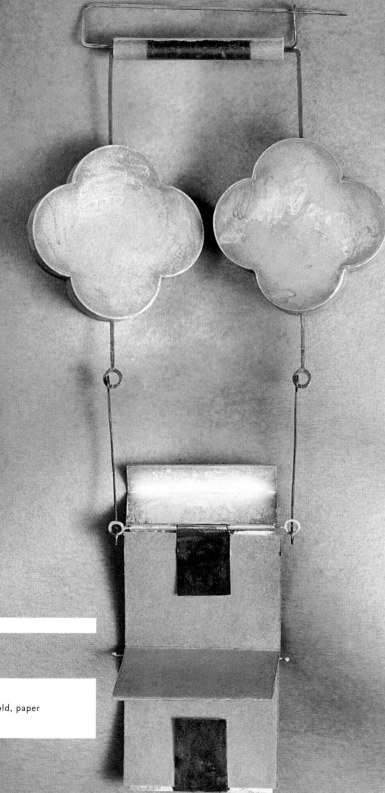

LUCY SARNEEL

Fortuna
brooch
silver, zinc, steel, gold, paper

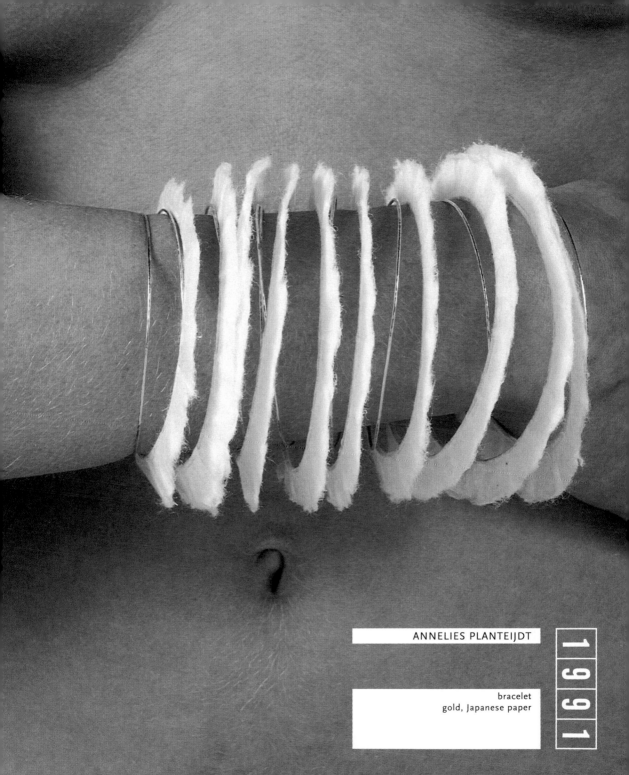

ANNELIES PLANTEIJDT

bracelet
gold, Japanese paper

1991

1991

MARION HERBST

Boat
ring
silver, glass, sodalith

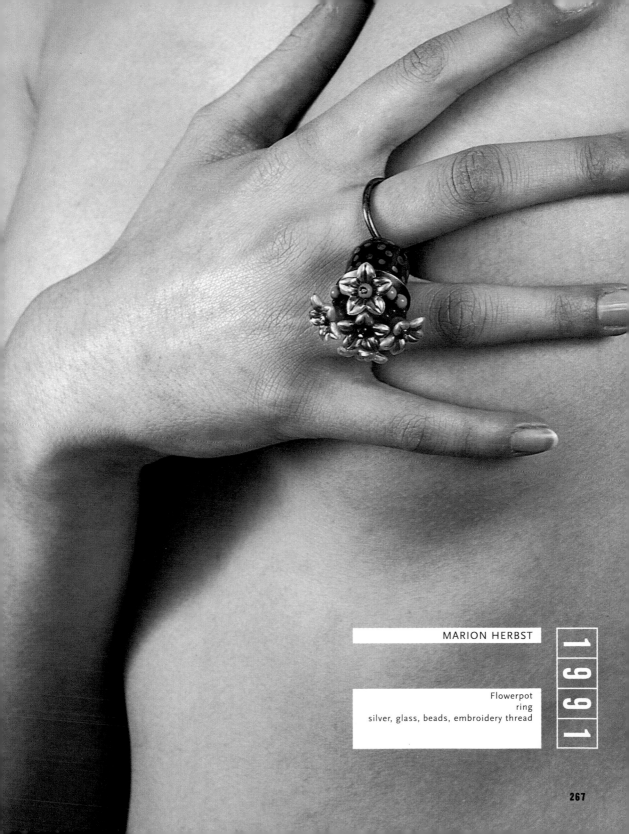

MARION HERBST

Flowerpot
ring
silver, glass, beads, embroidery thread

1 9 9 1

PHILIP SAJET

The red parasite
necklace
gold, glass beads, rock-crystal, ruby

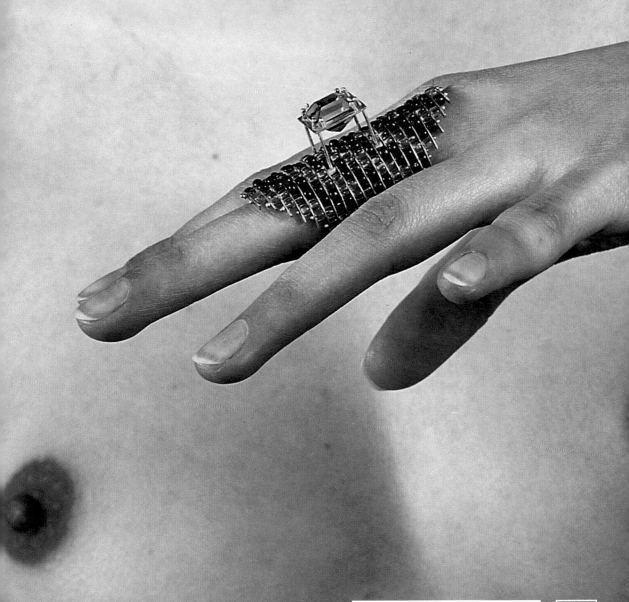

PHILIP SAJET

Ottoman ring I
silver, glass beads, rose quartz

1
9
9
2

MARION HERBST

Brooch no. 4
silver, glass, pearl

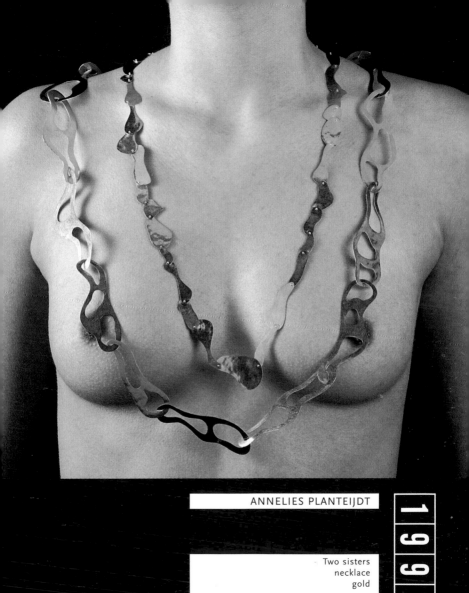

ANNELIES PLANTEIJDT

1993

Two sisters
necklace
gold

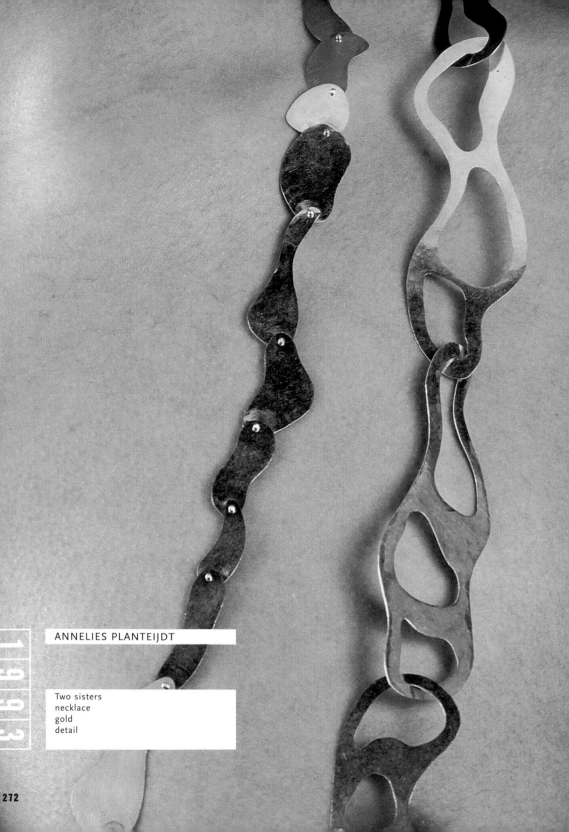

ANNELIES PLANTEIJDT

Two sisters
necklace
gold
detail

LUCY SARNEEL

1993

Chain of office
necklace
silver, steel, brass
collection Marie-José van den Hout

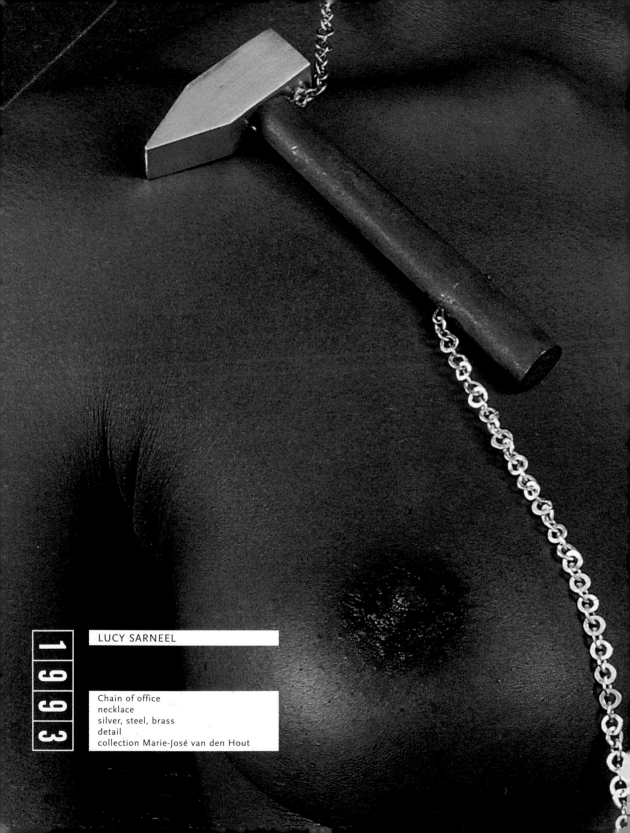

LUCY SARNEEL

1993

Chain of office
necklace
silver, steel, brass
detail
collection Marie-José van den Hout

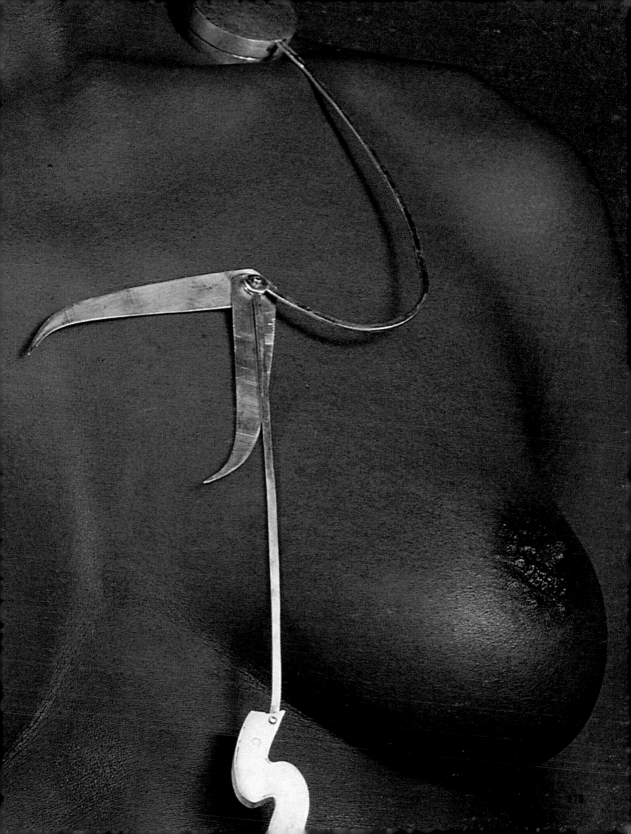

WILLEM HONING

bracelet
silver

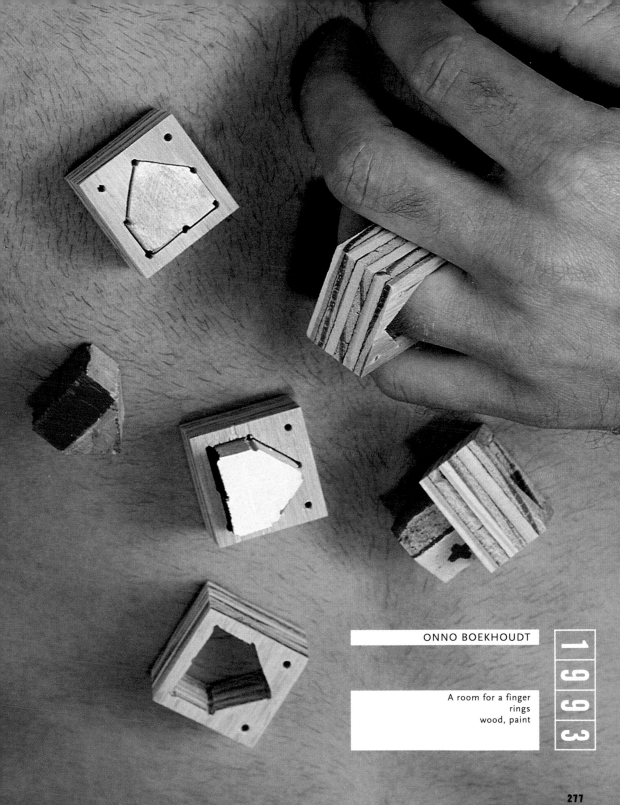

ONNO BOEKHOUDT

1
9
9
3

A room for a finger
rings
wood, paint

1994

MARION HERBST

Cake
brooch
silver, glass, plastic, rock-crystal,
embroidery thread, pearl, shell

DINIE BESEMS

1994

Chalk necklace
chalk
detail

1994

DINIE BESEMS

Chalk necklace
chalk

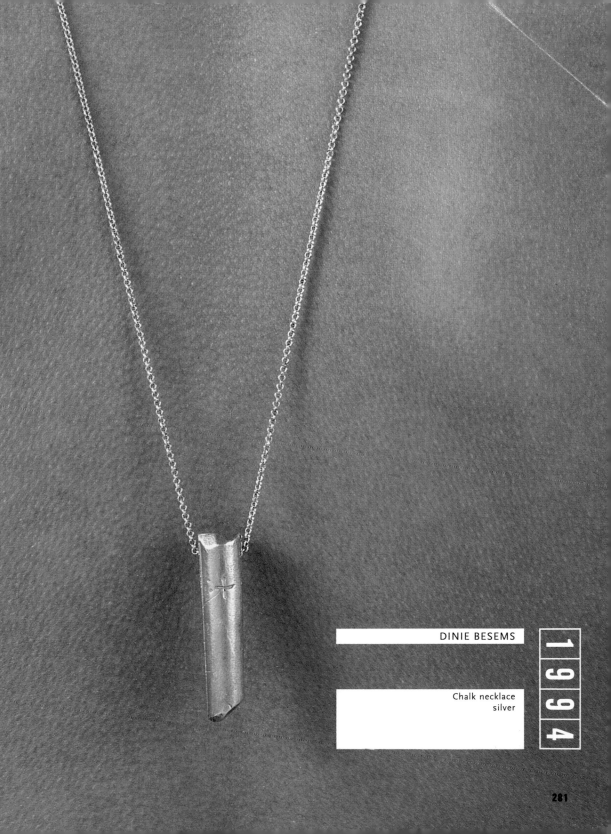

DINIE BESEMS

Chalk necklace
silver

LUCY SARNEEL

Jewel
necklace
silver, steel

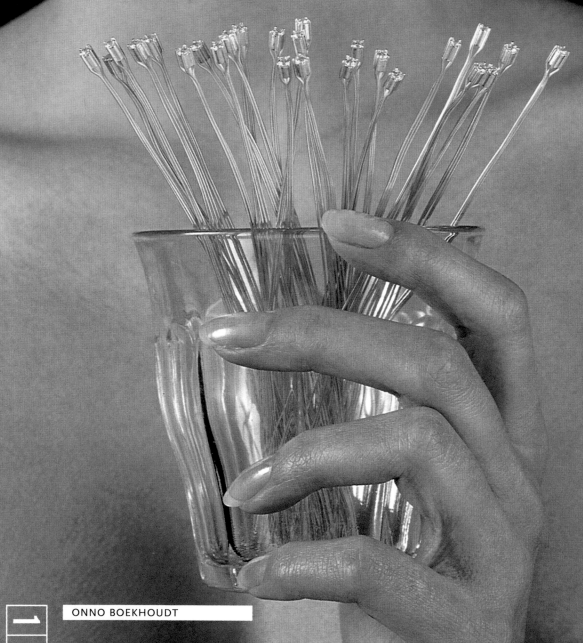

ONNO BOEKHOUDT

glass with 25 pieces of jewelry
silver thread, zircon, drinking glass

DINIE BESEMS

This space is mine
necklace/object
gold-plated silver
detail

1996

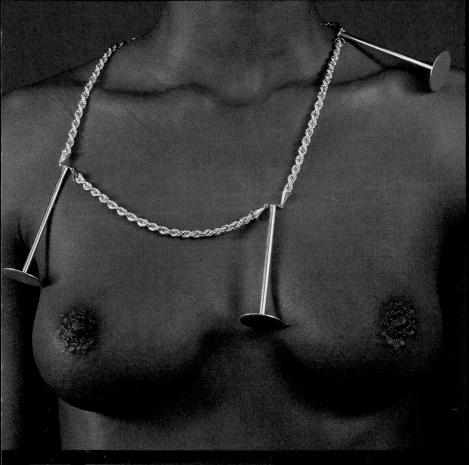

1996

DINIE BESEMS

This space is mine
necklace/object
gold-plated silver

PHILIP SAJET

necklace
various materials/found objects

1996

287

PHILIP SAJET

Buttons
necklace
mother-of-pearl, pearl, gold

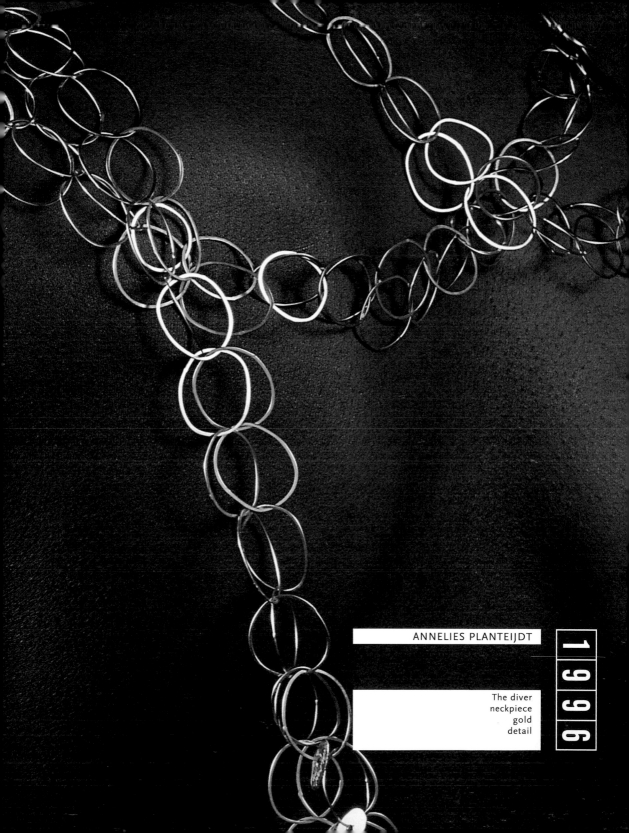

ANNELIES PLANTEIJDT

The diver
neckpiece
gold
detail

ANNELIES PLANTEIJDT

The diver
neckpiece
gold

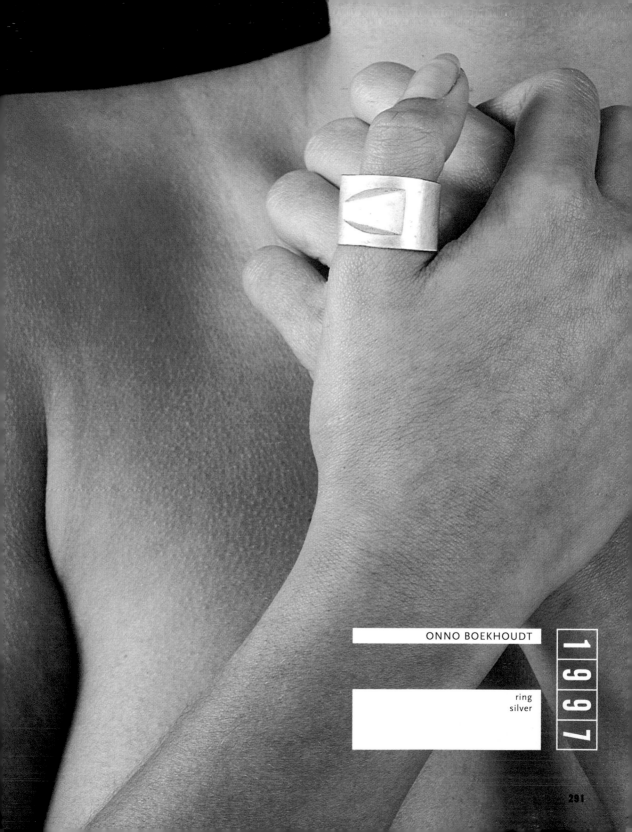

ONNO BOEKHOUDT

ring
silver

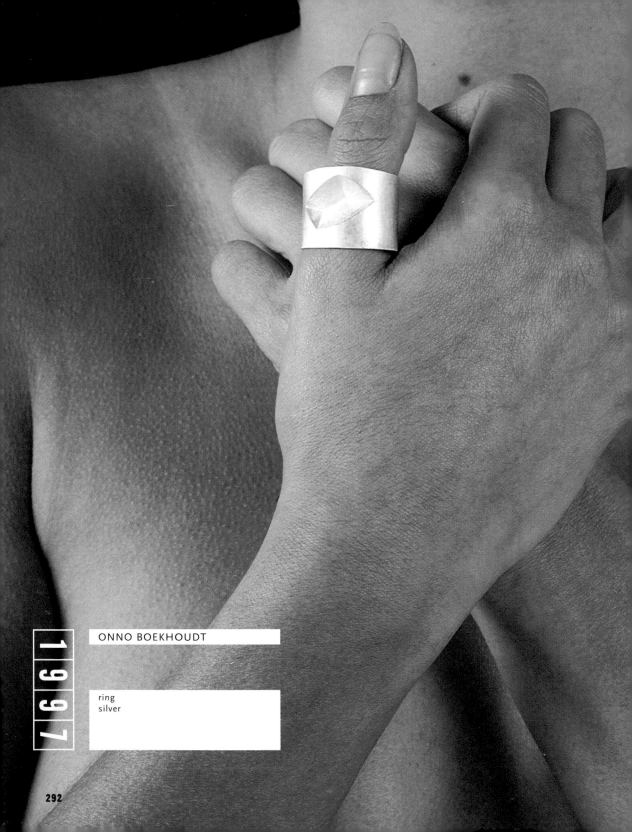

ONNO BOEKHOUDT

1997

ring
silver

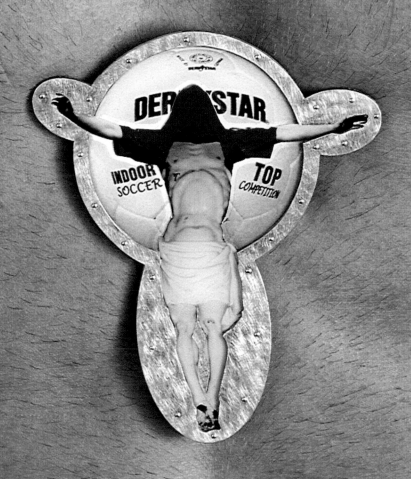

GIJS BAKKER

Praha Der Star
brooch
silver, computer manipulated photograph,
plexiglass

1998

GIJS BAKKER

Münster da Vinci
brooch
silver, gold leaf, computer manipulated
photograph

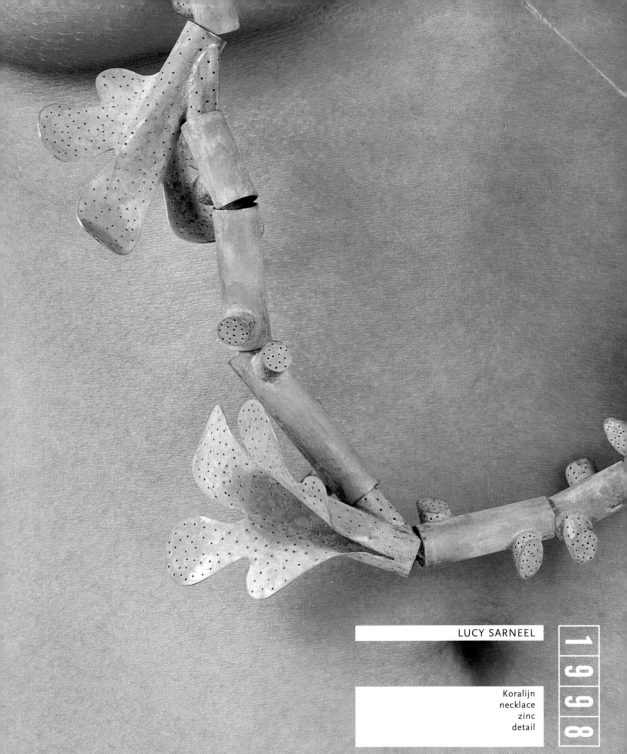

LUCY SARNEEL

1998

Koralijn
necklace
zinc
detail

1998

LUCY SARNEEL

Koralijn
necklace
zinc

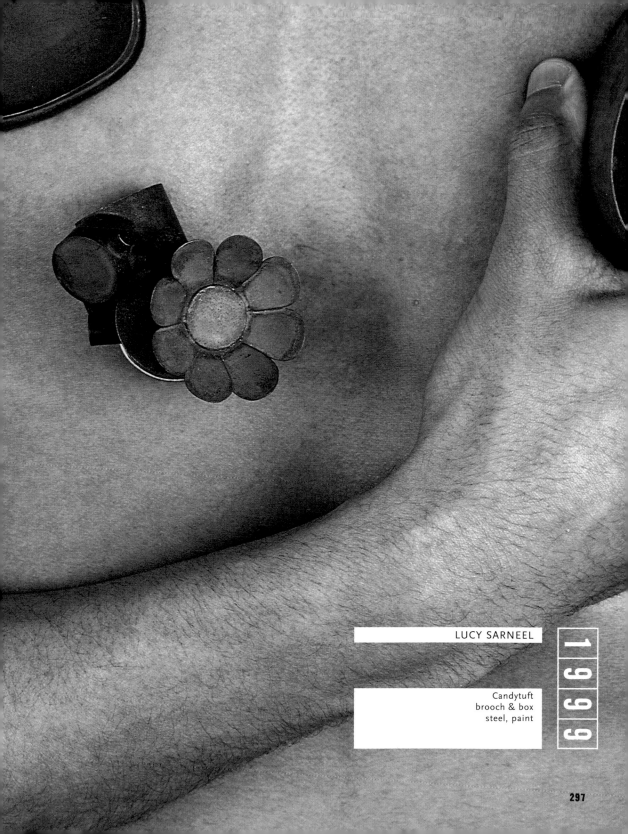

1999

Candytuft
brooch & box
steel, paint

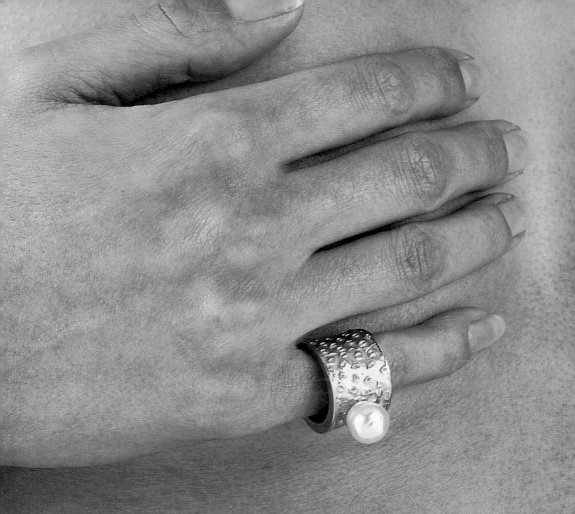

1999

DINIE BESEMS

Oaeasrtbeeri
ring
gold-plated silver, pearl

DINIE BESEMS

Als u mij haten wilt wacht dan nièt
Shakespeare, sonnet no. 90
chain
alpaca
detail

1999

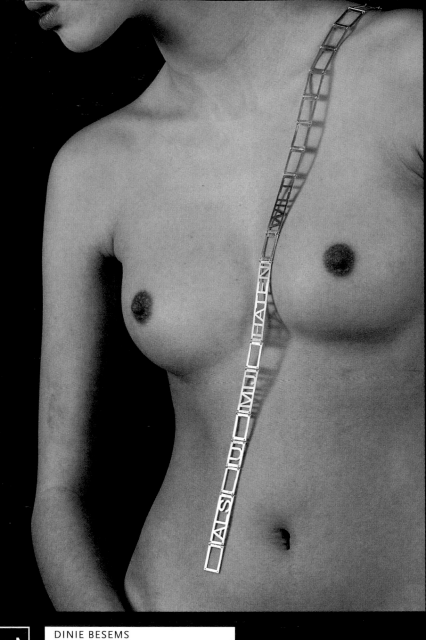

DINIE BESEMS

Als u mij haten wilt wacht dan niet
Shakespeare, sonnet no. 90
chain
alpaca

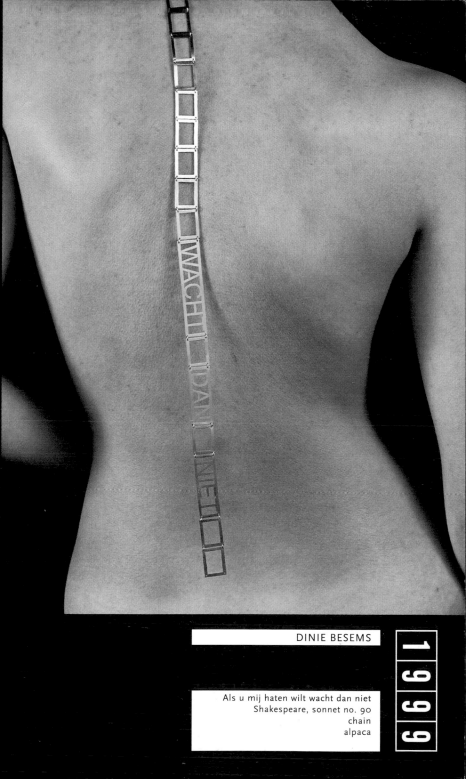

DINIE BESEMS

Als u mij haten wilt wacht dan niet
Shakespeare, sonnet no. 90
chain
alpaca

1999

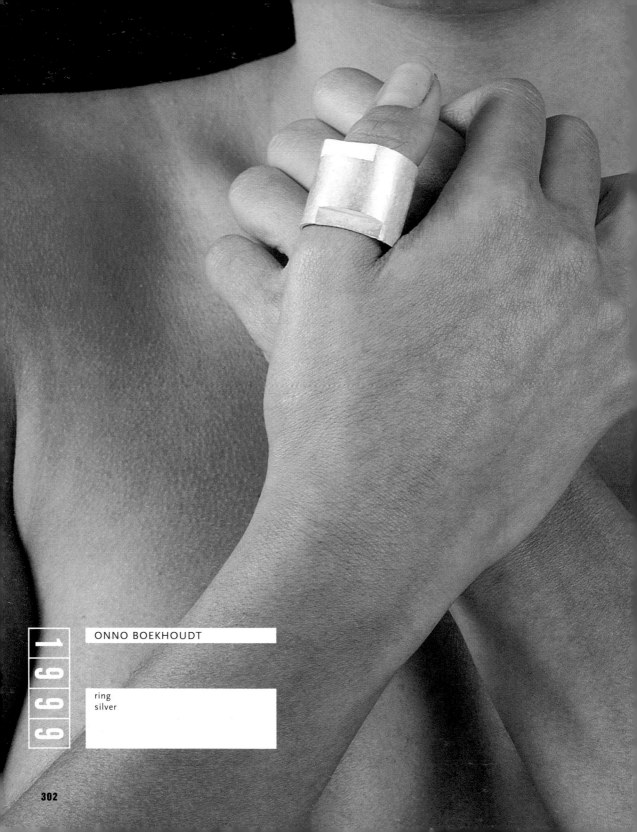

ONNO BOEKHOUDT

1999

ring
silver

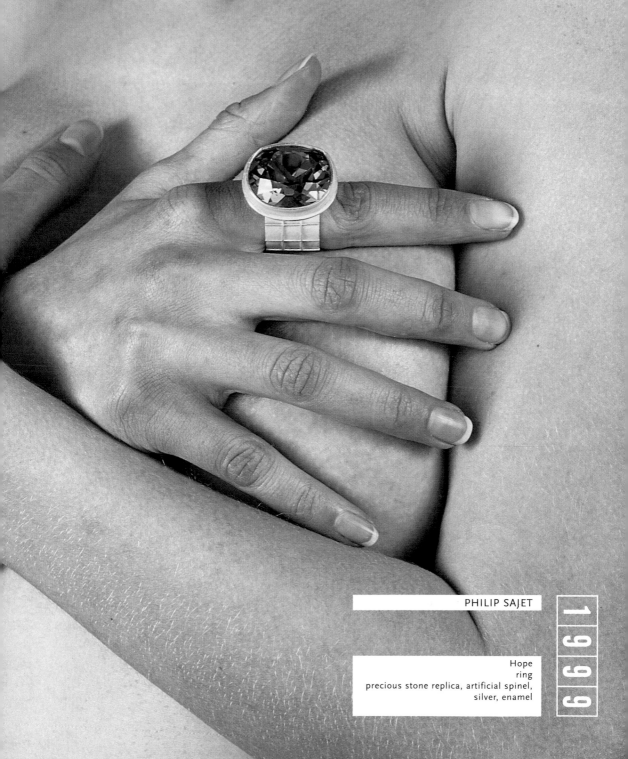

PHILIP SAJET

1
9
9
9

Hope
ring
precious stone replica, artificial spinel,
silver, enamel

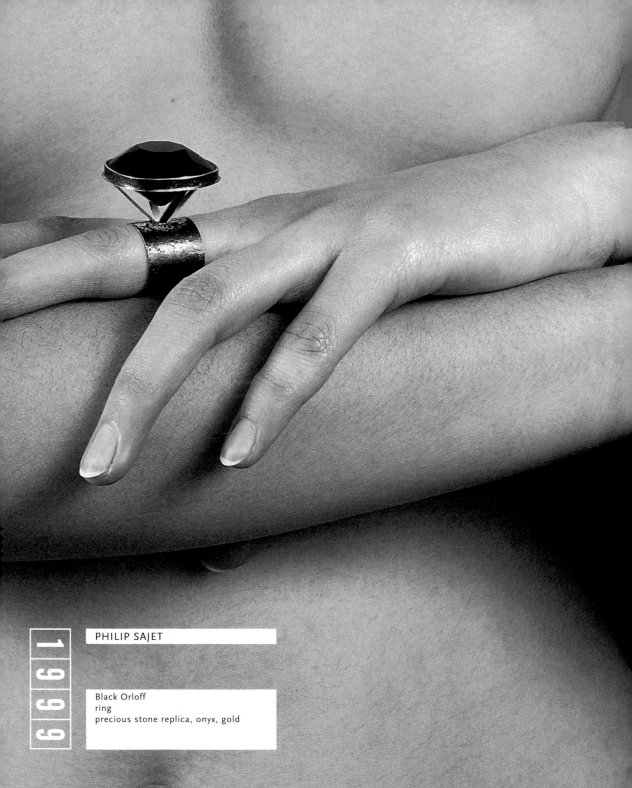

PHILIP SAJET

Black Orloff
ring
precious stone replica, onyx, gold

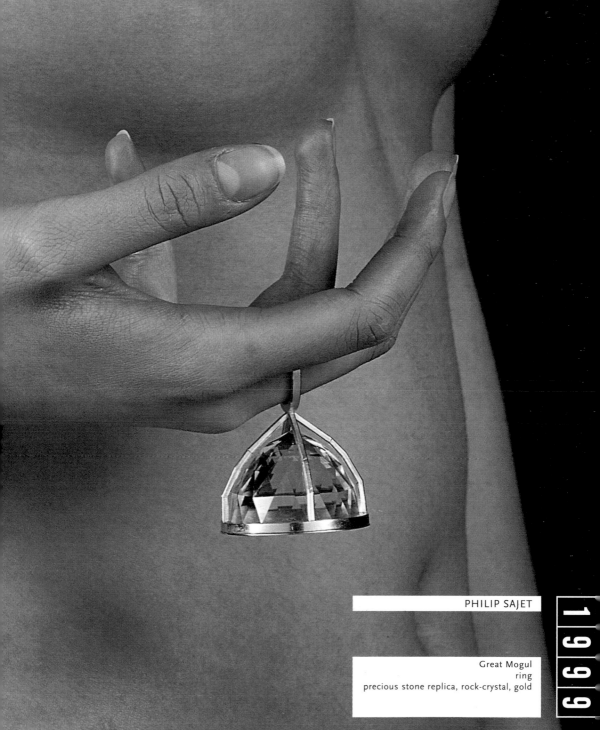

PHILIP SAJET

Great Mogul
ring
precious stone replica, rock-crystal, gold

1999

DUTCH

JEWELRY

DESIGN

1950
—
2000

JEWELS
of Mind and Mentality

JEWELS
of Mind and Mentality

DUTCH JEWELRY DESIGN
1950 – 2000

BIOGRAPHIES AND BIBLIOGRAPHIES

The book includes a biography and bibliography for each of the featured designers.

DUTCH

JEWELRY

DESIGN

1950 — 2000

HANS APPENZELLER
Born: 1949 Amsterdam/NL

EDUCATION:
1966-1970 Gerrit Rietveld Academie Amsterdam/NL

RELATED PROFESSIONAL EXPERIENCE:
1994   Organisation Art & Design, Sonsbeek, Arnhem/NL
1983-1991 Established Hans Appenzeller Inc., New York/USA
1975-   Established first location Hans Appenzeller Inc., Amsterdam/NL
1970-1977 Lecturer Akademie voor Beeldende Vorming, Amersfoort/NL
1969-1975 Co-founder/Director with Lous Martin, Gallery Sieraad, Amsterdam/NL

PUBLIC COLLECTIONS
Het Kruithuis, Stedelijk Museum voor Hedendaagse Kunst, 's-Hertogenbosch/NL
Stedelijk Museum, Amsterdam/NL

SELECTED EXHIBITIONS
2000 Jewels of Mind and Mentality Museum Het Kruithuis, 's-Hertogenbosch/NL travelling
1999 30 Years Hans Appenzeller Singer Museum, Laren/NL
1993 The Appenzeller Road Show travelling collection
1998 Allen Brown Gallery, Staffordshire/GB
1994 A Moveable Feast Stedelijk Museum, Amsterdam/NL
1993 Voorzien: Benno Premsela Applied Art Collection Stedelijk Museum, Amsterdam/NL
1991 Getooid en Versierd Rijksdienst Beeldende Kunst, The Hague/NL
1987 Concepts, Comments, Process: Dutch Jewellery 1967-1987 Rijksdienst Beeldende Kunst, The Hague/NL travelling
1987 Holland in Vorm, sieraden 1945-1987 Gemeentemuseum Arnhem, Arnhem/NL
1986 Sieraad 1986, Draagteken? Museum Het Kruithuis, 's-Hertogenbosch/NL
1985 New Tradition British Crafts Centre, London/GB
1982 Visies op sieraden 1965-1982 Stedelijk Museum, Amsterdam/NL
1979 56 Bracelets, 17 Rings, 2 Necklaces Gemeentelijk Van Reekummuseum, Apeldoorn/NL
1976 Hans Appenzeller/Jan Aarntzen Stedelijk Museum, Amsterdam/NL
1973 Amulets and Talisman New York/USA
1973 Jewelry as Sculpture as Jewelry Institute of Contemporary Arts, Boston/USA

SELECTED BIBLIOGRAPHY
30 Years Hans Appenzeller. CD-Rom, 1999 • Jewelry in Europe and America/Ralph Turner. – London: Thames and Hudson, 1996 • Jewelry of our time : art, ornament and obsession/Helen W. Drutt English and Peter Dormer. – London: Thames and Hudson, 1995 • Mode en Sieraad/Marjan Unger, Gert Staal. – Amsterdam: Vormgevingsinstituut, 1994 • Hans Appenzeller: 20 years/ed. Thomas Connors. – Amsterdam, 1989 • Concepts, Comments, Process: Dutch Jewellery 1967-1978. – Amsterdam: Rijksdienst Beeldende Kunst, 1987 • Holland in Vorm: vormgeving in Nederland 1945-1987/Gert Staal en Hester Wolters. - 's-Gravenhage: Stichting Holland in Vorm, 1987 • Nederlandse Sieraden 1945-1987: beschrijving bij de gelijknamige diaserie/Paul Derrez. – Utrecht: LOKV, 1987 • Hans Appenzeller: songs of adventure/Hans Appenzeller. – Amsterdam, 1986 • Sieraad 1986: draagteken?/Yvònne G.J.M. Joris. – 's-Hertogenbosch: Museum voor Hedendaagse Kunst Het Kruithuis, 1986 • Hans Appenzeller. – Amsterdam, 1985 • New Tradition: the evolution of jewellery 1966-1985/Caroline Broadhead. – London: British Crafts Centre, 1985 • Hans Appenzeller. – Amsterdam, 1984 • The Jewellery project: new departures in British and European work 1980-83. – London: Crafts Council Gallery, 1983 • Hans Appenzeller: sieraden, zijn visie op sieraden/Gert Staal. – Amsterdam, 1982 • Bracelets, Rings, Necklaces. – Amsterdam: Visual Arts office for abroad, 1979 • Sier in serie: sieraden. – Amsterdam: Nederlandse Kunststichting, 1973

GIJS BAKKER

Born: 1942 Amersfoort/NL

EDUCATION
1958-1962 Gerrit Rietveld Academie Amsterdam/NL
1962 Konstfack Skolen Stockholm/S

AWARDS
1965 2nd Van de Rijn Award for sculptors
1968 Gold and Silver Medal Jablonec, CZ
1988 Françoise van den Bosch Award
1995 Prins Bernhard Fonds Award for Applied Arts and Architecture
1996 Ra Award 1996

RELATED PROFESSIONAL EXPERIENCE
1992- Design Consultant, Cor Unum Ceramics, 's-Hertogenbosch/NL
1987- Senior Lecturer, Academie voor Industriële Vormgeving, Eindhoven/NL

PUBLIC COLLECTIONS
Centraal Museum, Utrecht/NL
Cleveland County Museum, Middlesborough/GB
Gemeentelijk Van Reekummuseum, Apeldoorn/NL
Gemeentemuseum Den Haag, The Hague/NL
Museum Boijmans van Beuningen, Rotterdam/NL
Museum voor Moderne Kunst, Arnhem/NL
Het Kruithuis, Stedelijk Museum voor Hedendaagse Kunst, 's-Hertogenbosch/NL
National Museum of Modern Art, Kyoto/J
Nordenfjeldske Kunstindustrimuseum, Trondheim/N
Power House Museum, Sydney/AUS
Stedelijk Museum, Amsterdam/NL

SELECTED SOLO EXHIBITIONS
1998 Holysport/Shot Project Helen Drutt, Philadelphia/USA
1994 Gijs Bakker: Holes Project a.o. Gallery RA, Amsterdam/NL
1989 Gijs Bakker, vormgever Centraal Museum, Utrecht/NL
1978 The Industrial Art of Gijs Bakker Crafts Advisory Committee Gallery, London/GB

SELECTED GROUP EXHIBITIONS
2000 Jewels of Mind and Mentality Museum Het Kruithuis, 's-Hertogenbosch/NL travelling
1998 Ad Dekkers in zijn tijd Stedelijk Museum, Amsterdam/NL
1998 Brooching it Diplomatically Helen Drutt, Philadelphia/USA travelling
1997 Chi ha paura...? Museum Het Kruithuis, 's- Hertogenbosch/NL
1994 A moveable Feast Stedelijk Museum, Amsterdam/NL
1993 Voorzien: Benno Premsela Applied Art Collection Stedelijk Museum, Amsterdam/NL
1990 Fremdkörper, Schmuck der Avantgarde Wilhelm Hack-Museum, Ludwigshafen/D
1990 L'Arte della Gioia, Gioiello Olandese d'Autore Pedrocchi, Padua/I
1990 Novidades da Holanda Fundaçao Calouste Gulbenkian, Lisbon/P travelling
1989 Jewelry: Means: Meaning University of Tennessee, Knoxville/USA travelling
1989 Ornamenta I Schmuckmuseum, Pforzheim/D
1987 Concepts, Comments, Process: Dutch Jewellery 1967-1987 Rijksdienst Beeldende Kunst, The Hague/NL

1987	Holland in Vorm, sieraden 1945-1987 Gemeentemuseum Arnhem, Arnhem/NL
1986	Sieraad 1986, Draagteken? Museum Het Kruithuis, 's-Hertogenbosch/NL
1986	Sieraad Vorm en Idee Gemeentelijk Van Reekummuseum, Apeldoorn/NL
1982	Jewellery Redefined British Crafts Centre, London/GB
1982	Visies op sieraden 1965-1982 Stedelijk Museum, Amsterdam/NL
1979	56 Bracelets, 17 Rings, 2 Necklaces Gemeentelijk Van Reekummuseum, Apeldoorn/NL
1972	Sieraad 1900-1972 De Zonnehof, Amersfoort/NL
1967	Sculpture to wear by Emmy van Leersum & Gijs Bakker Ewan Philips Gallery, London/GB

SELECTED BIBLIOGRAPHY

Gijs Bakker: holysport/shot/Yvonne Brentjes. - S.l.: s.n., 1998 • Brooching it Diplomatically: a tribute to Madeleine K. Albright/Helen W. Drutt English. – Philadelphia: Helen Drutt, 1998 • Jewelry in Europe and America/Ralph Turner. – London: Thames and Hudson, 1996 • Çhi ha paura...?. – Amsterdam: Stichting Çhi ha paura...?, 1996 • Jewelry of our time: art, ornament and obsession/Helen W. Drutt English and Peter Dormer. – London: Thames and Hudson, 1995 • Gebroken lijnen/Broken lines: Emmy van Leersum 1930-1984/ed. Yvònne G.J. M. Joris. -'s-Hertogenbosch: Museum Het Kruithuis, 1993 • Gijs Bakker: about the holes project/Renny Ramakers. - [Amsterdam]: [Gijs Bakker], 1993 • The best in contemporary jewellery/David Watkins. – London: B.T. Bradsford Ltd., 1993 • Getooid & Versierd/Liesbeth den Besten. – [The Hague]: [Rijksdienst Beeldende Kunst], 1991 • International Crafts/Martina Margetts. – London: Thames and Hudson, 1991 • De feestdis ontworpen door 39 kunstenaars The Banqueting table/Martijn van Ooststroom. – Amsterdam: Galerie Ra, 1991 • Novidades da Holanda: estudo sobre jóias/Marjan Unger. - Lisbon/Amsterdam: Fundaçao Calouste Gulbenkian/Dutch Form Foundation, 1990 • Fremdkörper: Schmuck der Avantgarde/Lida von Mengden. – Ludwigshafen: Wilhelm-Hack-Museum, 1990 • Jewelry: Means: Meaning/M. Tomlinson. - Knoxville Tennesee: Ewing Gallery of Art and Architecture, 1989 • Gijs Bakker, vormgever: solo voor een solist/Gert Staal. - The Hague: SDU Uitgeverij, 1989 • Holland in Vorm: vormgeving in Nederland 1945-1987/Gert Staal en Hester Wolters. – 's-Gravenhage: Stichting Holland in Vorm, 1987 • Concepts, Comments, Process: Dutch Jewellery 1967-1978. – Amsterdam: Rijksdienst Beeldende Kunst, 1987 • Sieraad 1986: draagteken?/Yvònne G.J.M. Joris. - 's-Hertogenbosch: Museum voor Hedendaagse Kunst Het Kruithuis, 1986 • Images: Sieraden Schmuck Jewellery/Marjan Unger, Renny Ramakers, Monique Mokveld...et al. – Amsterdam: VES, 1986 • Sieraden: vorm en idee/Liesbeth den Besten. – Apeldoorn: Gemeentelijk Van Reekummuseum, 1986 • Tien jaar Ra/Liesbeth Crommelin en Paul Derrez. – Amsterdam: Galerie Ra, 1986 • The New Jewelry: trends and traditions/Peter Dormer and Ralph Turner. – London: Thames and Hudson, 1985 • Twentieth-Century Jewelry/Barbara Cartlidge. - New York: Harry N. Abrams, 1985 • Bracelets, Rings, Necklaces. – Amsterdam: Visual Arts office for abroad, [1979] • Gijs Bakker, Bob Bonies, Storck van Besouw, Benno Premsela/Jerven Ober. – Apeldoorn: Gemeentelijke Van Reekumgalerij, 1977 • Sieraad 1975: 4e manifestatie van Nederlandse edelsmeden en sieradenontwerpers in Amersfoort. – Amersfoort: Galerie Het Kapelhuis, 1975 • Sier in serie: sieraden. – Amsterdam: Nederlandse Kunststichting, 1973 • Sieraad 1900-1972: eerste triënnale onder auspiciën van de Amersfoortse Culturele Raad/K. A. Citroen en Ralph Turner. – Amersfoort: De Zonnehof, 1972 • Objects to wear: by five Dutch jewelry designers. – Eindhoven: Van Abbemuseum, 1969 • Sieraad '69: werk van 22 Nederlandse edelsmeden in Het Kapelhuis. – Amersfoort: Het Kapelhuis, 1969 • Sieraad '67: tentoonstelling 30 Nederlandse edelsmeden. – Amersfoort: Het Kapelhuis, 1967

DUTCH

JEWELRY

DESIGN

1950
–
2000

312

JEWELS
of Mind and Mentality

NICOLAAS VAN BEEK

Born: 1938 The Hague/NL

EDUCATION

1967-1969 Academie voor Beeldende Kunst en Kunstnijverheid, Arnhem/NL

AWARDS

1969 AICA-award
1968 Bronze Medal Jablonec/CZ
1966 Academy-award Arnhem/NL

PUBLIC COLLECTIONS

Gemeentemuseum Schiedam, Schiedam/NL
Het Kruithuis, Stedelijk Museum voor Hedendaagse Kunst, 's-Hertogenbosch/NL
Museum voor Moderne Kunst, Arnhem/NL
Schmuckmuseum, Pforzheim/D

SELECTED EXHIBITIONS

2000 Jewels of Mind and Mentality Museum Het Kruithuis, 's-Hertogenbosch/NL travelling
1970 AICA prijs 1969, Stedelijk Museum, Amsterdam/NL
1970 Schmuck 1970: Tendenzen Schmuckmuseum, Pforzheim/D
1970 Objects to wear, USA travelling
1969 Gallery Sieraad, Amsterdam/NL
1969 Objects to wear, Van Abbemuseum, Eindhoven/NL travelling
1969 Sieraad 69, Gallery Het Kapelhuis, Amersfoort/NL
1967 Edelsmeden 3, Stedelijk Museum, Amsterdam/NL
1967 Expo, Montreal/CDN
1967 Sieraad '67, Gallery Het Kapelhuis, Amersfoort/NL
1966 Gallery Swart, Amsterdam/NL
1965 Schmuckmuseum, Pforzheim/D

SELECTED BIBLIOGRAPHY

Made in Holland: Design aus den Niederlanden/Gabriele Lueg...et al. – Tübingen: Ernst Wasmuth Verlag, 1994 •
Rijksaankopen 1991: Nederlandse kunst/Gijs van Tuyl. - 's-Gravenhage: Rijksdienst Beeldende Kunst, 1992 • Fremdkörper:
Schmuck der Avantgarde/Lida von Mengden. – Ludwigshafen: Wilhelm-Hack-Museum, 1990 • Holland in Vorm:
vormgeving in Nederland 1945-1987/Gert Staal en Hester Wolters. - 's-Gravenhage: Stichting Holland in Vorm, 1987 •
Sieraad 1900-1972: eerste triënnale onder auspiciën van de Amersfoortse Culturele Raad/K. A. Citroen en Ralph Turner. –
Amersfoort: De Zonnehof, 1972 • Nicolaas van Beek, sieraden/Bernardine de Neeve. – Amsterdam: Stedelijk Museum, 1970
• Objects to wear: by five Dutch jewelry designers. – Eindhoven: Van Abbemuseum, 1969 • Sieraad '69: werk van 22
Nederlandse edelsmeden in Het Kapelhuis. – Amersfoort: Het Kapelhuis, 1969 • Sieraad '67: tentoonstelling 30
Nederlandse edelsmeden. – Amersfoort: Het Kapelhuis, 1967

DUTCH

JEWELRY

DESIGN

1950
2000

JEWELS
of Mind and Mentality

DINIE BESEMS
Born: 1966

EDUCATION
Hogeschool voor de Kunsten, Arnhem/NL
1992 Gerrit Rietveld Academie, Amsterdam/NL

AWARDS
1999 incentive prize Applied Arts, Amsterdams Fonds voor de Kunst, Amsterdam/NL

SELECTED EXHIBITIONS
2000 Jewels of Mind and Mentality Museum Het Kruithuis, 's-Hertogenbosch/NL travelling
1999 Presentation of the book 'Het Magisch Vierkant deel IX' Boekhandel Nijhof & Lee, Amsterdam /NL
1998 Gallery Ademloos, The Hague/NL
1997 Gallery Louise Smit, Amsterdam/NL
1997 Fog Gallery, Boston/USA
1996 Kordaat, ferm, nobel, schoon Museum Aemstelle, Amstelveen/NL
1995 Everything should fit Gallery Ra, Amsterdam/NL

SELECTED BIBLIOGRAPHY
Premsela Present: designers design for a designer/Liesbeth den Besten...et al. – Amsterdam: Stichting Vormgevings-tentoonstellingen, 1998 • Passion and Profession: twintig jaar Ra sieraden toen nu straks/Paul Derrez. – Amsterdam: Galerie Ra, 1996 • Mode en Sieraad/Marjan Unger, Gert Staal. – Amsterdam: Vormgevingsinstituut, 1994

DUTCH

JEWELRY

DESIGN

1950 – 2000

JEWELS
of Mind and Mentality

312

MARIA BLAISSE

Born: 1944 Amsterdam/NL

EDUCATION

1968   Gerrit Rietveld Academie, Amsterdam/NL

RELATED PROFESSIONAL EXPERIENCE

1974-1987   teacher Gerrit Rietveld Academie, Amsterdam/NL
1989-1990   guest teacher in France, Switzerland and the USA

SELECTED EXHIBITIONS

1991   De feestdis Gallery Ra, Amsterdam/NL
1990   Novidades da Holanda Fundaçao Calouste Gulbenkian, Lisbon/P
1986   Images, Singer Museum, Laren/NL travelling
1986   Tien jaar Ra Gallery Ra, Amsterdam/NL
1985   Vormgevers in beweging: zes presentaties rond het lichaam Gemeentemuseum Den Haag, The Hague/NL
1984   Variaties op een hoofdthema Gallery Ra, Amsterdam/NL

SELECTED BIBLIOGRAPHY

Premsela Present: designers design for a designer/Liesbeth den Besten...et al. - Amsterdam: Stichting Vormgevings-tentoonstellingen, 1998 • De Feestdis ontworpen door 39 kunstenaars The Banqueting table/Martijn van Ooststroom. - Amsterdam: Galerie Ra, 1991 • Novidades da Holanda: estudo Sobre jóias/Marjan Unger. - Lisbon/Amsterdam: Fundaçao Calouste Gulbenkian/Dutch Form Foundation, 1990 • Imitation and Inspiration: Japanese Influence on Dutch Art/ed. Stefan van Raay. - Amsterdam: D'Arts, 1989 • Images: sieraden Schmuck jewellery/Marjan Unger, Renny Ramakers, Monique Mokveld...et al. - Amsterdam: VES, 1986 • Tien jaar Ra/Liesbeth Crommelin, Paul Derrez. - Amsterdam: Galerie Ra, 1986 • Vormgevers in beweging: zes presentaties rond het lichaam/Paul Derrez...et al. - The Hague: Gemeentemuseum Den Haag, 1985

DUTCH

JEWELRY

DESIGN

1950
2000

JEWELS
of Mind and Mentality

313

ONNO BOEKHOUDT

Born: 1944 Hellendoorn/NL

EDUCATION

1966-1968 Staatliche Kunst und Werkschule Pforzheim/D
1963-1966 Vakschool Schoonhoven, Schoonhoven/NL
1963-1966 Academie Artibus, Utrecht/NL

AWARDS

1966 1st prize Vakschool Schoonhoven, Schoonhoven/NL
1967 1st prize Vakschool Schoonhoven, Schoonhoven/NL
1996 Françoise van den Bosch Award

RELATED PROFESSIONAL EXPERIENCE

1998 external examiner Gerrit Rietveld Academie, Amsterdam/NL
1990- teacher Royal College of Art, London/GB
1985 teacher Hogeschool voor de Kunsten, Kampen/NL
1977-1979 external examiner Kunst Academie, Maastricht/NL
1974-1990 teacher Gerrit Rietveld Academie, Amsterdam/NL

PUBLIC COLLECTIONS

Centraal Museum, Utrecht/NL
Fries Museum, Leeuwarden/NL
Gemeentelijk Van Reekummuseum, Apeldoorn/NL
Het Kruithuis, Stedelijk Museum voor Hedendaagse Kunst, 's-Hertogenbosch/NL
Museum voor Moderne Kunst, Arnhem/NL
Power House Museum, Sydney/AUS
Schmuckmuseum, Pforzheim/D
Stedelijk Museum, Amsterdam/NL

SELECTED SOLO EXHIBITIONS

1997 Groninger Museum, Groningen/NL
1995 Gallery Marzee, Nijmegen/NL
1991 Gallery RA, Amsterdam/NL
1987 Gallery Nouvelles Images, The Hague/NL
1987 Gallery RA, Amsterdam/NL

SELECTED GROUP EXHIBITIONS

2000 Jewels of Mind and Mentality Museum Het Kruithuis, 's-Hertogenbosch/NL travelling
1998 Jewellery moves National Museum of Scotland, Edinburgh/GB
1991 Bedels aan banden Gemeentemuseum Arnhem, Arnhem/NL
1990 30 jaar Het Kapelhuis Gallery Het Kapelhuis, Amersfoort/NL
1990 Novidades da Holanda Fundaçao Calouste Gulbenkian, Lisbon/P
1989 Ornamenta I Schmuckmuseum, Pforzheim/D
1987 Concepts, Comments, Process: Dutch Jewellery 1967-1987 Rijksdienst Beeldende Kunst, The Hague/NL travelling
1987 Gemengd nieuws Centraal Museum, Utrecht/NL
1987 Holland in Vorm, sieraden 1945-1987 Gemeentemuseum Arnhem, Arnhem/NL
1986 10 jaar galerie RA Gallery RA, Amsterdam/NL
1986 Sieraad 1986, Draagteken? Museum Het Kruithuis, 's-Hertogenbosch/NL

1979   Sieraad in Singer Singer Museum, Laren/NL
1972   Sieraad 1900-1972 De Zonnehof, Amersfoort/NL
1969   Sieraad '69 Gallery Het Kapelhuis, Amersfoort/NL

SELECTED BIBLIOGRAPHY

Onno Boekhoudt: why not jewellery?/David Watkins en Koos van Zomeren. – Groningen: Groninger Museum, 1997 •
Jewelry in Europe and America/Ralph Turner. – London: Thames and Hudson, 1996 • Schmücken: the art of
adornment/Marga Anstett-Janssen...et al. – Stuttgart: Arnoldsche, 1995 • The best in contemporary Jewellery/David
Watkins. – London: B.T. Bradsford Ltd., 1993 • Sieraden: Centrum Beeldende Kunst Groningen/Gerard Lakke. – Groningen:
Centrum Beeldende Kunst, 1992 • Bedels aan banden: hedendaagse interpretaties van de bedelarmband/Ietse Meij. –
Arnhem: Stichting Nieuwstad, 1991 • De feestdis ontworpen door 39 kunstenaars The Banqueting table/Martijn van
Ooststroom. – Amsterdam: Galerie Ra: 1991 • Novidades da Holanda: estudo sobre jóias/Marjan Unger. - Lisbon: Fundaçao
Calouste Gulbenkian, 1990 • Autori del gioiello Olandese contemporaneo/Liesbeth Crommelin. - [Vicenza]: [Torri di
Arcugnano], 1990 • L'Arte della Gioia: gioiello Ollandese d'autore l'oro di Padova/Liesbeth Crommelin. - Padova/The Hague:
Assessorato Cultura e beni culturali/Ministerie van WVC, 1990 • Ornamenta I: internationale Schmuckkunst/Michael
Erlhoff. – München: Prestel Verlag, 1989 • Concepts, Comments, Process: Dutch Jewellery 1967-1978. – Amsterdam:
Rijksdienst Beeldende Kunst, 1987 • Holland in Vorm: vormgeving in Nederland 1945-1987/Gert Staal, Hester Wolters. - 's-
Gravenhage: Stichting Holland in Vorm, 1987 • The New Jewelry: trends and traditions/Peter Dormer and Ralph Turner. –
London: Thames and Hudson, 1985 • Sieraad 1900-1972: eerste triënnale onder auspiciën van de Amersfoortse Culturele
Raad/K. A. Citroen en Ralph Turner. – Amersfoort: De Zonnehof, 1972 • Sieraad '69: werk van 22 Nederlandse edelsmeden
in Het Kapelhuis. – Amersfoort: Het Kapelhuis, 1969

DUTCH

JEWELRY

DESIGN

1950
2000

JEWELS
of Mind and Mentality

FRANÇOISE VAN DEN BOSCH

1944-1977

EDUCATION
1964-1969 Hogeschool voor de Kunsten Arnhem/NL

PUBLIC COLLECTIONS
Centraal Museum, Utrecht/NL
Gemeentelijk Van Reekummuseum, Apeldoorn/NL
Gemeentemuseum Den Haag, The Hague/NL
Het Kruithuis, Stedelijk Museum voor Hedendaagse Kunst, 's-Hertogenbosch/NL
Museum Boijmans van Beuningen, Rotterdam/NL
Rijksdienst Beeldende Kunst, The Hague/NL
Schmuckmuseum, Pforzheim/D
Stedelijk Museum, Amsterdam/NL

SELECTED SOLO EXHIBITIONS
1990 Françoise van den Bosch, sieraden en objecten... Stedelijk Museum, Amsterdam/NL
1989 Françoise van den Bosch, een overzicht Stedelijk Museum, Amsterdam/NL
1978 Françoise van den Bosch 1944-1977 Stedelijk Museum, Amsterdam/NL
1972 Aluminium objekten Gallery Het Kapelhuis, Amersfoort/NL
1972 Objekten Gallery Het Kapelhuis, Amersfoort/NL
1971 Sieraden van Françoise van den Bosch Gallery Sieraad, Amsterdam/NL

SELECTED GROUP EXHIBITIONS
2000 Jewels of Mind and Mentality Museum Het Kruithuis, 's-Hertogenbosch/NL travelling
1988 Keuze uit de kollektie Stedelijk Museum, Amsterdam/NL
1987 Holland in Vorm, sieraden 1945-1987 Gemeentemuseum Arnhem, Arnhem/NL
1979 Het Nederlandse Sieraad Gemeentelijk Van Reekummuseum, Apeldoorn/NL
1976 Zomeropstelling/recente aanwinsten Stedelijk Museum, Amsterdam/NL
1975 Sieraad 1975 Gallery Het Kapelhuis, Amersfoort/NL
1974 5 jaar Sieraad Gallery Sieraad, Amsterdam/NL
1974 Contemporary Dutch Jewellery CRM/NKS, Rijswijk/NL travelling
1974 Gemeente-aankopen 1973 Stedelijk Museum, Amsterdam/NL
1974 Nederlandse sieraden Stedelijk Museum, Amsterdam/NL
1974 Sieraden in het Kapelhuis Gallery Het Kapelhuis, Amersfoort/NL
1973 Expositie sieraden Gallery Het Kapelhuis, Amersfoort/NL
1973 International Jewelry Arts Exhibition Tokyo/J
1973 Jewelry as Sculpture as Jewelry Sculpture to Wear Gallery, New York/USA
1973 Sier in serie CRM/NKS, Rijswijk/NL
1972 Sieraad 1900-1972 De Zonnehof, Amersfoort/NL
1970 Gallery Sieraad, Amsterdam/NL
1969 Objects to wear Van Abbemuseum, Eindhoven/NL travelling
1969 Sieraad '69 Gallery Het Kapelhuis, Amersfoort/NL

SELECTED BIBLIOGRAPHY
Jewelry in Europe and America/Ralph Turner. – London: Thames and Hudson, 1996 • Françoise van den Bosch (1944-1977) over de grenzen heen/Jerven Ober. – Naarden: Stichting Françoise van den Bosch, 1990 • Holland in Vorm: vormgeving in Nederland 1945-1987/Gert Staal en Hester Wolters. - 's-Gravenhage: Stichting Holland in Vorm, 1987 • Concepts, Comments, Process: Dutch Jewellery 1967-1978. – Amsterdam: Rijksdienst Beeldende Kunst, 1987 • Sieraden: vorm en

idee/Liesbeth den Besten. – Apeldoorn: Gemeentelijk Van Reekummuseum, 1986 • Bracelets, Rings, Necklaces. – Amsterdam: Visual Arts office for abroad, [1979] • Françoise van den Bosch. – Amsterdam: Nederlandse Kunststichting, 1978 • Sieraad 1975: 4e manifestatie van Nederlandse edelsmeden en sieradenontwerpers in Amersfoort. – Amersfoort: Galerie Het Kapelhuis, 1975 • Sier in serie: sieraden. – Amsterdam: Nederlandse Kunststichting, 1973 • Sieraad 1900-1972: eerste triënnale onder auspiciën van de Amersfoortse Culturele Raad/K. A. Citroen en Ralph Turner. – Amersfoort: De Zonnehof, 1972 • Objects to wear: by five Dutch jewelry designers. – Eindhoven: Van Abbemuseum, 1969 • Sieraad '69: werk van 22 Nederlandse edelsmeden in Het Kapelhuis. – Amersfoort: Het Kapelhuis, 1969

DUTCH

JEWELRY

DESIGN

1950
–
2000

JEWELS
of Mind and Mentality

317

JOKE BRAKMAN
Born: 1946 Wassenaar/NL

EDUCATION
1963-1966 Vakschool Schoonhoven, Schoonhoven/NL
1971-1976 Gerrit Rietveld Academie, Amsterdam/NL

AWARDS
1983 International Jewellery Art Prize, Tokyo/J

RELATED PROFESSIONAL EXPERIENCE
1979-1997 teacher Jewellery Design Gerrit Rietveld Academie, Amsterdam/NL
1985-1989 member Committee Fonds voor Beeldende Kunsten, Vormgeving en Bouwkunst, Amsterdam/NL
1997- supervisor parttime Foundation Course Gerrit Rietveld Academie, Amsterdam/NL

PUBLIC COLLECTIONS
Centraal Museum, Utrecht/NL
Gemeentelijk Van Reekum Museum, Apeldoorn/NL
Gemeentemuseum Den Haag, The Hague/NL
Het Kruithuis, Stedelijk Museum voor Hedendaagse Kunst, 's-Hertogenbosch/NL
Museum voor Moderne Kunst, Arnhem/NL
Museum of Applied Art, Trondheim/N
Stedelijk Museum, Amsterdam/NL

SELECTED EXHIBITIONS
2000 Jewels of Mind and Mentality Museum Het Kruithuis, 's-Hertogenbosch/NL travelling
1994 In en uit balans Gemeentemuseum Den Haag, The Hague/NL
1986 Sieraad vorm en idee Gemeentelijk Van Reekummuseum, Apeldoorn/NL
1986 10 Jaar Ra Gallery Ra, Amsterdam/NL
1986 Images, Singer Museum, Laren/NL travelling
1986 Sieraad 1986 Draagteken? Museum Het Kruithuis, 's-Hertogenbosch/NL
1985 Decoration in Design Gemeentelijk Van Reekummuseum, Apeldoorn/NL
1985 New Tradition British Craft Center, London/GB
1984 Cross Currents Power House Museum, Sydney/Aus
1983 The Jewellery Project Crafts Council Gallery, London/GB
1982 Visions on Jewellery 1965-1982 Stedelijk Museum, Amsterdam/NL
1981 VES exhibition Stedelijk Museum, Amsterdam/NL
1980 Gallery Ra, Amsterdam/NL
1977 Gallery Ra, Amsterdam/NL

SELECTED BIBLIOGRAPHY
Jewelry in Europe and America/Ralph Turner. – London: Thames and Hudson, 1996 • Concepts, Comments, Process: Dutch Jewellery 1967-1978. - Amsterdam: Rijksdienst Beeldende Kunst, 1987 • Sieraad 1986: draagteken?/ Yvònne G.J. M. Joris. - 's-Hertogenbosch: Museum voor Hedendaagse Kunst Het Kruithuis, 1986 • Sieraden: vorm en idee/Liesbeth den Besten. - Apeldoorn: Gemeentelijk Van Reekummuseum, 1986 • Tien jaar Ra/Liesbeth Crommelin en Paul Derrez. – Amsterdam: Galerie Ra, 1986 • The New Jewelry: trends and traditions/Peter Dormer and Ralph Turner. - London: Thames and Hudson, 1985 • The Jewellery project: new departures in British and European work 1980-83. - London: Crafts Council Gallery, 1983 • VES. - Amsterdam: Vereniging van Edelsmeden en Sieraadontwerpers, 1981

PAUL DERREZ

Born: 1950 Sittard/NL

EDUCATION
1968-1970 Academie voor Industriële Vormgeving, Eindhoven/NL
1972-1975 Vakschool Schoonhoven, Schoonhoven/NL

AWARDS
1980 Françoise van den Bosch Award

RELATED PROFESSIONAL EXPERIENCE
1996- Member committee individual grants Fonds Beeldende Kunsten, Vormgeving en Bouwkunst, Amsterdam/NL
1990-1996 Royal appointment to Board Raad voor de Kunst
1985-1989 Member Amsterdamse Kunstraad
1976 Opening Gallery RA, Amsterdam NL

PUBLIC COLLECTIONS
Centraal Museum, Utrecht/NL
Cleveland County Museum, Middlesborough/GB
Gemeentelijk Van Reekummuseum, Apeldoorn/NL
Gemeentemuseum Den Haag, The Hague/NL
Het Kruithuis, Stedelijk Museum voor Hedendaagse Kunst, 's-Hertogenbosch/NL
Museum voor Moderne Kunst, Arnhem/NL
National Museum of Modern Art, Kyoto/J
Nordenfjeldske Kunstindustrimuseum, Trondheim/N
Power House Museum, Sydney/AUS
Rijksdienst Beeldende Kunst, The Hague/NL
Stedelijk Museum, Amsterdam/NL

SELECTED SOLO EXHIBITIONS
1997 Paul Derrez, Cool Creator Gallery Biró, Munich/D
1996 Risky Business Gallery RA, Amsterdam/NL
1985 Paul Derrez, Jewellery, Bowls and Plates Apects Gallery, London/GB
1980 Paul Derrez, winnaar Françoise van den Boschprijs Stedelijk Museum, Amsterdam/NL

SELECTED GROUP EXHIBITIONS
2000 Jewels of Mind and Mentality Museum Het Kruithuis, 's-Hertogenbosch/NL travelling
1997 Spectacles: A Recent History Crafts Council Gallery, London/GB travelling
1996 Jewellery in Europe and America, New Times, New Thinking Crafts Council Gallery, London/GB
1993 Tekens en Ketens Museum van der Togt, Amstelveen/NL
1991 Point of View, Contemporary Dutch Jewelry and Design USA/CDN travelling
1990 Fremdkörper, Schmuck der Avantgarde Wilhelm Hack-Museum, Ludwigshafen/D
1990 Autori del gioiello Olandese contemporaneo Torri di Arcugnano, Vicenza/I
1990 L'Arte delle Gioia Pedrocchi, Padua/I
1990 Novidades da Holanda Fundaçao Calouste Gulbenkian Lisbon/P travelling
1989 Jewelry: Means: Meaning University of Tennessee, Knoxville/USA travelling
1987 Concepts, Comments, Process: Dutch Jewellery 1967-1987 Rijksdienst Beeldende Kunst, The Hague/NL travelling
1986 Images Singer Museum, Laren/NL travelling
1986 International Jewellery Art Exhibition National Museum of Modern Art, Kyoto/J

DUTCH
JEWELRY
DESIGN
1950
2000

JEWELS
of Mind and Mentality

319

1985   Body Works and Wearable Sculpture Visual Arts Centre of Alaska, Anchorage/USA
1984   Contemporary Jewellery: The Americas, Australia, Europe and Japan The National Museum of Modern Art, Kyoto/J
1984   Cross Currents: Jewellery from Australia, Britain, Germany and Holland Power House Museum, Sydney/ AUS travelling
1984   Jewellery International American Craft Museum II, New York/USA
1983   The Jewellery Project Crafts Council Gallery, London/GB
1982   Visies op sieraden 1965-1982 Stedelijk Museum, Amsterdam/NL
1975   Sieraad 1975 Gallery Het Kapelhuis Amersfoort/NL

SELECTED BIBLIOGRAPHY

The Ring: design past en present/Sylvie Lambert. - Crans-Près-Céligny: Rotovision, 1998 • Premsela Present: designers design for a designer/Liesbeth den Besten...et al. – Amsterdam: Stichting Vormgevingstentoonstellingen, 1998 • Paul Derrez: cool creator/Liesbeth den Besten. – Amsterdam: Galerie Ra, 1997 • Jewelry in Europe and America/Ralph Turner. – London: Thames and Hudson, 1996 • Passion and Profession: twintig jaar Ra sieraden toen nu straks/Paul Derrez. – Amsterdam: Galerie Ra, 1996 • Jewelry of our time: art, ornament and obsession/Helen W. Drutt English and Peter Dormer. – London: Thames and Hudson, 1995 • VES View Review. – Amsterdam: VES, 1991 • Novidades da Holanda: estudo sobre jóias/Marjan Unger. - Lisbon/Amsterdam: Fundaçao Calouste Gulbenkian/Dutch Form Foundation, 1990 • Autori del gioiello Olandese contemporaneo/Liesbeth Crommelin. - [Vicenza]: [Torri di Arcugnano], 1990 • L'Arte della Gioia: gioiello Ollandese d'autore l'oro di Padova/Liesbeth Crommelin. - Padova/The Hague: Assessorato Cultura e beni culturali/ Ministerie van WVC, 1990 • Fremdkörper: Schmuck der Avantgarde/Lida von Mengden. – Ludwigshafen: Wilhelm-Hack-Museum, 1990 • Point of view: Dutch contemporary jewelry and design/Charon Kransen. - S.l.: s.n., 1990 • Jewelry: Means: Meaning/ M. Tomlinson. - Knoxville Tennesee: Ewing Gallery of Art and Architecture, 1989 • Première Biennale du Bijou 1987/Françoise-Claire Prodhon. - S.l.: s.n., 1987 • Concepts, Comments, Process: Dutch Jewellery 1967-1978. – Amsterdam: Rijksdienst Beeldende Kunst, 1987 • Images: Sieraden Schmuck Jewellery/Marjan Unger...et al. – Amsterdam: VES, 1986 • Tien jaar Ra/Liesbeth Crommelin en Paul Derrez. – Amsterdam: Galerie Ra, 1986 • Multiples: heden en verleden. – Amsterdam: VES, 1986 • The New Jewelry: trends and traditions/Peter Dormer and Ralph Turner. – London: Thames and Hudson, 1985 • New Tradition: the evolution of jewellery 1966-1985/Caroline Broadhead. – London: British Crafts Centre, 1985 • Twentieth-Century Jewelry/Barbara Cartlidge. - New York: Harry N. Abrams, 1985 • The Jewellery project: new departures in British and European work 1980-83. – London: Crafts Council Gallery, 1983 • Sieraad 1975: 4e manifestatie van Nederlandse edelsmeden en sieradenontwerpers in Amersfoort. – Amersfoort: Galerie Het Kapelhuis, 1975

DUTCH
JEWELRY
DESIGN
1950
2000

JEWELS
of Mind and Mentality

320

JACOMIJN VAN DER DONK
Born: 1963

EDUCATION
1986-1991 Gerrit Rietveld Academie, Amsterdam/NL

AWARDS
1993 Puntgaaf Award, Groningen/NL

PUBLIC COLLECTIONS
Centraal Museum, Utrecht/NL
Fonds National d'Art Contemporain, Paris/F
Museum voor Moderne Kunst, Arnhem/NL
Stedelijk Museum, Amsterdam/NL

SELECTED SOLO EXHIBITIONS
1996 Gallery Louise Smit, Amsterdam/NL
1995 Gallery Art Box, Waregem/B
1994 Gallery Helene Poree, Paris/F
1993 Gallery Louise Smit, Amsterdam/NL

SELECTED GROUP EXHIBITIONS
1995 Parels Gallery Marzee, Nijmegen/NL
1995 Nouvelles Images, The Hague/NL
1993 Gallery Puntgaaf, Groningen/NL
1993 De kracht van heden, Amsterdam/NL
1993 Facet I Kunsthal, Rotterdam/NL
1993 Gallery Louise Smit, Amsterdam/NL
1992 Gevoel voor Ringen Gallery Louise Smit, Amsterdam/NL
1991 Sieraad als objekt – Objekt als sieraad De Librije, Zwolle/NL
1990 Kammen Gallery Marzee, Nijmegen, NL
1990 Jewellery Joint Exhibition Hiko Mizuno Jewellery College, Tokyo/J

SELECTED BIBLIOGRAPHY
Jacomijn van der Donk/Onno Boekhoudt. – Waregem: Art Box, 1995 ● The Best in Contemporary Jewellery/David Watkins.
- London: B.T. Batsford Ltd., 1993. ● Facet I: internationale sieradenbiënnale/Martita Slewe. - Rotterdam: Kunsthal, 1993 ●
De Kracht van heden: 45 individuele presentaties/Hester Wolters(red). - Amsterdam: Stichting Fonds voor Beeldende
kunsten, vormgeving en bouwkunst, 1993

DUTCH

JEWELRY

DESIGN

1950
–
2000

JEWELS
of Mind and Mentality

321

ARCHIBALD DUMBAR
1916-1988

EDUCATION
Gerrit Rietveld Academie, Amsterdam/NL

SELECTED EXHIBITIONS
2000   Jewels of Mind and Mentality Museum Het Kruithuis, 's-Hertogenbosch/NL travelling
1991   Getooid & Versierd Rijksdienst Beeldende Kunst, The Hague/NL
1973   Sier in serie: sieraden Nederlandse Kunststichting, Amsterdam/NL
1967   Sieraad '67 Het Kapelhuis, Amersfoort/NL

SELECTED BIBLIOGRAPHY
Genootschap van samenwerkende Ambachtskunstenaars/J. Koenraads. - Utrecht: Vereniging Genootschap Samenwerkende Ambachtskunstenaars • Getooid & Versierd/Liesbeth den Besten. - Haarlem: [The Hague]: [Rijksdienst Beeldende Kunst], 1991 • Sier in serie: sieraden. - Amsterdam: Nederlandse Kunststichting, 1973 • Sieraad '67: tentoonstelling 30 Nederlandse edelsmeden. - Amersfoort: Het Kapelhuis, 1967

DUTCH

JEWELRY

DESIGN

1950
–
2000

JEWELS
of Mind and Mentality

322

MARIJKE DE GOEY

Born: 1947 Utrecht/NL

EDUCATION
1974-1979 Gerrit Rietveld Academie, Amsterdam/NL

AWARDS
1986 Françoise van den Bosch Award
1985 Gouda City Award

PUBLIC COLLECTIONS
Het Kruithuis, Stedelijk Museum voor Hedendaagse Kunst, 's-Hertogenbosch/NL
Stedelijk Museum, Amsterdam/NL

SELECTED SOLO EXHIBITIONS
1999 Gallery Louise Smit, Amsterdam/NL
1995 Gallery Ademloos, The Hague/NL
1990 De Zonnehof, Amersfoort/NL
1989 Stedelijk Museum, Amsterdam/NL
1989 Nederlands Textielmuseum, Tilburg/NL
1986 Museum Boijmans van Beuningen, Rotterdam/NL
1985 Stedelijk Museum, Gouda/NL
1984 Museum De Beyerd, Breda/NL
1980 Stedelijk Van Abbemuseum, Eindhoven/NL
1979 Museum Fodor, Amsterdam/NL

SELECTED GROUP EXHIBITIONS
1998 La renaissance du bijou Gallery Piltzer, Paris/F
1998 Zes hedendaagse Nederlandse kunstenaars Gallery Zuidwaarts, Brasschaat/B
1998 Repetitions II travelling exhibition USA
1997 Chi ha Paura...? Museum Het Kruithuis, 's-Hertogenbosch/NL
1996 Stedelijk Museum, Amsterdam/NL
1996 Gallery Marzee, Nijmegen/NL
1995 Body Language Cooper-Hewitt Museum, New York/USA
1994 Salone de Mobile, Milan/I
1993 International Sculpture Biennial, Toyamura/J
1990 Nederlandse Beeldende Kunst Textiel De Zonnehof, Amersfoort/NL

SELECTED BIBLIOGRAPHY

Premsela Present: designers design for a designer/Liesbeth den Besten...et al. – Amsterdam: Stichting Vormgevings-tentoonstellingen, 1998 • Zes hedendaagse Nederlandse kunstenaars. – Brasschaat: Galerie Zuidwaarts, 1998 Marijke de Goey/Maurits Schmidt. – Blaricum: V + K Publishing, 1997 • Chi ha paura...?. – Amsterdam: Stichting Çhi ha paura...?, 1996 • Sierbeelden: sieraden ontworpen door beeldend kunstenaars/Hadewych Martens. – Arnhem: Museum voor Moderne Kunst, 1995 • Textiel in het Stedelijk/Liesbeth Crommelin. – Amsterdam: Stedelijk Museum, 1993 • Kunst bij rijksgebouwen: 8 jaar kunstopdrachten van de Rijksgebouwendienst/Th. van Krieken. - 's-Gravenhage: Staatsuitgeverij, 1986 • Standpunten/Marjan Unger. – Tilburg: Nederlands Textielmuseum, 1986

DUTCH

JEWELRY

DESIGN

1950
2000

JEWELS
of Mind and Mentality

MARIA HEES
Born: 1948 Bergeijk/NL

EDUCATION
1977 Hogeschool voor de Kunsten, Arnhem/NL

RELATED PROFESSIONAL EXPERIENCE
1980- External examiner Akademie voor Beeldende Kunsten, Kampen/NL
1980- Guest lecturer several Art Academies
1980- External examiner Gerrit Rietveld Academie, Amsterdam/NL

PUBLIC COLLECTIONS
Israël Museum, Jerusalem/IL
Het Kruithuis, Stedelijk Museum voor Hedendaagse Kunst, 's-Hertogenbosch/NL
Museum für Kunsthandwerk, Frankfurt/D
Museum of Modern Art, New York/USA
Museum voor Moderne Kunst, Arnhem/NL
Stedelijk Museum, Amsterdam/NL

SELECTED SOLO EXHIBITIONS
1998 Kunstuitleen Zwolle, Zwolle/NL
1997 Soft power Gallery RA, Amsterdam/NL
1993 Maria Hees 15 jaar ontwerpen Gemeentemuseum Arnhem, Arnhem/NL
1991 Gallery RA, Amsterdam/NL
1986 VO Gallery Washington/USA
1982 Gallery Marzee, Nijmegen/NL
1982 Gallery RA, Amsterdam/NL
1979 Gallery RA, Amsterdam/NL

SELECTED GROUP EXHIBITIONS
2000 Jewels of Mind and Mentality Museum Het Kruithuis, 's-Hertogenbosch/NL travelling
1998 A matter of materials USA travelling
1994 A moveable Feast Stedelijk Museum, Amsterdam/NL
1994 Sieraden 1964-1994 Stedelijk Museum, Amsterdam/NL
1994 Symfonie voor Solisten Gemeentemuseum Arnhem, Arnhem/NL
1993 Tekens en Ketens Museum van der Togt, Amstelveen/NL travelling
1991 Point of View, Contemporary Dutch Jewelry and Design USA/CDN travelling
1990 L'Arte della Gioia, Gioiello Olandese d'Autore Pedrocchi, Padua/I
1990 Novidades da Holanda Fundaçao Calouste Gulbenkian, Lisbon/P travelling
1987 Holland in Vorm, sieraden 1945-1987 Gemeentemuseum Arnhem, Arnhem/NL
1986 Sieraad 1986, Draagteken? Museum Het Kruithuis, 's-Hertogenbosch/NL
1984 Modern Jewelry USA travelling
1984 Kleding/mode Gemeentelijk Van Reekummuseum, Apeldoorn/NL
1983 Some dutch jewellers Arnolfini Gallery, Bristol/GB
1980 Stedelijk Museum, Amsterdam/NL

SELECTED BIBLIOGRAPHY

Premsela Present: designers design for a designer/Liesbeth den Besten...et al. – Amsterdam: Stichting Vormgevings-
tentoonstellingen, 1998 • Passion and Profession: twintig jaar Ra sieraden toen nu straks/Paul Derrez. – Amsterdam:
Galerie Ra, 1996 • Jewelry of our time: art, ornament and obsession/Helen W. Drutt English and Peter Dormer. – London:

Thames and Hudson, 1995 • Symfonie voor solisten/Jeroen N.M. van den Eynde. – Wageningen: H. Veerman & Zn., 1994 • Tekens & Ketens/Erik Beenker. – Amsterdam: Voetnoot Publishers, [1994] • De feestdis ontworpen door 39 kunstenaars The Banqueting table/Martijn van Ooststroom. – Amsterdam: Galerie Ra, 1991 • Novidades da Holanda: estudo sobre jóias/Marjan Unger. - Lisbon/Amsterdam: Fundaçao Calouste Gulbenkian/Dutch Form Foundation, 1990 • L'Arte della Gioia: gioiello Ollandese d'autore l'oro di Padova/Liesbeth Crommelin. - Padova/The Hague: Assessorato Cultura e beni culturali/Ministerie van WVC, 1990 • Autori del gioiello Olandese contemporaneo/Liesbeth Crommelin. - [Vicenza]: [Torri di Arcugnano], 1990 • Point of view: Dutch contemporary jewelry and design/Charon Kransen. - S.l.: s.n., 1990 • Sieraad en mode: tien jaar Galerie Beeld & Aambeeld/Lisette Pelgers (red.). – Enschede: Galerie Beeld & Aambeeld, 1989 • Holland in Vorm: vormgeving in Nederland 1945-1987/Gert Staal en Hester Wolters. – 's-Gravenhage: Stichting Holland in Vorm, 1987 • Concepts, Comments, Process: Dutch Jewellery 1967-1978. – Amsterdam: Rijksdienst Beeldende Kunst, 1987 • Sieraad 1986: draagteken?/Yvònne G.J.M. Joris. - 's-Hertogenbosch: Museum voor Hedendaagse Kunst Het Kruithuis, 1986 • Tien jaar Ra/Liesbeth Crommelin en Paul Derrez. – Amsterdam: Galerie Ra, 1986 • Multiples: heden en verleden. – Amsterdam: VES, 1986 • The New Jewelry: trends and traditions/Peter Dormer and Ralph Turner. – London: Thames and Hudson, 1985 • Some Dutch Jewellery. – Bristol: Arnolfini, 1984

DUTCH

JEWELRY

DESIGN

1950
–
2000

JEWELS
of Mind and Mentality

MARION HERBST
1944-1995

EDUCATION

1962-1968   Gerrit Rietveld Academie, Amsterdam NL

RELATED PROFESSIONAL EXPERIENCE

          Teacher Nieuwe Lerarenopleiding Tilburg/NL
1992   Guest teacher Fachhochschule Pforzheim/D
1990-1992   member supervisory board Dutch Form, Amsterdam/NL
1988-1991   member committee Fonds voor Beeldende Kunst, Design en Bouwkunde, Amsterdam/NL
1984-1990   member Raad voor de Kunst
1981-1992   teacher Gerrit Rietveld Academie, Amsterdam/NL
1974   Co-founder Bond van Oproerige Edelsmeden

PUBLIC COLLECTIONS

Angermuseum, Erfurt/D
Centraal Museum, Utrecht/NL
Frans Halsmuseum, Haarlem/NL
Gemeentelijk Van Reekummuseum, Apeldoorn/NL
Het Kruithuis, Stedelijk Museum voor Hedendaagse Kunst, 's-Hertogenbosch/NL
Museum Boijmans van Beuningen, Rotterdam/NL
Museum voor Moderne Kunst, Arnhem/NL
Museo Universitario de Ciencias y Arte, Mexico City/MEX
Nederlands Kostuummuseum, The Hague/NL
Rijksdienst Beeldende Kunst, The Hague/NL
Stedelijk Museum, Amsterdam/NL

SELECTED SOLO EXHIBITIONS

1981   5 keer Marion Herbst, 5 jaar Galerie RA Gallery RA, Amsterdam/NL
1982   Marion Herbst, een overzicht 1969-1982 Gemeentelijk Van Reekummuseum, Apeldoorn/NL travelling
1976   Nieuw werk Gallery RA, Amsterdam/NL

SELECTED GROUP EXHIBITIONS

2000   Jewels of Mind and Mentality Museum Het Kruithuis, 's-Hertogenbosch/NL travelling
1993   Stedelijk Museum, Amsterdam/NL
1992   Schmuck und Objectkunst Angermuseum, Erfurt/D
1991   Bedels aan banden Gemeentemuseum Arnhem, Arnhem/NL
1991   De Feestdis Gallery RA, Amsterdam/NL
1991   Getooid en Versierd Rijksdienst Beeldende Kunst, The Hague/NL
1990   Autori del gioiello Olandese contemporaneo Torri di Arcugnano, Vicenza/I
1990   L'Arte della Gioia, Gioiello Olandese d'Autore Pedrocchi, Padua/I
1990   Novidades da Holanda Fundaçao Calouste Gulbenkian, Lisbon/P
1989   Kunstobject als onderscheiding II Stedelijk Museum, Amsterdam/NL
1989   Ornamenta I Schmuckmuseum, Pforzheim/D
1988   London - Amsterdam: new art objects...Gallery RA/Crafts Council Amsterdam, London/GB
1987   Concepts, Comments, Process: Dutch Jewellery 1967-1987 Rijksdienst Beeldende Kunst, The Hague/NL travelling
1987   Holland in Vorm, sieraden 1945-1987 Gemeentemuseum Arnhem, Arnhem/NL
1986   10 jaar galerie RA Gallery RA, Amsterdam/NL

DUTCH

JEWELRY

DESIGN

1950
2000

JEWELS
of Mind and Mentality

1986 Sieraad 1986, Draagteken? Museum Het Kruithuis, 's-Hertogenbosch/NL
1985 Body Works and Wearable Sculpture Visual Arts Centre of Alaska, Anchorage/USA
1984 Cross Currents: Jewellery from Australia, Britain, Germany and Holland Power House Museum, Sydney/
       AUS travelling
1984 Some Dutch Jewellery Arnolfini Gallery, Bristol/GB
1983 The Jewellery Project Crafts Council Gallery, London/GB
1982 Jewellery Redefined British Crafts Centre, London/GB
1982 Visies op sieraden 1965-1982 Stedelijk Museum, Amsterdam/NL
1979 Sieraad in Singer Singer Museum, Laren/NL
1975 Sieraad 1975 Gallery Het Kapelhuis, Amersfoort/NL
1974 5 jaar Sieraad Gallery Sieraad, Amsterdam/NL
1974 Revolt in Jewellery by Five Dutch Artists Electrum Gallery, London/GB
1973 Jewelry as Sculpture as Jewelry Institute of Contemporary Art, Bosten/USA
1972 Sieraad 1900-1972 De Zonnehof, Amersfoort/NL
1969 Sieraad '69 Gallery Het Kapelhuis, Amersfoort/NL

SELECTED BIBLIOGRAPHY

The Ring: design past en present/Sylvie Lambert. - Crans-Près-Céligny: Rotovision, 1998 • Jewelry in Europe and America/Ralph Turner. – London: Thames and Hudson, 1996 • Mode en Sieraad/Marjan Unger, Gert Staal. – Amsterdam: Vormgevingsinstituut, 1994 • Mag het iets meer zijn? Marion Herbst 1968-1993/Ans van Berkum...et al. – Wijk en Aalburg: Pictures Publishers, 1993 • Sieraden: Centrum Beeldende Kunst Groningen/Gerard Lakke. – Groningen: Centrum Beeldende Kunst, 1992 • De feestdis ontworpen door 39 kunstenaars The Banqueting table/Martijn van Ooststroom. – Amsterdam: Galerie Ra, 1991 • Bedels aan banden: hedendaagse interpretaties van de bedelarmband/Ietse Meij. – Arnhem: Stichting Nieuwstad, 1991 • Getooid & Versierd/Liesbeth den Besten. – [The Hague]: [Rijksdienst Beeldende Kunst], 1991 • Novidades da Holanda: estudo sobre jóias/Marjan Unger. - Lisbon/Amsterdam: Fundaçao Calouste Gulbenkian/Dutch Form Foundation, 1990 • L'Arte della Gioia: gioiello Ollandese d'autore l'oro di Padova/Liesbeth Crommelin. - Padova/The Hague: Assessorato Cultura e beni culturali/Ministerie van WVC, 1990 • Autori del gioiello Olandese contemporaneo/Liesbeth Crommelin. - [Vicenza]: [Torri di Arcugnano], 1990 • London Amsterdam: new objects from Britain and Holland/Gert Staal en Martina Margetts. – Amsterdam: Galerie Ra, 1988 • Holland in Vorm: vormgeving in Nederland 1945-1987/Gert Staal en Hester Wolters. - 's-Gravenhage: Stichting Holland in Vorm, 1987 • Concepts, Comments, Process: Dutch Jewellery 1967-1978. – Amsterdam: Rijksdienst Beeldende Kunst, 1987 • Sieraad 1986: draagteken?/Yvònne G.J.M. Joris. - 's-Hertogenbosch: Museum voor Hedendaagse Kunst Het Kruithuis, 1986 • Sieraden: vorm en idee/Liesbeth den Besten. – Apeldoorn: Gemeentelijk Van Reekummuseum, 1986 • Tien jaar Ra/Liesbeth Crommelin en Paul Derrez. – Amsterdam: Galerie Ra, 1986 • The New Jewelry: trends and traditions/Peter Dormer and Ralph Turner. – London: Thames and Hudson, 1985 • Twentieth-Century Jewelry/Barbara Cartlidge. - New York: Harry N. Abrams, 1985 • Some Dutch Jewellery. – Bristol: Arnolfini, 1984 • The Jewellery project: new departures in British and European work 1980-83. – London: Crafts Council Gallery, 1983 • Marion Herbst: een overzicht 1969-1982. – Apeldoorn: Gemeentelijke Van Reekumgalerij, 1982 • VES. – Amsterdam: Vereniging van Edelsmeden en Sieraadontwerpers, 1981 • Sieraad 1975: 4e manifestatie van Nederlandse edelsmeden en sieradenontwerpers in Amersfoort. – Amersfoort: Galerie Het Kapelhuis, 1975 • Sieraad '69: werk van 22 Nederlandse edelsmeden in Het Kapelhuis. – Amersfoort: Het Kapelhuis, 1969

DUTCH

JEWELRY

DESIGN

1950
2000

JEWELS
of Mind and Mentality

327

HERMAN HERMSEN

Born: 1950 Nijmegen/NL

EDUCATION
1974-1979 Hogeschool voor de Kunsten, Arnhem/NL

RELATED PROFESSIONAL EXPERIENCE
1993- teacher Fachhochschule Düsseldorf/D
1990-1992 teacher Hogeschool voor de Kunsten, Arnhem/NL
1985-1990 teacher Hogeschool voor de Kunsten, Utrecht/NL

PUBLIC COLLECTIONS
Bauhaus Archiv, Berlin/D
Centraal Museum, Utrecht/NL
Cleveland County Museum, Middlesborough/GB
Cooper-Hewitt Museum, New York/USA
Gemeentelijk Van Reekummuseum, Apeldoorn/NL
Gemeentemuseum Den Haag, The Hague/NL
Musée des Arts Décoratifs, Montreal/CDN
Museum Boijmans van Beuningen, Rotterdam/NL
Museum für Angewandte Kunst, Munich/D
Museum voor Moderne Kunst, Arnhem/NL
Het Kruithuis, Stedelijk Museum voor Hedendaagse Kunst, s-Hertogenbosch/NL
Museum voor Kunsthandwerk, Oslo/N
Rijksdienst Beeldende Kunst, The Hague/NL
Stedelijk Museum, Amsterdam/NL
Victoria and Albert Museum, London/GB

SELECTED SOLO EXHIBITIONS
1998 Gallery Marzee, Nijmegen/NL
1996 Gallery V & V, Vienna/A
1995 Gallery RA, Amsterdam/NL
1989 Gallery V & V, Vienna/A
1989 Gallery RA, Amsterdam/NL
1986 TC Design Centre, Schiedam/NL
1986 Gallery Marzee, Nijmegen/NL
1985 VO Gallery, Washington/USA
1984 Overzicht 1978-1984 Gemeentemuseum Arnhem, Arnhem/NL
1982 Gallery Marzee, Nijmegen/NL
1982 Apects Gallery, London/GB

SELECTED GROUP EXHIBITIONS
1995 Pareltentoonstelling Gallery Marzee, Nijmegen/NL
1994 Made in Holland Museum für Angewandte Kunst, Cologne/D
1994 Symfonie voor Solisten Gemeentemuseum Arnhem, Arnhem/NL
1993 Tekens en Ketens Museum van der Togt, Amstelveen/NL travelling
1991 De Feestdis Gallery RA, Amsterdam/NL
1987 Holland in Vorm, sieraden 1945-1987 Gemeentemuseum Arnhem, Arnhem/NL
1987 Joieria Europea Contemporània Fundació Caixa de Pensions, Barcelona/E
1984 Some Dutch Jewellers Arnolfini Gallery, Bristol/GB

1982   Jewellery Redefined British Crafts Centre, London/GB
1982   Visies op sieraden 1965-1982 Stedelijk Museum, Amsterdam/NL

SELECTED BIBLIOGRAPHY

The Ring: design past en present/Sylvie Lambert. - Crans-Près-Céligny: Rotovision, 1998 • Premsela Present: designers design for a designer/Liesbeth den Besten...et al. – Amsterdam: Stichting Vormgevingstentoonstellingen, 1998 • Passion and Profession: twintig jaar Ra sieraden toen nu straks/Paul Derrez. – Amsterdam: Galerie Ra, 1996 • Symfonie voor solisten/Jeroen N.M. van den Eynde. – Wageningen: H. Veerman & Zn., 1994 • Tekens & Ketens/Erik Beenker. – Amsterdam: Voetnoot Publishers, [1994] • Bedels aan banden: hedendaagse interpretaties van de bedelarmband/Ietse Meij. – Arnhem: Stichting Nieuwstad, 1991 • De feestdis ontworpen door 39 kunstenaars The Banqueting table/Martijn van Ooststroom. – Amsterdam: Galerie Ra, 1991 • L'Arte della Gioia: gioiello Ollandese d'autore l'oro di Padova/Liesbeth Crommelin. - Padova/The Hague: Assessorato Cultura e beni culturali/Ministerie van WVC, 1990 • Autori del gioiello Olandese contemporaneo/Liesbeth Crommelin. - [Vicenza]: [Torri di Arcugnano], 1990 • Fremdkörper: Schmuck der Avantgarde/Lida von Mengden. – Ludwigshafen: Wilhelm-Hack-Museum, 1990 • Point of view: Dutch contemporary jewelry and design/Charon Kransen. - S.l.: s.n., 1990 • Herman Hermsen: jewellery, Schmuck, sieraden/Egon Kuhn. - S.l.: Herman Hermsen, 1989 • Jewellery: makers motifs history techniques/Diana Scarisbrick. – London: Thames and Hudson, 1989 • Concepts, Comments, Process: Dutch Jewellery 1967-1978. – Amsterdam: Rijksdienst Beeldende Kunst, 1987 • Holland in Vorm: vormgeving in Nederland 1945-1987/Gert Staal en Hester Wolters. - 's-Gravenhage: Stichting Holland in Vorm, 1987 • Images: Sieraden Schmuck Jewellery/Marjan Unger, Renny Ramakers, Monique Mokveld...et al. – Amsterdam: VES, 1986 • Multiples: heden en verleden. – Amsterdam: VES, 1986 • Tien jaar Ra/Liesbeth Crommelin en Paul Derrez. – Amsterdam: Galerie Ra, 1986 • The New Jewelry: trends and traditions/Peter Dormer and Ralph Turner. – London: Thames and Hudson, 1985 • Some Dutch Jewellery. – Bristol: Arnolfini, 1984 • Herman Hermsen: Werk. - S.l.: Vormgeversassociatie, 1984 • The Jewellery project: new departures in British and European work 1980-83. - London: Crafts Council Gallery, 1983 • Jewellery redefined: the 1st international exhibition of multi-media non-precious jewellery 1982. – London: British Crafts Centre, 1982

JEWELS
of Mind and Mentality

WILLEM HONING

Born: 1955 Rotterdam/NL

EDUCATION

1977-1981 Gerrit Rietveld Academie, Amsterdam/NL

AWARDS

1987 Herbert-Hofmann Award, Internationale Handwerksmesse, Munich/D

PUBLIC COLLECTIONS

Cleveland County Museum, Middlesborough/GB
Collectie Culturele Raad Zuid-Holland/NL
Gemeentelijk Van Reekummuseum, Apeldoorn/NL
Het Kruithuis, Stedelijk Museum voor Hedendaagse Kunst, 's-Hertogenbosch/NL
Kunstindustriemuseet, Oslo/N
Musée des Arts Décoratifs, Montreal/CDN
Museum für Kunstgewerbe, Berlin/D
Museum voor Moderne Kunst, Arnhem/NL
National Museum of Modern Art, Kyoto/J
Power House Museum, Sydney/AUS
Rijksdienst Beeldende Kunst, The Hague/NL

SELECTED SOLO EXHIBITIONS

1993 Studio Ton Berends, The Hague/NL
1981 Gallery RA, Amsterdam/NL

SELECTED GROUP EXHIBITIONS

2000 Jewels of Mind and Mentality Museum Het Kruithuis, 's-Hertogenbosch/NL travelling
1993 Voorzien: Benno Premsela Applied Art Stedelijk Museum Collection, Amsterdam/NL
1992 Sieraden Centrum Beeldende Kunst, Groningen/NL
1991 De Feestdis Gallery RA, Amsterdam/NL
1991 Getooid en Versierd Museum de Vishal, Haarlem/NL
1991 View, Review, 15 jaar VES Stedelijk Museum, Amsterdam/NL
1990 Fremdkörper, Schmuck der Avantgarde aus Wilhelm Hack-Museum, Ludwigshafen/D
1990 L'Arte della Gioia, Gioiello Olandese d'Autore Pedrocchi, Padua/I
1988 London – Amsterdam British Crafts Council London/GB
1987 Concepts, Comments, Process: Dutch Jewellery 1967-1987 Rijksdienst Beeldende Kunst The Hague/NL travelling
1987 Holland in Vorm, sieraden 1945-1987, Gemeentemuseum Arnhem, Arnhem/NL
1986 10 jaar RA Gallery RA, Amsterdam/NL
1986 Sieraden: vorm en idee Gemeentelijk Van Reekummuseum, Apeldoorn/NL
1985 New Tradition British Crafts Council, London/GB
1984 Cross Currents: Jewellery from Australia, Britain, Germany and Holland Power House Museum Sydney/ AUS travelling
1982 Jewellery Redefined British Crafts Centre, London/GB
1982 Visies op sieraden 1965-1982 Stedelijk Museum, Amsterdam/NL
1981 VES tentoonstelling Stedelijk Museum, Amsterdam/NL

DUTCH

JEWELRY

DESIGN

1950
–
2000

JEWELS
of Mind and Mentality

330

SELECTED BIBLIOGRAPHY

Passion and Profession: twintig jaar Ra sieraden toen nu straks/Paul Derrez. – Amsterdam: Galerie Ra, 1996 • Sieraden: Centrum Beeldende Kunst Groningen/Gerard Lakke. – Groningen: Centrum Beeldende Kunst, 1992 • De feestdis ontworpen door 39 kunstenaars The Banqueting table/Martijn van Ooststroom. – Amsterdam: Galerie Ra, 1991 • L'Arte della Gioia: gioiello Ollandese d'autore l'oro di Padova/Liesbeth Crommelin. - Padova/The Hague: Assessorato Cultura e beni culturali/Ministerie van WVC, 1990 • Autori del gioiello Olandese contemporaneo/Liesbeth Crommelin. - [Vicenza]: [Torri di Arcugnano], 1990 • Perth InternationalCrafts Triennial/Robert Bell. – Perth: Art Gallery of Western Australia, 1989 London Amsterdam: new objects from Britain and Holland/Gert Staal en Martina Margetts. – Amsterdam: Galerie Ra, 1988 • Concepts, Comments, Process: Dutch Jewellery 1967-1978. – Amsterdam: Rijksdienst Beeldende Kunst, 1987 • Holland in Vorm: vormgeving in Nederland 1945-1987/Gert Staal en Hester Wolters. - 's-Gravenhage: Stichting Holland in Vorm, 1987 • Tien jaar Ra/Liesbeth Crommelin en Paul Derrez. – Amsterdam: Galerie Ra, 1986 • The New Jewelry: trends and traditions/Peter Dormer and Ralph Turner. – London: Thames and Hudson, 1985 • Jewellery redefined: the 1st international exhibition of multi-media non-precious jewellery 1982. – London: British Crafts Centre, 1982

DUTCH
JEWELRY
DESIGN
1950
2000

331

RIAN DE JONG

Born: 1951 Zoeterwoude/NL

EDUCATION

1979-1985 Gerrit Rietveld Academie, Amsterdam/NL

RELATED PROFESSIONAL EXPERIENCE

1989   teacher Mimar Sinan Universitesi, Istanbul/T
1989-   teacher Art Academy HKU, Utrecht/NL
1992-1993   teacher Fachhochschule Pforzheim, Pforzheim/D

PUBLIC COLLECTIONS

Het Kruithuis, Stedelijk Museum voor Hedendaagse Kunst, 's-Hertogenbosch/NL
Museum Boijmans van Beuningen, Rotterdam/NL
Rijksdienst Beeldende Kunst, The Hague/NL
Stedelijk Museum, Amsterdam/NL

SELECTED SOLO EXHIBITIONS

1999   Reisgenoten Gallery Ra, Amsterdam/NL
1996   Vanity Tables Gallery Ra, Amsterdam/NL
1992   Echo Gallery Ra, Amsterdam/NL

SELECTED GROUP EXHIBITIONS

1992   Sieraden Centrum Beeldende Kunst, Groningen/NL
1991   Bedels aan banden Gemeentemuseum Arnhem, Arnhem/NL
1991   De Feestdis, Gallery Ra, Amsterdam/NL
1991   Sieraad als objekt, objekt als sieraad, Librije, Zwolle/NL
1991   Point of view USA/CDN travelling
1991   VES View Review Stedelijk Museum, Amsterdam/NL
1990   Novidades da Hollanda Gulbenkian Museum, Lisbon/P
1989   Ornamenta I, Schmuckmuseum, Pforzheim/D
1989   Contemporary Dutch Jewellery City Art Gallery, Leeds/GB
1988   Le Bijou contemporain en Hollande Gallery Neon, Brussels/B
1988   Unica Stedelijk Museum, Amsterdam/NL
1987   Concepts, comments, Progress: Dutch Jewellery 1967-1987 Rijksdienst Beeldende Kunst, The Hague/NL
1986   Images Singer Museum, Laren /NL travelling
1986   10 Jaar Ra Gallery Ra, Amsterdam/NL

SELECTED BIBLIOGRAPHY

Jewelry in Europe and America/Ralph Turner. – London: Thames and Hudson, 1996 • Passion and Profession: twintig jaar Ra sieraden toen nu straks/Paul Derrez. – Amsterdam: Galerie Ra, 1996 • Tekens & Ketens/Erik Beenker. – Amsterdam: Voetnoot Publishers, [1994] • Echo: Rian de Jong/Heide Hinterthür. – Amsterdam: Rian de Jong, 1992 • Sieraden: Centrum Beeldende Kunst Groningen/Gerard Lakke. – Groningen: Centrum Beeldende Kunst, 1992 • De feestdis ontworpen door 39 kunstenaars: The Banqueting table/Martijn van Ooststroom. – Amsterdam: Galerie Ra, 1991 • Bedels aan banden: hedendaagse interpretaties van de bedelarmband/Ietse Meij. – Arnhem: Stichting Nieuwstad, 1991 • VES View Review. – Amsterdam: VES, 1991 • Novidades da Holanda: estudo sobre jóias/Marjan Unger. - Lisbon/Amsterdam: Fundaçao Calouste Gulbenkian/Dutch Form Foundation, 1990 • Unica. – Amsterdam: VES, 1987 • Concepts, Comments, Process: Dutch Jewellery 1967-1978. – Amsterdam: Rijksdienst Beeldende Kunst, 1987 • Images: Sieraden Schmuck Jewellery/Marjan Unger, Renny Ramakers, Monique Mokveld...et al. – Amsterdam: VES, 1986 • Tien jaar Ra/Liesbeth Crommelin en Paul Derrez. – Amsterdam: Galerie Ra, 1986

DUTCH

JEWELRY

DESIGN

1950
—
2000

JEWELS
of Mind and Mentality

BEPPE KESSLER

Born: 1952 Amsterdam/NL

EDUCATION
1974-1979 Gerrit Rietveld Academie, Amsterdam/NL

PUBLIC COLLECTIONS
Gemeentelijk Van Reekummuseum, Apeldoorn/NL
Gemeentemuseum Den Haag, The Hague/NL
Musée des Arts Décoratifs, Montreal/CDN
Museum für Angewandte Kunst, Vienna/A
Museum voor Moderne Kunst, Arnhem/NL
Nederlands Textielmuseum, Tilburg/NL
Nordenfjeldske Kunstindustrimuseum, Trondheim/N
Rijksdienst Beeldende Kunst, The Hague/NL
Stedelijk Museum, Amsterdam/NL

SELECTED SOLO EXHIBITIONS
1998 Gallery Hipotesí, Barcelona/E
1992 Gallery RA, Amsterdam/NL
1988 Gallery RA, Amsterdam/NL
1985 Gallery Eewal, Leeuwarden/NL

SELECTED GROUP EXHIBITIONS
1998 Brooching it Diplomatically Helen Drutt, Philadelphia/USA travelling
1998 Jewellery moves National Museum of Scotland, Edinburgh/GB
1996 Briljant en gevat Nederlands Kostuummuseum, The Hague/NL
1993 Tekens en Ketens Museum van der Togt, Amstelveen/NL
1993 Voorzien: Benno Premsela Applied Art Collection Stedelijk Museum, Amsterdam/NL
1991 Bedels aan banden Gemeentemuseum Arnhem, Arnhem/NL
1991 Point of View, Contemporary Dutch Jewelry and Design USA/CDN travelling
1990 Novidades da Holanda Fundaçao Calouste Gulbenkian Lisbon/P travelling
1989 Ornamenta I Schmuckmuseum, Pforzheim/D
1987 Holland in Vorm, sieraden 1945-1987 Gemeentemuseum Arnhem, Arnhem/NL
1986 Images Singer Museum, Laren/NL travelling
1982 Jewellery Redefined British Crafts Centre, London/GB

SELECTED BIBLIOGRAPHY

Premsela Present: designers design for a designer/Liesbeth den Besten...et al. — Amsterdam: Stichting Vormgevings-tentoonstellingen, 1998 • Brooching it Diplomatically: a tribute to Madeleine K. Albright/Helen W. Drutt English. — Philadelphia: Helen Drutt, 1998 • Passion and Profession: twintig jaar Ra sieraden toen nu straks/Paul Derrez. — Amsterdam: Galerie Ra, 1996 • Beppe Kessler/Michaja Langelaan. —Amsterdam: Beppe Kessler, 1996 • Tekens & Ketens/Erik Beenker. — Amsterdam: Voetnoot Publishers, [1994] • De feestdis ontworpen door 39 kunstenaars: The Banqueting table/ Martijn van Ooststroom. — Amsterdam: Galerie Ra, 1991 • Novidades da Holanda: estudo sobre jóias/Marjan Unger. - Lisbon/Amsterdam: Fundaçao Calouste Gulbenkian/Dutch Form Foundation, 1990 • Point of view: Dutch contemporary jewelry and design/Charon Kransen. - S.l.: s.n., 1990 • Unica. — Amsterdam: VES, 1987 • Concepts, Comments, Process: Dutch Jewellery 1967-1978. — Amsterdam: Rijksdienst Beeldende Kunst, 1987 • Images: Sieraden Schmuck Jewellery/Marjan Unger, Renny Ramakers, Monique Mokveld...et al. — Amsterdam: VES, 1986 • Tien jaar Ra/Liesbeth Crommelin en Paul Derrez. — Amsterdam: Galerie Ra, 1986 • Jewellery redefined: the 1st international exhibition of multi-media non-precious jewellery 1982. — London: British Crafts Centre, 1982

JEWELS
of Mind and Mentality

EMMY VAN LEERSUM

1930-1984

EDUCATION
1958-1962 Instituut voor Kunstnijverheidsonderwijs Amsterdam/NL
1962-1963 Konstfack Skolen Stockholm/S

PUBLIC COLLECTIONS
Centraal Museum, Utrecht/NL
Cleveland County Museum, Middlesborough/GB
Gemeentelijk Van Reekummuseum, Apeldoorn/NL
Museum voor Moderne Kunst, Arnhem/NL
Gemeentemuseum Den Haag, The Hague/NL
Museo Universitario de Ciencias y Arte, Mexico City/MEX
Het Kruithuis, Stedelijk Museum voor Hedendaagse Kunst, 's-Hertogenbosch/NL
Nordenfjeldske Kunstindustrimuseum, Trondheim/N
Power House Museum, Sydney/AUS
Rijksdienst Beeldende Kunst, The Hague/NL
Stedelijk Museum, Amsterdam/NL
Victoria and Albert Museum, London/GB

SELECTED SOLO EXHIBITIONS
1993 Broken Lines: Emmy van Leersum, 1930-1984 Museum Het Kruithuis, 's-Hertogenbosch/NL   travelling
1982 Emmy van Leersum. Sieraden en Breisels Gemeentelijk Van Reekummuseum, Apeldoorn/NL
1982 Gallery RA, Amsterdam/NL
1979 Emmy van Leersum Stedelijk Museum, Amsterdam/NL travelling
1979 Emmy van Leersum, sieraden en objecten 1964-1979 Stedelijk Museum, Amsterdam/NL

SELECTED GROUP EXHIBITIONS
2000 Jewels of Mind and Mentality Museum Het Kruithuis, 's-Hertogenbosch/NL travelling
1994 A moveable Feast Stedelijk Museum, Amsterdam/NL
1989 Ornamenta I Schmuckmuseum, Pforzheim/D
1987 Concepts, Comments, Process: Dutch Jewellery 1967-1987 Rijksdienst Beeldende Kunst The Hague/NL
      travelling
1987 Holland in Vorm, sieraden 1945-1987 Gemeentemuseum Arnhem, Arnhem/NL
1986 Sieraad 1986, Draagteken? Museum Het Kruithuis, 's-Hertogenbosch/NL
1986 Images, Singer Museum, Laren/NL travelling
1985 Body Works and Wearable Sculpture Visual Arts Center of Alaska, Anchorage/USA
1985 New Tradition British Crafts Centre, London/GB
1984 Cross Currents: Jewellery from Australia, Britain, Germany and Holland Power House Museum, Sydney/
      AUS travelling
1984 Jewelry International American Craft Museum II, New York/USA
1983 Sieren en Versieren Gemeentelijk Van Reekummuseum, Apeldoorn/NL
1982 Jewellery Redefined British Crafts Centre, London/GB
1982 Visies op sieraden 1965-1982 Stedelijk Museum, Amsterdam/NL
1979 56 Bracelets, 17 Rings, 2 Necklaces Gemeentelijk Van Reekummuseum, Apeldoorn/NL
1976 Sieraden C.R.M., Rijswijk/NL travelling
1975 Contemporary Dutch Jewellery Bureau Beeldende Kunst Buitenland, Amsterdam/NL travelling
1975 Sieraad 1975 Gallery Het Kapelhuis, Amersfoort/NL
1974 18 Orfèvres d'aujourd'hui Musée des Arts Décoratifs de la Ville de Lausanne, Lausanne/CH

1973 Sier in serie CRM/NKS, Rijswijk/NL travelling
1972 Objects to wear, Emmy van Leersum en Gijs Bakker Electrum Gallery, London/GB
1972 Sieraad 1900-1972 De Zonnehof, Amersfoort/NL
1971 Schmuck - Objekte Museum Bellerive, Zurich/CH
1971 Stedelijk '60-'70 Paleis voor Schone Kunsten, Brussels/B
1969 Objects to wear Van Abbemuseum, Eindhoven/NL travelling
1969 Sieraad '69 Gallery Het Kapelhuis, Amersfoort/NL
1967 Sieraad '67 Gallery Het Kapelhuis, Amersfoort/NL

SELECTED BIBLIOGRAPHY

The Ring: design past en present/Sylvie Lambert. - Crans-Près-Céligny: Rotovision, 1998 • Jewelry in Europe and America/Ralph Turner. - London: Thames and Hudson, 1996 • Jewelry of our time: art, ornament and obsession/Helen W. Drutt English and Peter Dormer. - London: Thames and Hudson, 1995 • Gebroken lijnen/Broken Lines: Emmy van Leersum 1930-1984/ed. Yvònne G.J. M. Joris. - 's-Hertogenbosch: Museum Het Kruithuis, 1993 • Fremdkörper: Schmuck der Avantgarde/Lida von Mengden. - Ludwigshafen: Wilhelm-Hack-Museum, 1990 • Sieraad 1986: draagteken?/Yvònne G.J.M. Joris. - 's-Hertogenbosch: Museum voor Hedendaagse Kunst Het Kruithuis, 1986 • Holland in Vorm: vormgeving in Nederland 1945-1987/Gert Staal en Hester Wolters. - 's-Gravenhage ; Stichting Holland in Vorm, 1987 • Concepts, Comments, Process: Dutch Jewellery 1967-1978. - Amsterdam: Rijksdienst Beeldende Kunst, 1987 • Sieraden: vorm en idee/Liesbeth den Besten. - Apeldoorn: Gemeentelijk Van Reekummuseum, 1986 • The New Jewelry: trends and traditions/Peter Dormer and Ralph Turner. – London: Thames and Hudson, 1985 • Twentieth-Century Jewelry/Barbara Cartlidge. - New York: Harry N. Abrams, 1985 • The Jewellery project: new departures in British and European work 1980-83. – London: Crafts Council Gallery, 1983 • Jewellery redefined: the 1st international exhibition of multi-media non-precious jewellery 1982. – London: British Crafts Centre, 1982 • Bracelets, Rings, Necklaces. – Amsterdam: Visual Arts office for abroad, [1979] • Sieraad 1975: 4e manifestatie van Nederlandse edelsmeden en sieradenontwerpers in Amersfoort. – Amersfoort: Galerie Het Kapelhuis, 1975 • Sier in serie: sieraden. – Amsterdam: Nederlandse Kunststichting, 1973 • Sieraad '69: werk van 22 Nederlandse edelsmeden in Het Kapelhuis. – Amersfoort: Het Kapelhuis, 1969 • Objects to wear: by five Dutch jewelry designers. – Eindhoven: Van Abbemuseum, 1969 • Sieraad '67: tentoonstelling 30 Nederlandse edelsmeden. – Amersfoort: Het Kapelhuis, 1967

For a complete survey see: Gebroken lijnen/Broken Lines: Emmy van Leersum 1930-1984/ed. Yvònne G.J. M. Joris. - 's-Hertogenbosch: Museum Het Kruithuis, 1993

DUTCH

JEWELRY

DESIGN

1950
—
2000

JEWELS
of Mind and Mentality

NEL LINSSEN

Born: 1935 Mook en Middelaar/NL

EDUCATION
Academie voor Beeldende Kunsten, Arnhem/NL

PUBLIC COLLECTIONS
Cleveland County Collection, Middlesborough/GB
Cooper-Hewitt Museum, New York/USA
Gemeentelijk Van Reekummuseum, Apeldoorn/NL
Kunstgewerbe Museum, Berlin/D
Musée des Arts Decoratifs, Lausanne/CH
Musée des Arts Decoratifs, Montreal/CDN
Museum Boijmans van Beuningen, Rotterdam/NL
Museum für Kunst und Gewerbe, Hamburg/D
Museum voor Moderne Kunst, Arnhem/NL
Museum De Zonnehof, Amersfoort/NL
Nederlands Textielmuseum, Tilburg/NL
Scottish Museum, Edinburgh/GB
Stedelijk Museum, Amsterdam/NL

SELECTED SOLO EXHIBITIONS
1995 Gallery Slavik, Vienna/A
1994 Gallery Marzee, Nijmegen/NL
1993 Gallery Ra, Amsterdam/NL
1991 Gallery Puntgaaf, Groningen/NL
1989 Gallery Trits, Delft/NL

SELECTED GROUP EXHIBITIONS
1996 Badisches Landesmuseum, Karlsruhe/D
1996 Gemeentemuseum Den Haag, The Hague/NL
1995 Gemeentelijk Van Reekummuseum, Apeldoorn/NL
1995 Museum Bellerive, Zürich/CH
1992 American Craft Museum, New York/USA
1990 Novidades da Hollanda Fundaçao Calouste Gulbenkian, Lisbon/P
1990 Le Bijou contemporain Brussels/B
1991 Point of View, USA/CDN travelling
1989 Ornamenta I Schmuckmuseum, Pforzheim/D

SELECTED BIBLIOGRAPHY

Passion and Profession: twintig jaar Ra sieraden toen nu straks/Paul Derrez. – Amsterdam: Galerie Ra, 1996 • Tekens & Ketens/Erik Beenker. – Amsterdam: Voetnoot Publishers, [1994] • Bedels aan banden: hedendaagse interpretaties van de bedelarmband/Ietse Meij. – Arnhem: Stichting Nieuwstad, 1991 • International Crafts/Martina Margetts. – London: Thames and Hudson, 1991 • Paper Jewelry 1986-1991/Paul Derrez. – Nijmegen: Nel Linssen, 1991 • VES View Review. – Amsterdam: VES, 1991 • Novidades da Holanda: estudo sobre jóias/Marjan Unger. - Lisbon/Amsterdam: Fundaçao Calouste Gulbenkian/Dutch Form Foundation, 1990 • Point of view: Dutch contemporary jewelry and design/Charon Kransen. - S.l.: s.n., 1990 • Ornamenta I: internationale Schmuckkunst/Michael Erlhoff. – München: Prestel Verlag, 1989 • Concepts, Comments, Process: Dutch jewellery 1967-1978. – Amsterdam: Rijksdienst Beeldende Kunst, 1987 • Unica. – Amsterdam: VES, 1987

DUTCH
JEWELRY
DESIGN
1950
2000

LOUS MARTIN

Born: 1945 Caracas/VEN

EDUCATION
1967 Gerrit Rietveld Academie Amsterdam/NL
1968 Hogeschool voor de Kunsten Arnhem/NL

RELATED PROFESSIONAL EXPERIENCE
1969-1975 Cofounder/Director with Hans Appenzeller, Gallery Sieraad, Amsterdam/NL
1996- Director Gallery Lous Martin, Delft/NL

PUBLIC COLLECTIONS
Centraal Museum, Utrecht/NL
Gemeentemuseum Den Haag, The Hague/NL
Kunstindustrimuseum, Kopenhagen/DN
Het Kruithuis, Stedelijk Museum voor Hedendaagse Kunst, 's-Hertogenbosch/NL
Museum voor Moderne Kunst, Arnhem/NL
Nederlands Textielmuseum, Tilburg/NL
Nordenfjeldske Kunstindustrimuseum, Trondheim/N
Schmuckmuseum, Pforzheim/D
Stedelijk Museum, Amsterdam/NL

SELECTED SOLO EXHIBITIONS
1995-1996 Eigen jubileumexpositie Delft, Ghent, Enschede/travelling
1975 Gallery Sieraad, Amsterdam/NL

SELECTED GROUP EXHIBITIONS
2000 Jewels of Mind and Mentality Museum Het Kruithuis, 's-Hertogenbosch/NL travelling
1996 Jewellery in Europe and America, New Times, New Thinking Crafts Council Gallery, London/ GB
1993 Tekens en Ketens Museum van der Togt, Amstelveen/NL
1991 View, Revlew, 15 jaar VES Stedelijk Museum, Amsterdam/NL
1991 Point of View, Contemporary Dutch Jewelry and Design USA/CDN travelling
1990 Novidades da Holanda Fundaçao Calouste Gulbenkian, Lisbon/P travelling
1989 Ornamenta I Schmuckmuseum, Pforzheim/D
1987 Concepts, Comments, Process: Dutch Jewellery 1967-1987 Rijksdienst Beeldende Kunst, The Hague/NL travelling
1987 Holland in Vorm, sieraden 1945-1987 Gemeentemuseum Arnhem/NL
1986 Images Singer Museum, Laren/NL travelling
1980 Mode - kleren - mode Stedelijk Museum, Amsterdam/NL
1975 Sieraad 1975 Gallery Het Kapelhuis, Amersfoort/NL
1972 Sieraad 1900-1972 De Zonnehof, Amersfoort/NL
1968 Gallery Nouvelles Images, The Hague/NL

SELECTED BIBLIOGRAPHY
Lous Martin 1965-1995: simpelweg sieraden. – Amsterdam: Lous Martin, 1995 • Tekens & Ketens/Erik Beenker. – Amsterdam: Voetnoot Publishers, [1994] • Vormgevers op locatie/Cees Straus. - [Amsterdam]: VES, 1992 • VES View Review. – Amsterdam: VES, 1991 • Novidades da Holanda: estudo sobre jóias/Marjan Unger. - Lisbon/Amsterdam: Fundaçao Calouste Gulbenkian/Dutch Form Foundation, 1990 • Point of view: Dutch contemporary jewelry and design/Charon Kransen. - S.l.: s.n., 1990 • Ornamenta I: internationale Schmuckkunst/Michael Erlhoff. – München: Prestel Verlag, 1989 • Unica. – Amsterdam: VES, 1987 • Concepts, Comments, Process: Dutch Jewellery 1967-1978. – Amsterdam: Rijksdienst

Beeldende Kunst, 1987 • Images: Sieraden Schmuck Jewellery/Marjan Unger, Renny Ramakers, Monique Mokveld...et al. – Amsterdam: VES, 1986 • Tien jaar Ra/Liesbeth Crommelin en Paul Derrez. – Amsterdam: Galerie Ra, 1986 • Multiples: heden en verleden. – Amsterdam: VES, 1986 • New Tradition: the evolution of jewellery 1966-1985/Caroline Broadhead. – London: British Crafts Centre, 1985 • VES op reis. – Amsterdam: VES, 1985 • Sieraad 1975: 4e manifestatie van Nederlandse edelsmeden en sieradenontwerpers in Amersfoort. – Amersfoort: Galerie Het Kapelhuis, 1975

JEWELS
of Mind and Mentality

RIET NEERINCX

Born: 1925

EDUCATION

1941-1946 Academy of Art, Arnhem/NL
1947-1951 Central School of Arts and Crafts, London/GB

PUBLIC COLLECTIONS

Stedelijk Museum, Amsterdam/NL

SELECTED EXHIBITIONS

2000 Jewels of Mind and Mentality Museum Het Kruithuis, 's-Hertogenbosch/NL travelling
1991 Getooid en versierd Rijksdienst Beeldende Kunst, The Hague/NL
1969 Sieraad '69 Het Kapelhuis, Amersfoort/NL
1967 Sieraad '67 Het Kapelhuis, Amersfoort/NL

SELECTED BIBLIOGRAPHY

Jewelry in Europe and America: new times, new thinking/Ralph Turner. – London: Thames and Hudson, 1996 • Getooid en versierd/Liesbeth den Besten. – [The Hague]: [Rijksdienst Beeldende Kunst, 1991 • Sieraad '69: werk van 22 Nederlandse edelsmeden in het Kapelhuis. – Amersfoort: Het Kapelhuis, 1969 • Sieraad '67: tentoonstelling 30 Nederlandse edelsmeden. – Amersfoort: Het Kapelhuis, 1967

DUTCH

JEWELRY

DESIGN

1950
2000

FRANS VAN NIEUWENBORG

Born: 1941 Venlo/NL

EDUCATION

1958-1963 Academie voor Industriële Vormgeving, Eindhoven/NL

MARTIJN WEGMAN

Born: 1955 The Hague/NL

EDUCATION

1973-1978 Gerrit Rietveld Academie, Amsterdam/NL

PUBLIC COLLECTIONS

Cooper-Hewitt Museum, New York/USA
Gemeentemuseum Den Haag, The Hague/NL
Musée des Arts Décoratifs, Montreal/CDN
Museo Universitario de Ciencias y Arte, Mexico City/MEX
Museum Boijmans van Beuningen, Rotterdam/NL
Museum of Modern Art, New York/USA
Museum voor Moderne Kunst, Arnhem/NL
Museum van Bommel van Dam, Venlo/NL
Nederlands Textielmuseum, Tilburg/NL
Rijksdienst Beeldende Kunst, The Hague/NL
Stedelijk Museum, Amsterdam/NL
The Saint Louis Art Museum, Missouri/USA

SELECTED EXHIBITIONS

2000 Jewels of Mind and Mentality Museum Het Kruithuis, 's-Hertogenbosch/NL travelling
1994 A Moveable Feast Stedelijk Museum, Amsterdam/NL
1986 Serie Sieraad Stedelijk Museum, Amsterdam/NL
1986 Sieraad 1986, Draagteken? Museum Het Kruithuis, 's-Hertogenbosch/NL
1985 New Tradition British Crafts Centre, London/GB
1979 56 Bracelets, 17 Rings, 2 Necklaces Gemeentelijk Van Reekummuseum, Apeldoorn/NL

SELECTED BIBLIOGRAPHY

Premsela Present: designers design for a designer/Liesbeth den Besten...et al. – Amsterdam: Stichting Vormgevings-tentoonstellingen, 1998 • Jewelry in Europe and America/Ralph Turner. – London: Thames and Hudson, 1996 • Jewelry of our time: art, ornament and obsession/Helen W. Drutt English and Peter Dormer. – London: Thames and Hudson, 1995 • Van Nieuwenborg/Wegman: industrial design consultancygroup/Ivo Wildenberg. - [Leiden]: [Van Nieuwenborg/Wegman], 1991 • Fremdkörper: Schmuck der Avantgarde/Lida von Mengden. – Ludwigshafen: Wilhelm-Hack-Museum, 1990 • New Tradition: the evolution of jewellery 1966-1985/Caroline Broadhead. – London: British Crafts Centre, 1985 • Concepts, Comments, Process: Dutch Jewellery 1967-1978. – Amsterdam: Rijksdienst Beeldende Kunst, 1987 • Holland in Vorm: vormgeving in Nederland 1945-1987/Gert Staal en Hester Wolters. - 's-Gravenhage: Stichting Holland in Vorm, 1987 • Tien jaar Ra/Liesbeth Crommelin en Paul Derrez. – Amsterdam: Galerie Ra, 1986 • Contemporary jewellery: The Americas, Australia, Europe. – Kyoto: The National Museum of Modern Art, 1984 • Bracelets, Rings, Necklaces. – Amsterdam: Visual Arts office for abroad, 1979 • Sieraad 1975: 4e manifestatie van Nederlandse edelsmeden en sieradenontwerpers in Amersfoort. – Amersfoort: Galerie Het Kapelhuis, 1975 • Sier in serie: sieraden. – Amsterdam: Nederlandse Kunststichting, 1973

DUTCH

JEWELRY

DESIGN

1950
2000

JEWELS
of Mind and Mentality

BRUNO NINABER VAN EYBEN

Born: 1950 Boxtel/NL

EDUCATION
1967-1971 Stadsacademie voor toegepaste Kunsten, Maastricht/NL

AWARDS
1979 first Kho Liang Ie-award

PUBLIC COLLECTIONS
Gemeentelijk Van Reekummuseum, Apeldoorn/NL
Het Kruithuis, Stedelijk Museum voor Hedendaagse Kunst, 's-Hertogenbosch/NL
Museum Boijmans van Beuningen, Rotterdam/NL
Museum of Modern Art, New York/USA
Museum voor Moderne Kunst, Arnhem/NL
Stedelijk Museum, Amsterdam/NL

SELECTED SOLO EXHIBITIONS
1980 Gemeentelijke van Reekumgalerij, Apeldoorn/NL

SELECTED GROUP EXHIBITIONS
2000 Jewels of Mind and Mentality Museum Het Kruithuis, 's-Hertogenbosch/NL travelling
1994 Made in Holland: Design aus den Niederlanden Museum für Angewandte Kunst, Cologne/D
1991 Ninaber/Peters/Krouwel Functie vormt stijl Stedelijk Museum, Amsterdam/NL
1981 Gallery Knoef, Arnhem/NL
1987 Concepts, Comments, Process: Dutch Jewellery 1967-1987, Rijksdienst Beeldende Kunst, The Hague/NL travelling
1987 Holland in Vorm, sieraden 1945-1987 Gemeentemuseum Arnhem, Arnhem/NL
1986 10 Jaar Ra Gallery Ra, Amsterdam/NL
1975 Sieraad 1975 Gallery Het Kapelhuis, Amersfoort/NL
1973 Sier in Serie CRM/NKS, Rijswijk/NL travelling

SELECTED BIBLIOGRAPHY
Made in Holland: Design aus den Niederlanden/ Gabriele Lueg...et al. – Tübingen: Ernst Wasmuth Verlag, 1994 • Ninaber/Peters/Krouwel: functie vormt stijl/Reyer Kras. – Amsterdam: Stedelijk Museum, 1991 • Fremdkörper: Schmuck der Avantgarde/Lida von Mengden. – Ludwigshafen: Wilhelm-Hack-Museum, 1990 • Concepts, Comments, Process: Dutch Jewellery 1967-1978. – Amsterdam: Rijksdienst Beeldende Kunst, 1987 • Holland in Vorm: vormgeving in Nederland 1945-1987/Gert Staal en Hester Wolters. - 's-Gravenhage: Stichting Holland in Vorm, 1987 • Tien jaar Ra/Liesbeth Crommelin en Paul Derrez. – Amsterdam: Galerie Ra, 1986 • Nieuw werk: reizende tentoonstelling van aktuele Nederlandse sieraden.- Amsterdam: Vereniging van Edelsmeden en Sieraadontwerpers, 1979 • Sieraad 1975: 4e manifestatie van Nederlandse edelsmeden en sieradenontwerpers in Amersfoort. – Amersfoort: Galerie Het Kapelhuis, 1975 • Sier in serie: sieraden. – Amsterdam: Nederlandse Kunststichting, 1973

TED NOTEN

Born: 1956 Tegelen/NL

EDUCATION
1983-1986 Academie voor toegepaste Kunsten, Maastricht/NL
1986-1990 Gerrit Rietveld Academie, Amsterdam/NL

AWARDS
1992 Startstipendium, Fonds voor Beeldende Kunst, Vormgeving en Bouwkunst, Amsterdam/NL
1995 Basisstipendium, Fonds voor Beeldende Kunst, Vormgeving en Bouwkunst, Amsterdam/NL

PUBLIC COLLECTIONS
Musée des Arts Decoratifs, Montreal/CDN
Museum voor Moderne Kunst, Arnhem/NL

SELECTED SOLO EXHIBITIONS
1996 Gallery Marzee, Nijmegen/NL
1996 Art Box, Waregem/B
1994 Alter-Ego Gallery Louise Smit, Amsterdam/NL
1993 De Muzeval Gallery, Emmen/NL

SELECTED GROUP EXHIBITIONS
1998 Gallery Louise Smit, Amsterdam/NL
1995 Parelproject Gallery Marzee, Nijmegen/NL
1995 Schmuckkunst aus Holland Gallery Slavik, Vienna/A
1994 Een Confrontatie: 10 jaar Gallery Puntgaaf Gallery Puntgaaf, Groningen/NL
1993 De Oogst Stedelijk Museum, Amsterdam/NL
1992 Gevoel voor ringen Gallery Louise Smit, Amsterdam/NL
1991 Sieraad als Objekt - Objekt als Sieraad Museum voor Hedendaagse Kunst De Lijbrije, Zwolle /NL
1990 Jewellery Joint Exhibition Hiko Mizumo Jewelry College, Tokyo/J
1989 Drei dimensionale Vorstufen zur Schmuck Schmuckmuseum Pforzheim, Pforzheim/D

SELECTED BIBLIOGRAPHY
AEX Amsterdam Exposé/Leontine Coelewij. – Amsterdam: Stedelijk Museum, 1999 • The Ring: design past en present/Sylvie Lambert. - Crans-Près-Céligny: Rotovision, 1998 • Sieraden: de keuze van Amersfoort/Anja van Kessel. – Nijmegen: Galerie Marzee, 1997 • Ted Noten/ed. Veerle Wenes; tekst Liesbeth den Besten.- Amsterdam: Ted Noten, 1996

DUTCH

JEWELRY

DESIGN

1950
2000

JEWELS
of Mind and Mentality

342

RUUDT PETERS

Born: 1950 Naaldwijk/NL

EDUCATION

1970-1974 Gerrit Rietveld Academie Amsterdam/NL

AWARDS

1993 Only One-award for parfumflacon 'Passio'

RELATED PROFESSIONAL EXPERIENCE

1990- teacher Gerrit Rietveld Academie, Amsterdam/NL
1984-1990 teacher Hogeschool voor de Kunsten, Kampen/NL

PUBLIC COLLECTIONS

Angermuseum, Erfurt/D
Cleveland County Museum, Middlesborough/GB
Cooper-Hewitt Museum, New York/USA
Gemeentelijk Van Reekummuseum, Apeldoorn/NL
Hiko Mizuno Art School, Tokyo/J
Musée des Arts Décoratifs, Montreal/CDN
Museum Boijmans van Beuningen, Rotterdam /NL
Museum für Angewandte Kunst, Hamburg/D
Museum für Angewandte Kunst, Vienna/A
Museum voor Moderne Kunst, Arnhem/NL
Rijksdienst Beeldende Kunst, The Hague/NL
Schmuckmuseum, Pforzheim/D
Stedelijk Museum, Amsterdam/NL

SELECTED SOLO EXHIBITIONS

1997 Gallery Louise Smit, Amsterdam/NL
1997 Gallery Sofie Lachaert, Antwerp/B
1997 Lapis Harvard Club, New York/USA
1996 Art Box, Waregem/B
1995 Gallery Marzee, Nijmegen/NL
1991 Gallery Sofie Lachaert, Ghent/B
1991 Gemeentelijk Van Reekummuseum, Apeldoorn/NL
1984 Apects Gallery, London/GB
1983 Gallery RA, Amsterdam/NL

SELECTED GROUP EXHIBITIONS

1998 Brooching it Diplomatically Helen Drutt Philadelphia/USA travelling
1994 A Moveable Feast Stedelijk Museum, Amsterdam/NL
1993 Tekens en Ketens Museum van der Togt, Amstelveen/NL
1993 Voorzien: Benno Premsela Applied Art Collection Stedelijk Museum, Amsterdam/NL
1992 Triennale du Bijou Musée des Arts Décoratifs, Paris/F
1990 L'Arte della Gioia, Gioiello Olandese d'Autore Pedrocchi, Padua/I
1990 Novidades da Holanda Fundaçao Calouste Gulbenkian Lisbon/P travelling
1990 Triennale du Bijou Musée du Luxembourg, Paris/F
1989 An Art Collection of Combs Gallery Marzee, Nijmegen/NL travelling
1989 Ornamenta I Schmuckmuseum, Pforzheim/D

DUTCH

JEWELRY

DESIGN

1950
2000

JEWELS
of Mind and Mentality

1987   Holland in Vorm, sieraden 1945-1987 Gemeentemuseum Arnhem, Arnhem/NL
1985   New Tradition British Crafts Centre, London/GB
1984   Modern Jewelry USA/CDN travelling
1983   The Jewellery Project Crafts Council Gallery, London/GB
1982   Visies op sieraden 1965-1982 Stedelijk Museum, Amsterdam/NL

SELECTED BIBLIOGRAPHY

The Ring: design past en present/Sylvie Lambert. - Crans-Près-Céligny: Rotovision, 1998 • Brooching it Diplomatically: a tribute to Madeleine K. Albright/Helen W. Drutt English. – Philadelphia: Helen Drutt, 1998 • Ruudt Peters: Lapis/Gert Staal. –Amsterdam: Uitgeverij De Voetnoot, 1997 • Jewelry in Europe and America/Ralph Turner. – London: Thames and Hudson, 1996 • Jewelry of our time: art, ornament and obsession/Helen W. Drutt English and Peter Dormer. – London: Thames and Hudson, 1995 • Mode en Sieraad/Marjan Unger, Gert Staal. – Amsterdam: Vormgevingsinstituut, 1994 • Tekens & Ketens/Erik Beenker. – Amsterdam: Voetnoot Publishers, [1994] • The best in contemporary jewellery/David Watkins. – London: B.T. Bradsford Ltd., 1993 • Ruudt Peters: Passio/Marjan Unger. – Amsterdam: Uitgeverij De Voetnoot, 1992 • Sieraden: Centrum Beeldende Kunst Groningen/Gerard Lakke. – Groningen: Centrum Beeldende Kunst, 1992 • International Crafts/Martina Margetts. – London: Thames and Hudson, 1991 • Ruudt Peters: Interno/Ans van Berkum. – Amsterdam: Ruudt Peters, 1991 • L'Arte della Gioia: gioiello Ollandese d'autore l'oro di Padova/Liesbeth Crommelin. - Padova/The Hague: Assessorato Cultura e beni culturali/MinisterieWVC, 1990 • Autori del gioiello Olandese contemporaneo/Liesbeth Crommelin.- [Vicenza]: [Torri di Arcugnano], 1990 • Novidades da Holanda: estudo sobre jóias/Marjan Unger. - Lisbon/Amsterdam: Fundaçao Calouste Gulbenkian/Dutch Form Foundation, 1990 • Ruudt Peters: dedicated to/Ans van Berkum. – Amsterdam: Ruudt Peters, 1989 • Holland in Vorm: vormgeving in Nederland 1945-1987/Gert Staal en Hester Wolters. – 's-Gravenhage: Stichting Holland in Vorm, 1987 • Tien jaar Ra/Liesbeth Crommelin en Paul Derrez. – Amsterdam: Galerie Ra, 1986 • Multiples: heden en verleden. – Amsterdam: VES, 1986 • Some Dutch Jewellery. – Bristol: Arnolfini, 1984 • The Jewellery project: new departures in British and European work 1980-83. – London: Crafts Council Gallery, 1983 • Jewellery redefined: the 1st international exhibition of multi-media non-precious jewellery 1982. – London: British Crafts Centre, 1982 • Sieraad 1975: 4e manifestatie van Nederlandse edelsmeden en sieradenontwerpers in Amersfoort. – Amersfoort: Galerie Het Kapelhuis, 1975

DUTCH

JEWELRY

DESIGN

1950
2000

JEWELS
of Mind and Mentality

344

ANNELIES PLANTEIJDT

Born: 1956 Rotterdam/NL

EDUCATION

1978-1983   Gerrit Rietveld Academie Amsterdam/NL
1974-1978   Vakschool Schoonhoven, Schoonhoven/NL

AWARDS

1990   Emmy van Leersum Award
1993   Stipendium, Fonds voor Beeldende Kunsten, Vormgeving en Bouwkunst, Amsterdam/NL

PUBLIC COLLECTIONS

Gemeentelijk Van Reekummuseum, Apeldoorn/NL
Gemeentemuseum Den Haag, The Hague/NL
Museum Boijmans van Beuningen, Rotterdam/NL
Het Kruithuis, Stedelijk Museum voor Hedendaagse Kunst, 's-Hertogenbosch/NL
Museum voor Moderne Kunst, Arnhem/NL
National Gallery, Bratislava/CS
Nederlands Textielmuseum, Tilburg/NL
Rijksdienst Beeldende Kunst, The Hague/NL
Stedelijk Museum, Amsterdam/NL
Zeeuws Museum, Middelburg/NL

SELECTED SOLO EXHIBITIONS

1999   Gallery Slavik, Vienna/A
1997   Museum Het Kruithuis, 's-Hertogenbosch/NL
1996   Gallery Marzee, Nijmegen/NL

SELECTED GROUP EXHIBITIONS

2000   Jewels of Mind and Mentality Museum Het Kruithuis, 's-Hertogenbosch/NL travelling
1999   Gallery Piltzer Paris/F
1998   Jewellery moves National Museum of Scotland, Edinburgh/GB
1997   25 jaar Amsterdams Fonds voor de Kunst Stedelijk Museum, Amsterdam/NL
1994   Tekens en Ketens Museum van der Togt, Amstelveen/NL
1993   Het sieraad nu Centrum Beeldende Kunst, Rotterdam/NL
1992   III Triennale du Bijou Musée des Arts Décoratifs, Paris/F
1991   De Feestdis Gallery RA, Amsterdam/NL
1991   Sieraad als objekt, Objekt als sieraad Librije, Zwolle/NL
1990   30 jaar Nouvelles Images Gallery Nouvelles Images, The Hague/NL
1990   Novidades da Holanda Fundaçao Calouste Gulbenkian, Lisbon/P travelling
1989   Museum of Modern Art, Nottingham, Gloucester/GB
1989   Ornamenta I Schmuckmuseum, Pforzheim/D

SELECTED BIBLIOGRAPHY

The Ring: design past en present/Sylvie Lambert. - Crans-Près-Céligny :Rotovision, 1998 • Premsela Present: designers design for a designer/Liesbeth den Besten...et al. - Amsterdam: Stichting Vormgevingstentoonstellingen, 1998 • Passion and Profession: twintig jaar Ra sieraden toen nu straks/Paul Derrez. - Amsterdam: Galerie Ra, 1996 • Tekens & Ketens/Erik Beenker. - Amsterdam: Voetnoot Publishers, [1994] • Sieraden: Centrum Beeldende Kunst Groningen/Gerard Lakke. - Groningen: Centrum Beeldende Kunst, 1992 • IIIeme Triennale du bijou/Chantal Bizot...et al. - Paris: Musée des Arts Décoratifs, 1992 • De feestdis ontworpen door 39 kunstenaars The Banqueting table/Martijn van Ooststroom. -

DUTCH

JEWELRY

DESIGN

1950
2000

JEWELS
of Mind and Mentality

Amsterdam: Galerie Ra, 1991 • Novidades da Holanda: estudo sobre jóias/Marjan Unger. - Lisbon/Amsterdam: Fundaçao Calouste Gulbenkian/Dutch Form Foundation, 1990 • Autori del gioiello Olandese contemporaneo/Liesbeth Crommelin. - [Vicenza]: [Torri di Arcugnano], 1990 • L'Arte della Gioia: gioiello Ollandese d'autore l'oro di Padova/Liesbeth Crommelin. – Padova/The Hague: Assessorato Cultura e beni culturali/Ministerie van WVC, 1990 • Ornamenta I: internationale Schmuckkunst/Michael Erlhoff. - München: Prestel Verlag, 1989 • Concepts, Comments, Process: Dutch Jewellery 1967-1978. - Amsterdam: Rijksdienst Beeldende Kunst, 1987 • Tien jaar Ra/Liesbeth Crommelin en Paul Derrez. - Amsterdam: Galerie Ra, 1986 • The New Jewelry: trends and traditions/Peter Dormer and Ralph Turner. - London: Thames and Hudson, 1985 • New Tradition: the evolution of jewellery 1966-1985/Caroline Broadhead. - London: British Crafts Centre, 1985 • The Jewellery project: new departures in British and European work 1980-83. - London: Crafts Council Gallery, 1983

DUTCH
JEWELRY
DESIGN
1950
2000

JEWELS
of Mind and Mentality

346

PHILIP SAJET
Born: 1953 Amsterdam/NL

EDUCATION
1977-1981 Gerrit Rietveld Academie Amsterdam/NL

PUBLIC COLLECTIONS
Gemeentelijk Van Reekummuseum, Apeldoorn/NL
Het Kruithuis, Stedelijk Museum voor Hedendaagse Kunst, 's-Hertogenbosch/NL
Museum voor Moderne Kunst, Arnhem/NL
Stedelijk Museum, Amsterdam/NL

SELECTED SOLO EXHIBITIONS
1996 18 ringen Stedelijk Museum, Amsterdam/NL
1994 11 colliers Stedelijk Museum, Amsterdam/NL
1986 Gallery Louise Smit, Amsterdam/NL

SELECTED GROUP EXHIBITIONS
2000 Jewels of Mind and Mentality Museum Het Kruithuis, 's-Hertogenbosch/NL travelling
1997 Aanwinsten 1997 Museum voor Moderne Kunst, Arnhem/NL
1997 Chi Ha Paura...? Museum Het Kruithuis, 's-Hertogenbosch/NL
1996 Jewellery in Europe and America, New Times, New Thinking Crafts Council Gallery, London/GB
1995 Multiple Choice Museum Het Kruithuis, 's-Hertogenbosch/NL
1993 Facet 1, Kunsthal, Rotterdam/NL
1992 Sieraden expositie Centrum Beeldende Kunst, Groningen/NL
1991 Beauty is a story Museum Het Kruithuis, 's-Hertogenbosch/NL
1991 Neoteric Jewelry Newhouse Center for Contemporary Art, New York/USA
1990 L'Arte della Gioia, Gioiello Olandese d'Autore Padova/I
1989 Ornamenta I Schmuckmuseum, Pforzheim/D
1987 Holland in Vorm, sieraden 1945-1987 Gemeentemuseum Arnhem, Arnhem/NL

SELECTED BIBLIOGRAPHY
The Ring: design past en present/Sylvie Lambert. - Crans-Près-Céligny: Rotovision, 1998 • Sieraden: de keuze van Amersfoort/Anja van Kessel. - Nijmegen: Galerie Marzee, 1997 • Jewelry in Europe and America/Ralph Turner. - London: Thames and Hudson, 1996 • Jewelry of our time: art, ornament and obsession/Helen W. Drutt English and Peter Dormer. - London: Thames and Hudson, 1995 • Philip Sajet: elf colliers/Marjan Unger. - Amsterdam: Stedelijk Museum, 1994 • Facet I: internationale sieradenbiënnale/Martita Slewe. - Rotterdam: Kunsthal, 1993 • The best in contemporary jewellery/David Watkins. - London: B.T. Bradsford Ltd., 1993 • Sieraden: Centrum Beeldende Kunst Groningen/Gerard Lakke. - Groningen: Centrum Beeldende Kunst, 1992 • IIIeme Triennale du bijou/Chantal Bizot...et al. - Paris: Musée des Arts Décoratifs, 1992 • Beauty is a story/Gert Staal. - 's-Hertogenbosch: Museum Het Kruithuis, 1991 • Autori del gioiello Olandese contemporaneo/Liesbeth Crommelin. - [Vicenza]: [Torri di Arcugnano], 1990 • L'Arte della Gioia: gioiello Ollandese d'autore l'oro di Padova/Liesbeth Crommelin. - Padova/The Hague: Assessorato Cultura e beni culturali/Ministerie van WVC, 1990 • Ornamenta I: internationale Schmuckkunst/Michael Erlhoff. - München: Prestel Verlag, 1989 • Dutch jewellery designers. - Trondheim: Nordenfjelske Kunstindustrimuseum, 1985

DUTCH

JEWELRY

DESIGN

1950
2000

LUCY SARNEEL

Born: 1961 Maastricht/NL

EDUCATION
1985-1989 Gerrit Rietveld Academie, Amsterdam/NL
1982-1985 Stadsacademie Maastricht/NL

AWARDS
1999 Emmy van Leersum Award

RELATED PROFESSIONAL EXPERIENCE
1996 Guest Lecturer Gerrit Rietveld Academie, Amsterdam/NL

PUBLIC COLLECTIONS
Het Kruithuis, Stedelijk Museum voor Hedendaagse Kunst, 's-Hertogenbosch/NL

SELECTED SOLO EXHIBITIONS
1997 Gallery Marzee, Nijmegen/NL
1993 Gallery Marzee, Nijmegen/NL

SELECTED GROUP EXHIBITIONS
2000 Jewels of Mind and Mentality Museum Het Kruithuis, 's-Hertogenbosch/NL travelling
1999 Gallery Slavnik, Vienna/A
1998 Brooching it Diplomatically Helen Drutt Philadelphia/USA travelling
1997 Flessibellissimo Gallery Marzee, Nijmegen/NL
1994 Sign of Mine Museum für Angewandte Kunst, Cologne/D
1993 Facet 1, sieradenbiënnale Kunsthal, Rotterdam/NL
1993 Holandaise de Joieria Gallery Hipotesí, Barcelona/E
1993 Tekens en Ketens Museum van der Togt, Amstelveen/NL
1992 Centrum Beeldende Kunst, Groningen/NL
1991 Beauty is a story Museum Het Kruithuis, 's-Hertogenbosch/NL
1990 Novidades da Holanda Fundaçao Calouste Gulbenkian, Lisbon/P travelling
1990 Triennale du Bijou Musée du Luxembourg, Paris/F

SELECTED BIBLIOGRAPHY
AEX Amsterdam EXpos/Leontine Coelewij. - Amsterdam: Stedelijk Museum, 1999 ● Brooching it Diplomatically: a tribute to Madeleine K. Albright/Helen W. Drutt English. - Philadelphia: Helen Drutt, 1998 ● The Ring: design: past and present/Sylvie Lambert. - Crans-Près-Céligny: Rotovision, 1998 ● Sieraad Symbool Signaal/Jan Walgrave. - Antwerpen: Provinciebestuur van Antwerpen, 1995 ● Tekens & Ketens/Erik Beenker et al. - Amsterdam: Voetnoot Publishers, [1994] ● Sieraden: Centrum Beeldende Kunst Groningen/Gerard Lakke. - Groningen: Centrum Beeldende Kunst, 1992 ● Beauty is a Story/Gert Staal. - 's-Hertogenbosch: Museum Het Kruithuis, 1991 ● Novidades da Holanda: estudo Sobre jóias/Marjan Unger. - Lisbon: Fundaçao Calouste Gulbenkian, 1990

ROBERT SMIT

Born: 1941 Delft/NL

EDUCATION

1954-1957 Technische School, certificate in precision engineering Delft/NL
1963-1966 Staatliche Kunst und Werkschule Pforzheim/D

RELATED PROFESSIONAL EXPERIENCE

1980-1994 teacher at art schools and academies in the Netherlands, Belgium, Germany, Great Britain
and the United States
1999 member of the jury for the Danner Award

PUBLIC COLLECTIONS

Centraal Museum, Utrecht/NL
Danner-Stiftung, Munich/D
Gemeentelijk Van Reekummuseum, Apeldoorn/NL
Gemeentemuseum Den Haag, The Hague/NL
Het Kruithuis, Stedelijk Museum voor Hedendaagse Kunst, 's-Hertogenbosch/NL
Museum voor Moderne Kunst, Arnhem/NL
Rijksdienst Beeldende Kunst, The Hague/NL
Schmuckmuseum, Pforzheim/D
Stedelijk Museum, Amsterdam/NL
Stedelijk Museum 'Het Prinsenhof', Delft/NL

SELECTED SOLO EXHIBITIONS

1998 Kortsluiting Gallery Louise Smit, Amsterdam/NL
1994 Musée d'Art Moderne et d'Art Contemporain, Nice/F
1994 Gallery Louise Smit, Amsterdam/NL
1993 Contacto Dirercto Lissabon/P
1987 Beyond Reach Stedelijk Museum Het Prinsenhof Delft/NL
1984 Stedelijk Museum, Amsterdam/NL
1973 Different Information Gallery Riekje Swart, Amsterdam/NL
1973 De Volle Maan Stedelijk Museum, Delft/NL

SELECTED GROUP EXHIBITIONS

2000 Jewels of Mind and Mentality Museum Het Kruithuis, 's-Hertogenbosch/NL travelling
1998 Brooching it Diplomatically Helen Drutt, Philadelphia/USA travelling
1998 Jewellery moves National Museum of Scotland, Edinburgh/GB
1993 Facet 1, sieradenbiënnale Kunsthal, Rotterdam/NL
1992 III Trienale du Byou, Musée des Arts Décoratifs, Paris/F
1992 Sieraden Centrum Beeldende Kunst, Groningen/NL
1990 Biennale du Bijou Paris/F
1990 L'Arte della Gioia, Gioiello Olandese d'Autore Pedrocchi, Padua/I
1989 Triennale Perth Perth/AUS
1988 Tragezeichen Museum Morsbroich, Leverkusen/D
1987 Schmuck, Zeichen am Korper Linzer Institut für Gestaltung, Linz/A
1987 Holland in Vorm, sieraden 1945-1987 Gemeentemuseum Arnhem, Arnhem/NL
1975 Jewellery in Europe Scottish Arts Council Gallery, Edinburgh/GB
1972 Sieraad 1900-1972 De Zonnehof, Amersfoort/NL

DUTCH

JEWELRY

DESIGN

1950
2000

JEWELS
of Mind and Mentality

SELECTED BIBLIOGRAPHY

Robert Smit: Empty House/Gert Staal. – Stuttgart: Arnoldsche, 1999 • The Ring: design past en present/Sylvie Lambert. - Crans-Près-Céligny: Rotovision, 1998. • Brooching it Diplomatically: a tribute to Madeleine K. Albright/Helen W. Drutt English. - Philadelphia: Helen Drutt, 1998 • Jewelry in Europe and America/Ralph Turner. - London: Thames and Hudson, 1996 • Robert Smit/Robert Smit. Amsterdam: Robert Smit, 1995 • Schmücken: the art of adornment/Marga Anstett-Janssen...et al. - Stuttgart: Arnoldsche, 1995 • Jewelry of our time: art, ornament and obsession/Helen W. Drutt English and Peter Dormer. - London: Thames and Hudson, 1995. • Mode en Sieraad/Marjan Unger, Gert Staal. - Amsterdam: Vormgevingsinstituut, 1994 • Facet I: internationale sieradenbiënnale/Martita Slewe. - Rotterdam: Kunsthal, 1993 • The best in contemporary jewellery/David Watkins. - London: B.T. Bradsford Ltd., 1993 • Robertsmit/Marja Bloem...et al. - Zürich: Aurum Publishing AG, 1992 • L'Arte della Gioia: gioiello Ollandese d'autore l'oro di Padova/Liesbeth Crommelin. - Padova/The Hague: Assessorato Cultura e beni culturali/Ministerie van WVC, 1990 • Autori del gioiello Olandese contemporaneo/Liesbeth Crommelin. -[Vicenza]: [Torri di Arcugnano], 1990 • Holland in Vorm: vormgeving in Nederland 1945-1987/Gert Staal en Hester Wolters. - 's-Gravenhage: Stichting Holland in Vorm, 1987 • Concepts, Comments, Process: Dutch Jewellery 1967-1978. - Amsterdam: Rijksdienst Beeldende Kunst, 1987 • Robert Smit: beyond reach. - Delft: Stedelijk Museum 'Het Prinsenhof', 1987 • Sieraad 1900-1972: eerste triënnale onder auspiciën van de Amersfoortse Culturele Raad/K. A. Citroen en Ralph Turner. Amersfoort: De Zonnehof, 1972

DUTCH

JEWELRY

DESIGN

1950
2000

JEWELS
of Mind and Mentality

350

MARGA STAARTJES

Born: 1953

EDUCATION
Academie voor Beeldende Kunst, Arnhem/NL

PUBLIC COLLECTIONS
Gemeentelijk Van Reekummuseum, Apeldoorn/NL
Gemeentemuseum Den Haag, The Hague/NL
Israel Museum, Jerusalem/IL
Het Kruithuis, Stedelijk Museum voor Hedendaagse Kunst, 's-Hertogenbosch/NL
Rijksdienst Beeldende Kunst, The Hague/NL
Stedelijk Museum, Amsterdam/NL

SELECTED EXHIBITIONS
2000 Jewels of Mind and Mentality Museum Het Kruithuis, 's-Hertogenbosch/NL travelling
1994 Symfonie voor solisten, Gemeentemuseum Arnhem, Arnhem/ NL
1993 Objects of desire, Louisville/USA
1987 Holland Festival Canada: Sieraden, Rijksdienst Beeldende Kunst, The Hague/NL travelling
1986 Gemeentelijk Van Reekummuseum, Apeldoorn/NL
1986 Le Roi Plastique Musée des Arts Decoratifs, Lausanne/CH
1983 Gemeentemuseum Den Haag, The Hague/NL travelling
1981 The Shoe Show Gemeentelijk van Reekummuseum, Apeldoorn/NL
1980 Mode Kleren Mode Stedelijk Museum, Amsterdam/NL
1980 Sieraden in Singer Singer Museum, Laren/NL
1977 Sieraden, een keuze door Emmy van Leersum Kunstcentrum Badhuis, Gorinchem/NL

SELECTED BIBLIOGRAPHY
Symfonie voor solisten/Jeroen N.M. van den Eynde. – Wageningen: H. Veerman & Zn., 1994 • Concepts, Comments, Process: Dutch Jewellery 1967-1978. – Amsterdam: Rijksdienst Beeldende Kunst, 1987 • Sieraden: vorm en idee/Liesbeth den Besten. – Apeldoorn: Gemeentelijk Van Reekummuseum, 1986 • New Tradition: the evolution of jewellery 1966-1985/Caroline Broadhead. – London: British Crafts Centre, 1985

CHRIS STEENBERGEN
Born: 1920 Amsterdam/NL

EDUCATION

1939-1942 Instituut voor Kunstnijverheidsonderwijs, Amsterdam/NL

PUBLIC COLLECTIONS

Centraal Museum, Utrecht/NL
Het Kruithuis, Stedelijk Museum voor Hedendaagse Kunst, 's-Hertogenbosch/NL
Museum Boijmans van Beuningen, Rotterdam/NL
Museum voor Moderne Kunst, Arnhem/NL
Rijksdienst Beeldende Kunst, The Hague/NL
Stedelijk Museum, Amsterdam/NL

SELECTED EXHIBTIONS

2000 Jewels of Mind and Mentality Museum Het Kruithuis, 's-Hertogenbosch/NL travelling
1985 Museum Waterland, Purmerend/NL
1985 25 jaar Nouvelles Images Gemeentemuseum Den Haag, The Hague/NL
1985 Chris Steenbergen edelsmid Museum Boijmans van Beuningen, Rotterdam/NL
1981 Gallery Nouvelles Images, The Hague/NL
1981 Zeitgenossisches Deutsches und Niederländisches Kunsthandwerk Kunstgewerbe Museum, Frankfurt/D
1980 Gallery De Witte Voet, Amsterdam/NL
1980 20 jaar Nouvelles Images Gallery Nouvelles Images, The Hague/NL
1979 Gallery Nouvelles Images, The Hague/NL
1978 Gallery Inart, Amsterdam/NL
1978 Gallery Nouvelles Images, The Hague/NL
1978 Internationale Schmuckschau Munich/D
1977 Internationale Schmuckschau Munich/D
1976 International Jewelry Arts Exhibition Tokyo/J
1975 Gallery Nouvelles Images, The Hague/NL
1975 15 jaar Nouvelles Images Gallery Nouvelles Images, The Hague/NL
1975 Nederlandse pedellenstaven Museum Boijmans van Beuningen, Rotterdam/NL
1975 Sieraad 1975 Gallery Het Kapelhuis, Amersfoort/NL
1974 Gallery Ekster, Leeuwarden/NL
1973 International Jewelry Arts Exhibition Tokyo/J
1972 Sieraad 1900-1972 De Zonnehof, Amersfoort/NL
1972 Twintig Nederlandse edelsmeden Gallery Nouvelles Images, The Hague/NL
1969 Sieraad '69 Gallery Het Kapelhuis, Amersfoort/NL
1968 Rotterdamse Kunstkring, Rotterdam/NL
1968 Bijoux d'orfèvres Néerlandais contemporains Institut Néerlandais, Paris/F
1967 Ontwerpen en maken Stedelijk Museum, Amsterdam/NL
1967 Sieraad '67 Gallery Het Kapelhuis, Amersfoort/NL
1966 Gemeentelijke Van Reekumgalerij, Apeldoorn/NL
1965 Gallery Het Kapelhuis, Amersfoort/NL
1965 Nederlandse sieraden van nu Museum Boijmans van Beuningen, Rotterdam/NL
1960 Nederlands zilver 1815-1960 Gemeentemuseum Den Haag, The Hague/NL
1956 Rotterdamse Kunstkring, Rotterdam/NL
1954 Gemeentelijk Museum Het Princessehof, Leeuwarden/NL
1954 Kunstcentrum de Prinsentuin, Leeuwarden/NL
1953 Rotterdamse Kunstkring, Rotterdam/NL

SELECTED BIBLIOGRAPHY

The Ring: design past en present/Sylvie Lambert. - Crans-Près-Céligny: Rotovision, 1998 • Jewelry in Europe and America/Ralph Turner. - London: Thames and Hudson, 1996 • Getooid & Versierd/Liesbeth den Besten. – [The Hague]: [Rijksdienst Beeldende Kunst], 1991 • Holland in Vorm: vormgeving in Nederland 1945-1987/Gert Staal, Hester Wolters. - 's-Gravenhage: Stichting Holland in Vorm, 1987 • Chris Steenbergen: edelsmid/D.U. Kuyken-Schneider. - Rotterdam: Museum Boijmans van Beuningen, 1985 • Bracelets, Rings, Necklaces: Amsterdam: Visual Arts office for abroad, 1979 • Sieraad 1975: 4e manifestatie van Nederlandse edelsmeden en sieradenontwerpers in Amersfoort. - Amersfoort: Galerie Het Kapelhuis, 1975 • Sier in serie: sieraden. - Amsterdam: Nederlandse Kunststichting, 1973 • Sieraad 1900-1972: eerste triënnale onder auspiciën van de Amersfoortse Culturele Raad/K. A. Citroen en Ralph Turner. - Amersfoort: De Zonnehof, 1972 • Sieraad '69: werk van 22 Nederlandse edelsmeden in Het Kapelhuis. - Amersfoort: Het Kapelhuis, 1969 • Sieraad '67: tentoonstelling 30 Nederlandse edelsmeden. - Amersfoort: Het Kapelhuis, 1967

DUTCH

JEWELRY

DESIGN

1950
–
2000

JEWELS
of Mind and Mentality

RICHARD WALRAVEN

Born: 1950 Nijmegen/NL

EDUCATION

1971 Vakschool Schoonhoven, Schoonhoven/NL
1982 Gerrit Rietveld Academie, Amsterdam/NL

PUBLIC COLLECTIONS

Nordenfjeldske Kunstindustrimuseet, Trondheim/N
Rijksdienst Beeldende Kunst, The Hague/NL
Stedelijk Museum, Amsterdam/NL

SELECTED EXHIBITIONS

1994 Made in Holland Design aus den Niederlanden Museum für Angewandte Kunst, Cologne/D
1990 Novidades da Holanda Fundaçao Calouste Gulbenkian, Lisbon/P
1991 Point of view Dutch contemporary Jewelry and design USA/CDN travelling
1990 Gallery Puntgaaf, Groningen/NL
1988 Unica Stedelijk Museum, Amsterdam/NL
1987 Kunstobjekt als onderscheiding Gallery Het Kapelhuis, Amersfoort/NL
1986 10 Jaar Ra Gallery Ra, Amsterdam/NL
1986 Multiples Stedelijk Museum, Amsterdam/NL

SELECTED BIBLIOGRAPHY

Designprijs Rotterdam 1994/Christine de Baan (red). – Amsterdam: Uitgeverij BIS, 1994 • Made in Holland: Design aus den Niederlanden/Gabriele Lueg...et al. - Tübingen: Ernst Wasmuth Verlag, 1994 • Tekens & Ketens/Erik Beenker. - Amsterdam: Voetnoot Publishers, [1994] • VES View Review. – Amsterdam: VES, 1991 • Novidades da Holanda: estudo sobre jóias/Marjan Unger. - Lisbon/Amsterdam: Fundaçao Calouste Gulbenkian/Dutch Form Foundation, 1990 • Point of view: Dutch contemporary jewelry and design/Charon Kransen. - S.l.: s.n., 1990 • Unica. - Amsterdam: VES, 1987 • Tien jaar Ra/Liesbeth Crommelin en Paul Derrez. – Amsterdam: Galerie Ra, 1986 • Multiples: heden en verleden. - Amsterdam: VES, 1986.

DUTCH
JEWELRY
DESIGN
1950
-
2000

JEWELS
of Mind and Mentality

354

LAM DE WOLF
Born: 1949 Badhoevedorp/NL

EDUCATION
1978-1981 Gerrit Rietveld Academie Amsterdam/NL

PUBLIC COLLECTIONS
Centraal Museum, Utrecht/NL
Gemeentelijk Van Reekummuseum, Apeldoorn/NL
Gemeentemuseum Den Haag, The Hague/NL
Het Kruithuis, Stedelijk Museum voor Hedendaagse Kunst, 's-Hertogenbosch/NL
Nederlands Textielmuseum, Tilburg/NL
Nederlandse Kunst Stichting, Amsterdam/NL
Stedelijk Museum, Amsterdam/NL

SELECTED SOLO EXHIBITIONS
2000 50 Poppen Gallery Ra, Amsterdam/NL
1996 Leeg Gemeentemuseum Arnhem, Arnhem/NL
1990 Textilemuseum, Toronto/CDN
1987 Helen Drutt Gallery, Philadelphia/USA
1982 British Crafts Centre, London/GB

SELECTED GROUP EXHIBITIONS
2000 Jewels of Mind and Mentality Museum Het Kruithuis, 's-Hertogenbosch/NL travelling
1997 Handcomputer Arti et Amicitiae, Amsterdam/NL
1996 Aktie reaktie Museum voor Moderne Kunst, Arnhem/NL
1995 Overspel Nederlands Textielmuseum, Tilburg/NL
1994 A Moveable Feast Stedelijk Museum, Amsterdam/NL
1994 Signalement Nederlands Textielmuseum, Tilburg/NL
1993 A head of Fashion: Hats of the 20th Century Philadelphia Museum of Art, Philadelphia/USA
1993 The Art of Jewellery Setagaya Art Museum, Tokyo/J
1992 International Textile Biennial Musée des Arts Décoratifs de la Ville de Lausanne, Lausanne/CH
1992 Met vlag en wimpel Nederlands Textielmuseum, Tilburg/NL
1991 Sieraad als object, object als sieraad Librije, Zwolle/NL
1990 Novidades da Holanda Fundaçao Calouste Gulbenkian, Lisbon/P travelling
1989 Jewelry: Means: Meaning University of Tennessee, Knoxville/USA travelling
1989 Ornamenta I Schmuckmuseum, Pforzheim/D
1988 New Art objects from Britain and Holland Gallery RA, Crafts Council Amsterdam, London/GB
1987 Holland in Vorm, sieraden 1945-1987 Gemeentemuseum Arnhem, Arnhem/NL
1986 10 jaar galerie RA Gallery RA, Amsterdam/NL
1986 Sieraad 1986, Draagteken? Museum Het Kruithuis, 's-Hertogenbosch/NL
1986 Sieraden vorm en idee Gemeentelijk Van Reekummuseum, Apeldoorn/NL
1985 Body Works and Wearable Sculpture Visual Arts Center of Alaska, Anchorage/USA
1985 Contemporary Jewelry Redefined Pittsburgh Center for the Arts, Pittsburgh/USA
1984 Cross Currents: Jewellery from Australia, Britain, Germany and Holland Power House Museum, Sydney/AUS travelling
1984 Jewelry International American Craft Museum II, New York/USA
1984 Object and image Nederlandse Kunst Stichting, Amsterdam/NL
1984 Some Dutch Jewellery Arnolfini, Bristol/GB
1983 Sieraden Stedelijk Museum, Amsterdam/NL

1982 Jewellery Redefined British Crafts Centre, London/GB
1982 Visies op sieraden 1965-1982 Stedelijk Museum, Amsterdam/NL

SELECTED BIBLIOGRAPHY

Jewelry in Europe and America/Ralph Turner. - London: Thames and Hudson, 1996 ● Jewelry of our time: art, ornament and obsession/Helen W. Drutt English and Peter Dormer. - London: Thames and Hudson, 1995 ● The best in contemporary jewellery/David Watkins. - London: B.T. Bradsford Ltd., 1993 ● Sieraden: Centrum Beeldende Kunst Groningen/Gerard Lakke. Groningen: Centrum Beeldende Kunst, 1992 ● De feestdis ontworpen door 39 kunstenaars The Banqueting table/Martijn van Ooststroom. - Amsterdam: Galerie Ra, 1991 ● Novidades da Holanda: estudo sobre jóias/Marjan Unger. - Lisbon/Amsterdam :Fundaçao Calouste Gulbenkian/Dutch Form Foundation, 1990 ● Point of view: Dutch contemporary jewelry and design/Charon Kransen. - S.l.: s.n., 1990 ● Ornamenta I: internationale Schmuckkunst/Michael Erlhoff. - München: Prestel Verlag, 1989 ● London Amsterdam: new objects from Britain and Holland/Gert Staal en Martina Margetts. - Amsterdam: Galerie Ra, 1988 ● Holland in Vorm: vormgeving in Nederland 1945-1987/Gert Staal en Hester Wolters. -'s-Gravenhage: Stichting Holland in Vorm, 1987 ● Concepts, Comments, Process: Dutch Jewellery 1967-1978. - Amsterdam: Rijksdienst Beeldende Kunst, 1987 ● Images: Sieraden Schmuck Jewellery/Marjan Unger, Renny Ramakers, Monique Mokveld...et al. - Amsterdam: VES: 1986 ● Lam de Wolf. - Antwerpen: Internationaal Cultureel Centrum, 1986 ● Sieraad 1986: draagteken?/Yvònne G.J.M. Joris. - 's-Hertogenbosch: Museum voor Hedendaagse Kunst Het Kruithuis, 1986 ● Sieraden: vorm en idee/Liesbeth den Besten. - Apeldoorn: Gemeentelijk Van Reekummuseum, 1986 ● Standpunten/Marjan Unger. - Tilburg: Nederlands Textielmuseum, 1986 ● Tien jaar Ra/Liesbeth Crommelin en Paul Derrez. - Amsterdam: Galerie Ra, 1986 ● The New Jewelry: trends and traditions/Peter Dormer and Ralph Turner. - London: Thames and Hudson: 1985 ● Twentieth-Century Jewelry/Barbara Cartlidge. - New York: Harry N. Abrams, 1985 ● Lam de Wolf/Paul Derrez...et al. - Amsterdam: Lam de Wolf, 1984 ● Some Dutch Jewellery. - Bristol: Arnolfini, 1984 ● The Jewellery project: new departures in British and European work 1980-83. - London: Crafts Council Gallery, 1983 ● Jewellery redefined: the 1st international exhibition of multi-media non-precious jewellery 1982. - London: British Crafts Centre, 1982 ● Lam de Wolf. - S.l.: s.n., 1982

DUTCH
JEWELRY
DESIGN
1950
-
2000

JEWELS
of Mind and Mentality

356

FRANK VAN ZWICHT

Born: 1950 Blaricum/NL

EDUCATION

1974 Vakschool Schoonhoven, Schoonhoven/NL

SELECTED EXHIBITIONS

1996 Vormgevers op locatie, VES Amsterdam/NL
1994 Tekens & Ketens
1991 VES View review Stedelijk Museum Amsterdam/NL
1990 Novidades da Holanda Fundaçao Calouste Gulbenkian, Lisbon/P
1989 Oorigineel Gallery Trits, Delft/NL
1988 Unica Stedelijk Museum, Amsterdam/NL
1986 Multiples Stedelijk Museum, Amsterdam/NL travelling

SELECTED BIBLIOGRAPHY

Tekens & Ketens / Erik Beenker. – Amsterdam : Voetnoot Publishers, [1994] • VES View Review. – Amsterdam : VES, 1991 • Novidades da Holanda : estudo sobre jóias / Marjan Unger. - Lisbon / Amsterdam : Fundaçao Calouste Gulbenkian/Dutch Form Foundation, 1990 • Unica. – Amsterdam : VES, 1987 • Images : Sieraden Schmuck Jewellery / Marjan Unger, Renny Ramakers, Monique Mokveld...et al. – Amsterdam : VES, 1986 • Multiples : heden en verleden.- Amsterdam : VES, 1986

DUTCH
JEWELRY
DESIGN
1950
2000

JEWELS
of Mind and Mentality

357

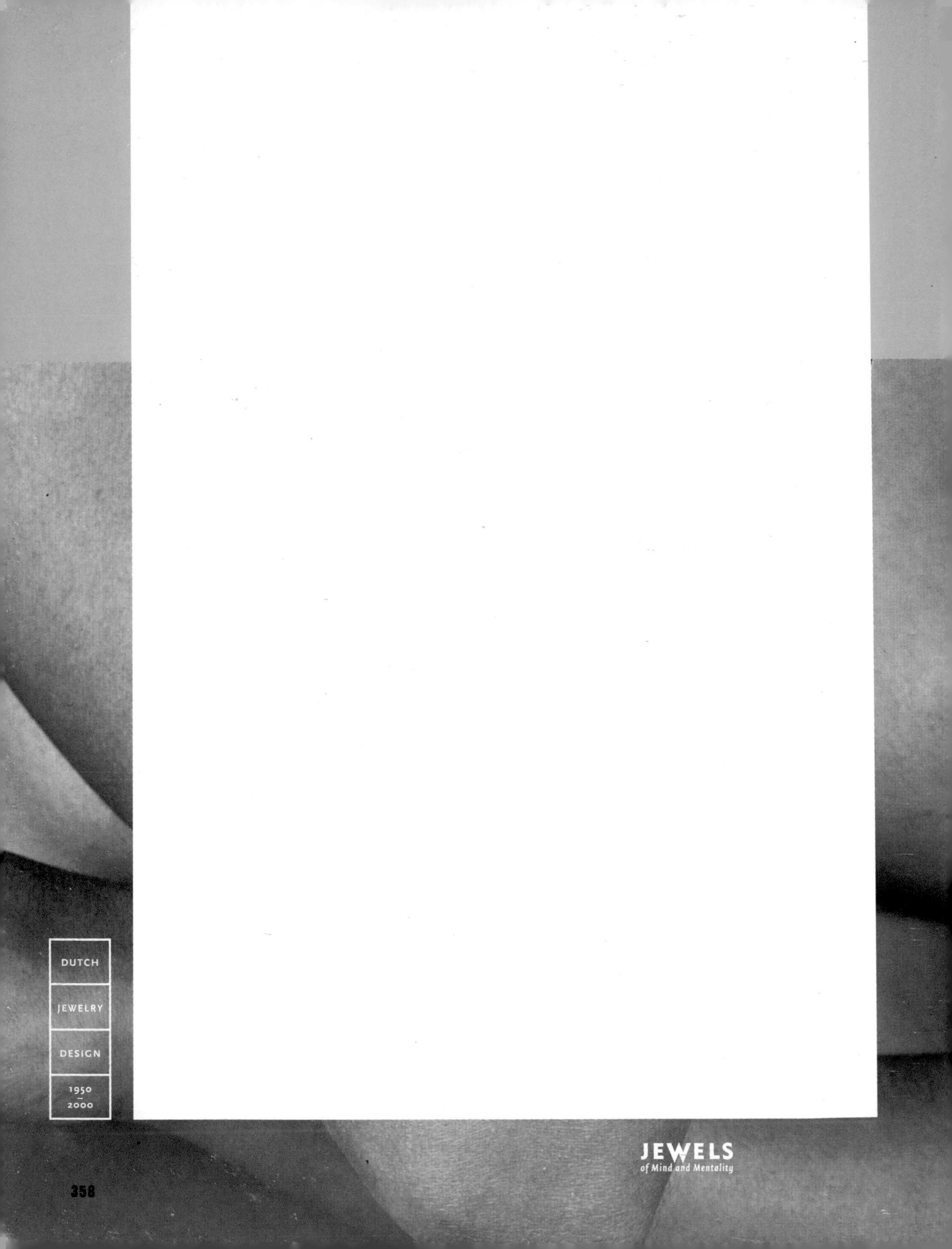

DUTCH

JEWELRY

DESIGN

1950
—
2000

JEWELS
of Mind and Mentality

JEWELS
of Mind and Mentality

DUTCH

JEWELRY

DESIGN

1950
–
2000

The publication was made possible with the support of the Mondriaan Foundation in Amsterdam/NL

EDITED BY
Yvònne G.J.M. Joris
Museum Het Kruithuis

TEXTS
Antje von Graevenitz, Amsterdam/NL
Jaap Huisman, Amsterdam/NL

TRANSLATIONS
Ted Alkins, Heverlee/B

BIOGRAPHIES/BIBLIOGRAPHIES
Wil van Gils
Museum Het Kruithuis

COPY EDITOR
Thea Sterken
Museum Het Kruithuis

PHOTOGRAPHY
Piek, Amsterdam/NL

DESIGN
Studio Roelof Mulder, Amsterdam/NL

LITHOGRAPHY/PRINTED BY
Snoeck-Ducaju & Zoon, Ghent/B

ISBN 90-6450-399-0 (hardcover) / 010 Publishers, Rotterdam (www.010publishers.nl)

DUTCH

JEWELRY

DESIGN

1950
~
2000

JEWELS
of Mind and Mentality